CW00673166

Going Under is funny, insightful an~~d~~ hanging out with a really brilliant friend who, you know, will make you a better person. Seana Smith is the real deal — a truth-teller and a writer of immense integrity.

KATHRYN HEYMAN
author of *Fury*

With a tender touch, Smith contemplates the two truths of her childhood: the wild island adventures and the brutal eruptions behind closed doors. Standing on the precipice of her own alcoholism, she realises that reckoning with the past is the only way to shape the future.

JENNY VALENTISH
author of *Woman of Substances*

With sparkling, musical prose and unflinching generosity of spirit, Seana Smith lays bare the facts of a life stalked by alcohol. A life that ricochets 'between privilege and terror, between adventure and fear'.

So much more than a book about the booze, *Going Under* is an intricate, often beautiful mosaic of family, the individuals caught inside its sharp-edged cracks, and the self-yearning to make sense of it all. The story of a woman emerging from the brokenness of the past and the never-ending pressures of the present to reclaim joy.

Honest. Tender. Laugh-cry funny. Walking with Seana through her year of *Going Under* is to make a new and wise friend.

KIM KELLY
author of *Ladies' Rest and Writing Room*

seana smith

going under

**A memoir of family secrets,
addiction and escape**

VENTURA
PRESS

VENTURA
PRESS

First published in 2024 by Ventura Press
PO Box 780, Edgecliff NSW 2027 AUSTRALIA
www.venturapress.com.au

All rights reserved. No part of this book may be reproduced or transmitted in
any form or by any means, electronic or mechanical, including photocopying,
recording or by any other information storage or retrieval system, without prior
permission in writing from the publisher.
Copyright © Seana Smith 2024

A catalogue record for this
book is available from the
National Library of Australia

Going Under
ISBN 9780645497236 (Print book)
ISBN 9780645497229 (ebook)

Cover and internal design: Deborah Parry Graphics
Managing editor: Amanda Hemmings
Printed and bound in Australia by Griffin Press

Ventura Press acknowledges the Traditional Owners of the country on which we
work, the Gadigal people of the Eora nation, and recognises their continuing
connection to the land, waters and culture. We pay our respects to their Elders
past, present and emerging.

The paper this book is printed on is certified against the
Forest Stewardship Council® Standards. Griffin Press holds
chain of custody certification SCS-COC-001185. FSC®
promotes environmentally responsible, socially beneficial
and economically viable management of the world's forests.

Author's Note

These stories are all true. I have changed names to protect the privacy of all who requested it, and some who did not.

Memory can be a fickle friend. Many of the stories from my younger childhood come from memory and I have tried to corroborate these by talking to other people who were present. Conversations have been recreated both from memory and from my diaries.

Orange, New South Wales

A frying-hot November day. I am hard at work building a new set of heavy-duty shelves in the garage of our house in Orange. I take out all the pieces, the shelves, the bolts, the slats, and lay them out neatly on the patch of floor I cleared of mess before I sliced the huge cardboard boxes with my Stanley knife.

It is almost a year since we moved into this house, yet the garage is still a disaster area. I have slithered in occasionally to retrieve particular items, but have often been startled by them, distressed, unable to take a deep breath and tidy up all the debris of our move. Flyscreen doors lean precariously against large cardboard boxes which could hold anything from my old TV shows from BBC Scotland on VHS to our son Ben's Warhammer figures, paints and glue. A pile of suitcases has slid sideways to rest against our bicycles, higgledy-piggledy against a wall.

Our twins are at school, just a ten-minute walk away. We bought this house for its proximity to their new high school. My husband Paul is in Sydney; he stays with our oldest son Jake a couple of nights a week while he studies a postgrad course.

I pick my way to the roller doors and heave one up, glad that the door does not stick, that the metal curtain slats smoothly curl around the barrel at the top. I throw the cardboard box that held the shelves outside. The sunlight that strikes me is ferocious so I pull the roller door back down fast, turning the lock bar so sharply my fingers burn with pain.

This chaos all around me is as stifling as the heat. The flowery red cushion I brought from Mum's house in Scotland is thick with dust; it lies askew on an old office chair. A garden fork is lying flat on top of a box, waiting to jab someone. A box of Christmas decorations has a crack along the side and tinsel spills out.

I need to build the shelves to start to create some order in here. I need to sort and tidy, bring some things into our house, recycle, donate, throw out the rest. But I need a scaffold first, secure, solid shelves, somewhere to place all the things we will keep, all the things we will use.

I scan the room again. That pile of old wellington boots. Yes, we need them, not at the moment when the drought is so severe, but once it breaks. The wellies can live on these shelves, once I build them.

And a thought darts in fast. I could hide bottles of wine in those wellies. I could pop in some sauvignon blanc; some local reds might be better though – to be drunk at room temperature. I could slide a plastic tumbler into a welly boot, too. The perfect hiding spot. I could sneak out to the garage during the day and in the evenings and just tipple away. No one would ever know.

I would know.

I would know.

ONE

January

Edinburgh: 21 January

On the morning of Mum's funeral, I get up early and set off
to climb Arthur's Seat, something I have never done before.
For Edinburgh folk, climbing to the top of Arthur's Seat is a
rite of spring; people go up and wash their faces in the dew
on May Day morning. This ancient volcano, which looks like
a sphinx or a restful lion, sits within Holyrood Park beside
Edinburgh's Old Town, Scottish Parliament and Holyrood
Palace. Holyrood Park is steeped in Scottish history and in our
family's story too.

I leave the large Victorian house in Duddingston which my
sisters Morag and Kirsty and I have let for these few days, open
the heavy iron gate and walk along to Duddingston Loch, then
I turn right to climb the Hundred Steps.

I am puffing at the top of the steps and set off slow and
steady along the path leading up the grassy hillside, passing
prickly gorse bushes dotted here and there. Clouds go
scudding by, chased by the January wind, their shadows and

weak sunbeams waltzing their way across the wide parklands. After leaning into the steeper sections of the path and with more huffing and puffing, I clamber though the huge rocks to get to the top and then, at the highest point, I can see it all.

Over there is the huge expanse of the Firth of Forth, its silvery sheen leading to the grey-blue horizon. The Kingdom of Fife rises to the north, the Pentland Hills to the west and to the east the rich rolling farmlands of East Lothian where Mum had made her home. I can see far over to the west, to Juniper Green where Mum spent all her school years, and down into George Square where she went to school and to university. I look over to the hospitals where she gave birth to three of us four children, all before she was twenty-nine years old. Along the south shores of the Firth of Forth are the beaches she took us to play at and inland are the Lammermuir Hills where we had picnics by streams and rivers.

Here at the very top of Arthur's Seat, I can see all of Holyrood Park, a place full of stories for our family; both sides lived in Scotland's capital city for generations. My paternal grandfather, Papa, was brought up in the Dumbiedykes, the tenement slums just below Salisbury Crags on the west side of the park. He used to climb the precipitous Cat's Nick route up the Crags at night when he was a teenager. Dad and Mum took us sledging on the little hillock called Haggis Knowe beside St Margaret's Loch on the north side of the park when we were little. We often went to Duddingston Loch on the south side of Holyrood Park to feed the ducks, back in the days when we all believed that white bread was the very thing that ducks delighted to dine upon.

Many times Dad told us the story of the huge rock that lies below Duddingston Low Road. The rock fell suddenly one day from the crags above and killed a milkmaid as she milked a cow in the field below. Thrilling! Might her bones still be there below the rock? And the cow's too, and the pail? Imagine the smell!

Dad had told us about the Bronze Age lake village at Duddingston Loch and the four ancient hill forts within Holyrood Park. He had pointed out the agricultural terraces on the east side of Whinny Hill, site of medieval farming. We had all thrown coins into the spring at the fifteenth-century St Margaret's Well.

Papa used to cycle up to the highest part of the Queen's Drive, to Dunsapie Loch. One day, in his seventies, he was feeling under the weather at home in Portobello. So Papa rode his bike up to Dunsapie where he immediately fell off and was taken to hospital in an ambulance. He had been feeling poorly because he was having a heart attack and his bike ride up that steep and winding road had not helped one bit. Papa survived and told that tale many times.

Duddingston Kirk was first built in the twelfth century and is still running Sunday services. Around the corner is the Sheep Heid Inn, the oldest pub in Scotland. An inn has been on this site since 1360, it is said; certainly Mary, Queen of Scots used to stay there. The Sheep Heid Inn has moved with the times though – I ate from the vegan menu when we met up with Mum's brother Uncle Peter and his family for dinner last night.

Over there, south of Duddingston Loch and beyond the park, is the luxurious Prestonfield House hotel. This very grand building dates from the late 1600s and has splendid views over Arthur's Seat. The hotel's furnishings are opulent with plenty of stags' heads on the walls and oil paintings. Prestonfield House was a favourite dining venue of Dad's, somewhere he loved taking clients and friends.

I turn around in a circle one last time before I start to walk down, looking out at the panorama of the places where Mum spent her life, where her life was so deeply rooted. I feel sad that Mum had to move far away to the north for the last eighteen months of her life. It was the right thing to do, but still sad. Today is a day for all the sadness. I wish and wish and wish that Paul was here for me and that our children could be present to farewell their Granny today.

I pick my way carefully through the gigantic rocks as I leave the summit of Arthur's Seat and set off slowly down the grassy path. Morag and family come walking up as I am walking down, strolling across the hillside on a different track, and we wave from afar. The walk down is harder than the walk up; I stumble as I go, wind in my face shifting my tears as they slide.

Our walks today add one more story to our family's store of Holyrood Park stories. It was fitting to climb this sleeping lion and gaze from its peak on the day that we lay Mum to rest.

I shower and dress, our brother Callum arrives from his care home, and we join the wider family to farewell our mother with poems, with Scottish songs, with friends and with flowers. There is no alcohol at the afternoon tea we have arranged at Prestonfield House. Mum had made that wish very clear. I feel jittery as I get to bed.

)F

Mum died on January 5th. Her decline and collapse into unconsciousness had happened fairly quickly. This year had not started at all as I had expected, although it did start in a way that was horribly familiar to me: New Year's Day, a hangover and anxiety.

Frenchs Forest, Sydney: 1 January

January 1st. I wake up with a cracking hangover and wish I had stayed sober last night. This is not the way I planned to start the New Year. I need to be on my best game today but how can I be now? My internal dialogue fires up and leaves the platform, starts to rattle along well-worn tracks.

You could have drunk nothing last night. What would have been wrong with just a couple of Diet Cokes? You knew you had a big day today.

And you knew it would be a hot day too – exactly what you don't need when you wake up dehydrated.

So, OK, I definitely will not drink tonight. I'll get everything I need to do done and then will pack up everything I need for the flight. I won't drink at all tonight. I can wait until I get onto that flight to Scotland.

Can you? Let's see.

My mother is dying in Scotland, and I have a flight booked for tomorrow, Sydney–London–Inverness. I will arrive on January 3rd and Mum may have died or she may still be alive. Mum dying was not the plan at all. When I left her to come back to Australia after a visit in late August last year, I was very firm indeed when saying goodbye to her at St Olaf Care Home in Nairn.

'Mum, I know I have come to visit the last three Januaries, but next year I just cannot come. We're moving house to Orange on the eighteenth of January and we need to pack up. I'll come in March, if I can. But not January.'

And Mum, back then in August, always wanting to be helpful, had said, 'I'll do my best to stay alive, dear. You come to see me again in March when the daffodils are out.'

Now I'm standing in the spacious kitchen of this house in Frenchs Forest in Sydney. I've pulled back the glass sliding doors so that the warm breeze can soothe me. My poor head is muzzy and my legs are shaky from the hangover and I am not sure at all what is the most important thing to pack. I've got this one day to do what I can. My husband Paul and our four kids are not going to fly to Scotland with me and it's likely that Paul will have to manage our coming house move on his own. What can I do to make it easy for him? How will he manage?

Mum had become more and more unwell after I left Scotland last August. In November and December she was having little strokes. By the time Christmas came, Mum could not talk and she could not walk.

My little sister Morag said to me, 'When I go to see Mum she is often sitting in the TV room and she turns to look at me and starts crying, but she can't say anything.'

Between Christmas and New Year, Mum started to choke when the care home staff tried to feed her. As the year ended, the decision was made to stop attempting to give her any food or liquid. She is unconscious now, dying. Yesterday, I booked the flight back to Scotland, then wired into a bottle of wine on an empty stomach.

This New Year's Day is hot and humid, and I spend it packing up boxes of our belongings, trying to help Paul just a bit. I pack warm clothes ready for the flight tomorrow. I chat to the four kids, ask them to be helpful to their dad when I am not here.

In the morning I had promised myself I'd stay sober tonight but, by the afternoon, my scalp is crawling and my heart is trying to thump its way out of my chest. Stressed. Anxious. I know there's a bottle of wine in the fridge. I pull it out fast – *don't think, don't think* – pour a glass and slip it down. I'll just have one or two.

By the time I get to bed, my head is swimming and the bottle is in the recycling.

Can't you just have one or two?

Why can't I just have one or two?

※

Next morning, a car picks me up at 4 am to go to the airport. I sit down in my seat at 6 am. The hostess glides to my side, holding a bottle of champagne with a napkin rolled around the top.

'Would you like a glass to welcome you aboard, madam?'

The flight takes off dead on time at 6.30 am, and I drink my second glass of champagne as the plane rises and banks, heading north, heading west, heading to Scotland, heading home.

Nairn, Scotland: 4 January

I place the CD into Mum's player and click forward to the song 'Now I'm Easy'.

My sisters and I are taking turns to sit with Mum's old and tired body. She isn't really here anymore, but her body still has some heartbeats to beat and breaths to breathe. I am sitting alone with Mum for a while; my elder sister Kirsty and younger sister Morag have gone back to Morag's house to sleep and look after the children. Jetlag is helpful – I am wakeful so I take the night watch.

We wish our brother Callum could be sitting with Mum too, but we just cannot manage to bring him here from his care home. It's a three-hour drive and the weather is bad. Callum has not spent a night away from that care home in ten years except during stays in psychiatric hospital wards. This is not the time to see how he goes sleeping elsewhere. We talk to him on the phone. He knows Mum is dying; she might die today, or tomorrow, none of us know.

The gentle, calm voice of Eric Bogle soothes me just as it had when I first heard his songs thirty years ago, newly arrived in Australia and feeling the loss and longing for the Scotland he sang of. Eric's song about his ceramic hot water bottle, 'Wee China Pig', made me laugh, and I remember my Gran telling me about her own wee china pig. His song 'Leaving Nancy' made me sob. Nancy was Eric's mum and she travelled with him to Waverley Station in Edinburgh to wave him off on his journey to Australia in the 1960s.

'Now I'm Easy' is a song about an old Australian farmer who has suffered terrible losses. As death comes, he lies at peace, accepting the end of a long, hard life.

Mum seems easy, at peace, at last. She is simply slipping away slowly, slowly.

I wipe away tears, silently thanking Eric for his songs, the soundtrack for my own messy life with its immigrant gratitude and emigrant regret.

'Now I'm Easy' ends and I jump the CD forward to 'Wee China Pig'. Then I sit back down beside Mum and pick up her cool pale hand. I stroke her old fingers as I sing along to the lyrics about Eric's ceramic hot water bottle which Mum and I had loved and sung together many times.

I chat to Mum as I sit beside her. I ask whether she can remember us going to see Eric Bogle live in a theatre in Edinburgh at least twenty years ago when I was on one of my trips home from Sydney. Eric is a generous and amusing performer and Mum enjoyed the show. I began to send her Eric Bogle CDs as Christmas presents. Mum played them often when she moved into St Olaf Care Home. I wonder if she can hear my words and the songs.

Mum's fingers are still and I am surprised by how soft they are. Mum always had strong gardener's hands – rough skin, dirt under her nails, however hard she scrubbed. They're clean now. Eighteen months in this care home have kept her safe.

Mum did like St Olaf well enough but she once said to me, 'It's a nice place, but it's not home.' How I wish Mum had been able to stay at home in Ormiston with her mind intact. I wish she had been able to keel over and die quickly of a heart attack while digging up potatoes in her own garden.

But who gets the death they hope for? Not Mum, and nor did Dad almost ten years before. If not the deaths, can we have the lives we wish for? I don't think my parents had the lives they would have wished for themselves.

And can I live the life I wish for now? Can the coming tree change to Orange help me get out of my own way and enjoy the freedom that is coming, finally? And what exactly, now, do I need to free myself from?

*

Mum lies propped up on pillows. She looks like herself from the top of her head to her nose, but, below her high cheekbones, her cheeks sag and her mouth is small and puckered, not like Mum at all.

She has a blue notebook in which she penned notes to herself years before when her own father was old.

'Do not be a burden to your family,' she wrote. 'Go into a care home when you need to. Do not make a fuss.'

She had written some specific requests and instructions too.

'Please keep my teeth in even when I am dying.'

Mum always kept her false teeth in. It was a rare person

who saw them out even as she became more and more unwell.

But now, when she is dying, when kindness is commonplace, voices are low and needs met, she is not allowed to wear her top and bottom plates in case they slip down her throat and choke her to death. Ironic. Maybe that was why she had wanted them left in, to shorten this stage of lifeless living limbo.

Over the three days my sisters and I spend sitting with Mum her legs and arms occasionally twitch, but for most of the time she is utterly still. Each evening she is given a small dose of morphine.

Now on this last day, Mum's breathing is shallow, a faint sigh in and out. We three daughters are seated around her, Kirsty in the chair by the window and Morag and I on larger armchairs wheeled into the room for this sitting-in.

It is dark by the late afternoon, the mustard yellow curtains are drawn and Mum's bedside lamp throws a splash of light onto her side table and the bed.

In the dim light I look over at her family photos, the edge of one small silver frame glinting. I move closer to look at that beautiful photo of our brother Callum as a little boy looking at the camera with a big smile, his brightly striped lifejacket half undone, the tones of the heather and the sea and the dinghy behind him the faded colours of 1970s film. Callum's smile is innocent, infectious, charming and full of promise, there is cheekiness, joy and pleasure in it. How comforting to feel that he is here with us in some way.

We three sisters sit in contented quiet. We recline the chairs, sleeping and waking, patiently waiting. We try not to talk of anything negative, nor of her will and all we will inherit or of what we've inherited in other ways. Every few hours care staff come in to move Mum a little, always chatting as if she is fully aware.

The rustle of pages turning as we read, the sucking of sweeties as we eat, wind blowing outside, the pinging of the beeper that calls the care staff to tend to another old person, the rolling by of the wheels of a trolley, the soft squeak as the door opens.

'Would you like a cup of tea?'

'Yes, we would, we'd love a cup of tea.'

The scent of sweet peas in a vase. Mum does not know the flowers are there and her sense of smell is almost non-existent anyway. But their dusty pinks and faded blues make the room look pretty and we can inhale their sugared almond scent. They remind me of the flowers in Mum's garden, the trellises alive with hundreds of sweet peas, their fragrance as we scampered past when we were kids.

Mum passes away on this Saturday night, approaching 8pm. I am sleeping in the reclining chair when Kirsty's voice wakes me.

'Seana, you need to wake up.'

'No, I'm happy asleep,' I mumble, feeling that dripping drag as the blanket of bemusement, heavy as mud, is dragged from me. 'Leave me alone, go away.'

'No, wake up. She's leaving; it's the end.'

Mum's final breaths are gentle, shallow, soft, and then she breathes no more. Her life passes out of her body.

There is no need to talk about what to do next. We pull aside the curtains and open the window just a little. We stand silent, allowing Mum's spirit to leave the room and slip away into the deep darkness of the Highland night.

Afterwards, we sit beside her body for some time then kiss her goodbye, a last kiss on her smooth cheeks with their peachy down. The care staff will look after Mum's body as it chills and stiffens. But her spirit is out there, flying or gliding or just hovering, we do not know. Mum is free.

We arrive at Morag's home and give her boys a hug. Children are the best balm for the death of an old person. In the cosy sitting room we talk and laugh and cry a little. There will be so many things to do: calls to make to friends and family, emails to send, an advert to be placed in the Scotsman, a funeral to be planned. But for this night, there is peace.

'I think I will absolutely demand to keep my teeth in when I'm dying,' I say as I reach once more for the biscuit tin then swig from my glass of wine. 'I think I will write in a wee book just the opposite of what Mum wrote. I will be a burden to my family.'

Then I ask, 'When you were a teenager, did Mum ever threaten that when you had your own place, she would come to your house and leave wet towels lying around on the floor like you did to her?'

'Haha! She did!' Morag replies.

'I used to laugh with her because she was very restrained and not once when she stayed with me did she leave those wet towels to moulder. She always hung them up.'

'Me too. And now I tell my own kids that I will one day come to their houses in the future and leave wet towels lying on the bathroom floors like they do.'

I pass around the bottle of wine, then go to get another. Am I behaving like a waiter, pouring wine into glasses before they're empty, without even asking if they would like some more? The thing is, I need more. Another biscuit, a glass of wine, pieces of shortbread, another glass of wine.

You won't sleep well tonight if you drink another glass, Seana. Be sensible, can't you?

I'll not sleep at all if I don't have another glass or two, how could I? I know we have a lot to do tomorrow but let me slake my sorrowful

thirst tonight. Don't nag, Seana.
I'm not nagging, I'm your voice of reason, you idiot.

)ƒ

'They both look about twelve years old, don't they?'

My sisters are taking down Mum and Dad's wedding photo which had hung above Mum's bed at St Olaf for the eighteen months she was there.

'Yes,' I reply, 'and so formal too. They look pleased but are holding themselves tight.'

'Dad has a truly cheerful smile. Mum looks wary.'

'Or are we just reading that in?'

In the wedding photo, Mum and Dad stand together outside the church. Dad wears a charcoal-grey morning coat with long tails, polished black shoes, and stripy trousers. He looks fit and very happy. Mum wears a white wedding dress. She is very slim: her waist was twenty-two inches at the time of her marriage.

This wedding photo hung on Mum and Dad's bedroom wall when I was a girl. I always knew they were both beautiful, but it was only in my thirties that their extreme youth struck me hard. Mum and Dad were twenty-one and twenty-two years old when they got married. That is not so very young compared with many others at that time, I know, but to us they look like babies. There is not a wrinkle on their faces, not a grey hair. Even our grandparents look young to us in that wedding photo as we lift it from its hook and wrap it in newspaper.

The differences between their marriage and those of their daughters are stark. Perhaps if my parents' marriage had looked like one to emulate we would have married in our early twenties too, but it didn't and we didn't. My elder sister Kirsty married when she was twenty-eight. My sister Morag met her husband in her thirties. I met Paul when I was thirty-one and it took four children, twenty-two years and a need to get a Saudi resident's visa before we actually did get married. And we never even used that visa.

'What do you think life would have been like if we'd married the boyfriends we had at twenty-one?' I ask.

'Very different. The marriages wouldn't have lasted long, that's for sure.'

'Thank God I was never the marrying kind,' I say to my sister.

We pack Mum and Dad's wedding photo carefully into a cardboard box, and then wrap and pack all of the photos and trinkets, the little china fox, the bronze rabbit with long ears and the mottled green seal made from marble from the Isle of Iona.

Fife, Scotland: 15 January

'So where is it we are going again?' my brother Callum asks; his short-term memory really has deteriorated.

'To the Kingsgate Shopping Centre, in Dunfermline. I've never been before though, have you?'

I'm finding it hard to keep my eye on Google Maps on my phone while paying attention to other cars on this busy road.

'Not sure. Maybe once or twice to go to the shops. Cannae mind.'

He twists in his seat, looks around as we arrive in the centre of Dunfermline. The streets are narrow and I am sure we should be heading in the opposite direction but we're stuck in a one-way system.

'Remember we are here to get a suit. Mum would love you to look very smart for her funeral.'

16

She would, wouldn't she? Mum often found Callum embarrassing to be with, especially when he had food stains down the front of his t-shirt or when his trousers drooped below the waist exposing his round, bulging belly. I always expected Mum to get over worrying about what other people thought, especially of Callum, but she never did.

'Oh aye, that's good. I need to go to the toilet though – could we stop?'

'Finding car parks and shopping centres is hard enough just now. Don't ask for a loo stop too! My brain will explode.'

There's a red light at the junction ahead and I am totally unsure of where to go. I wish Callum could help with the map-reading, but do not even ask. Too hard for him. A car toots loudly and makes me jump. Fuck!

'Just hang on. It won't be long. I'm in a one-way system and not sure where to find the car park entrance, but it can't be far. You can wait, can't you?'

'I really do need to go.'

'OK, just hang on, hang on.'

Trying not to cry or shriek in frustration, I turn left, see the entrance to a car park and turn sharply and speedily into it.

'Here we are, but it's busy. Bloody hell, give me strength.'

A whiff of urine floats up.

'Oh Callum, did you wet yourself?'

'Yes, looks like it, my jeans are soaking.'

The old stress training kicks in and I start taking long, slow breaths deep into my tummy as calming thoughts battle with panicked ones.

Oh my God, we are almost at the shops and his trousers are so wet. How can we still go shopping for this bloody suit? Should we turn around and go back to the care home to get cleaned up?

Now remember: nobody has died here, in fact no life is even

17

threatened. This is just an inconvenience.

Fuck, this is a hire car. How am I going to clean it?

A parking space materialises and we swing in. I stop the car and turn to Callum.

'This doesn't look familiar,' he says, not looking at all concerned that he is sitting in his own wee. That feels like a small mercy.

'Well, not to worry, we can work something out. Let's just get out of the car and find Top Shop and see if someone can be kind and help us. Let's stick to the plan. Would you like to find a toilet?

'Nah, it all came out.'

Callum opens the door and heaves himself around, putting his feet onto the ground. As he stands up, a rush of urine falls down his trouser legs and onto the car park floor. He steps around the pool and waits for me to finish getting my bag out of the boot.

I brave a look at the car seat. It is sopping. I throw a t-shirt and a jumper over it to try to soak up at least something. But then I stand up and decide to take Callum's lead and carry on regardless.

'Right then, let's go. It's not too far.'

Callum walks along very slowly, lumbering from side to side. He takes my hand, just as he did when we were children.

'Come on then, big sister Shoshi,' he says. 'Let's get this suit for Mum's funeral.'

And we do. A very kind man helps Callum try on suit jackets and guess at the right size of trousers. Then I take him home, borrow some cloths and a bucket of hot soapy water and clean the car seat as well as I can. In my hotel room that night, I drink a bottle of wine fast. I deserve it, surely?

Next morning, I feel sick when I wake up.

You drank that whole bottle of wine on your own, Seana. On your own. That's one more thing you said you'd never do. But you do it all the time at home and now you're doing it here too.

Look, when I'm at home with the kids I'm not really alone, am I?

Yes, you are – come on, don't be so dimwitted. When Paul's away, when the kids are in bed, you are definitely drinking alone. Telltale sign, telltale sign. Your dad sometimes claimed he wasn't an alcoholic because he drank with other people; he was adamant about it, until the days he did started drinking alone, sitting in his chair in that bloody sitting room. By then we'd all given up arguing with him about his drinking.

But here I am arguing with myself now.

Yes, Seana, here you are. And this is an argument that has been going on too long.

Glasgow, Scotland: 22 January

The limo stops at Glasgow Airport and the driver hops out as I fumble around getting my hand baggage in order. He has my suitcase ready for me and I wheel it to the business class check in. That driver was very discreet, not talking to me at all and ignoring my nose blowing and eye wiping as the road took us west from Edinburgh to Glasgow. I am booked on the old faithful 1 pm flight to Dubai which connects comfortably with the long onward flight to Sydney.

There's a glass of vintage champagne in my hand within seconds of me parking my posterior on my seat. Streams of tiny bubbles fly up through the tawny liquid, but not for long as I down it in two swallows and ask for another. Sleek and smart, the air hostess fills it up and asks if I would like some tissues. I take those with almost as much gratitude as the bubbly, but not quite.

I have drunk champagne and cried as I left Glasgow on the

way back to Sydney many times before. In the past years I have learned that being in business class really helps and not just because the bubbly is French. The flat beds, the never having to move as people come in and out of seats, the excellent nuts and snacks served in the bar area, not to mention any sort of drink I want for free. All that is soothing, and then there's the thrill of being quite so flash. It is dizzyingly posh to be in business class when you started out as a wee Scottish girl in a wee Scottish village. For anyone with airs and graces, business class is a thrill.

Business class flights will not be a feature of our lives going forward. Paul's retirement means living a simpler life and no more Emirates points from his flights to and from his work in the Middle East. So I'd better drink and eat as much as I can on this one. I'm a firm believer in comfort eating, only because it works. I am not sure that all the mid-air drinking is a comfort though. I know what it does to me.

On this flight, while I doze and wake and eat and drink, memories toss and turn as I do. All those family stories, all the reasons I had to leave that led me to be leaving again now. All the things we were never allowed to talk about.

That Scottish childhood, typical in so many ways, with an alcoholic father causing mayhem. But untypical in that we had so many ecstatic times, too. We kids ran wild over the islands of the Hebrides; we sailed among the rushing tides, past basking seals and seas made glassy by swarming jellyfish; we knew the lochs of Morvern and Argyll. Those are the memories that cause the ripping, tearing feeling of nostalgia in my mind and heart as I fly south and east. It's only the painful memories, the things that confused me so much as a child, that I am still glad to escape. I ask for another glass of wine and try to sleep again.

Ormiston, Scotland: Early 1970s

The back door slammed shut. Dad was home. There was a nanosecond of silence, just a beat, then came a thump and some bumps as he stotted off the walls on his erratic journey to the sitting room. He swung open the sitting room door and in came a rush of chilly outside air.

The fire was crackling, the room toasty warm, smelling faintly of smoke and the damp dog sleeping by the hearth. I'd been looking at books in the cabinet, a finely crafted piece of furniture with doors made with small glass panels, locked with a tiny key. Dad's favourite history books were here and in my hand I had *The Fortified House in Scotland,* volume 3.

Dad crashed through the doorway and sat with a humph in his easy chair. He was falling-about-drunk but not angry. He was excited, exuberant even. His cheeks were ruddy from windburn as he wrestled off his thick grey jumper with the suede shoulder patches that stopped his shotgun from slipping. He cleared his throat and I looked at him, saw the familiar glassy eyes, saw that he looked a bit wild, unsteady, excited.

'I have just made love to another woman two times,' he uttered. 'But by God I wish it had been your mother.'

I froze. I had heard the words, they had gone into my ears, but they were ricocheting around inside my skull, not making sense. I was only eight or nine.

'Pour me a drink, can you, Seana? There's water in the jug.'

I opened the door of the booze cupboard and poured a whisky into one of the heavy crystal glasses, then added the water. I was an expert at making drinks for Dad. He took a deep swig, sighed and tipped his head against the back of the chair, closed his eyes.

'I'm going to feed the rabbits,' I said as I darted out, still trying to make sense of what he had said.

On that blustery autumn day, sodden grey clouds covered the sky, low and lumpy as they moved slowly to the west, dropping rain here and there. Not a chink of blue sky all day. Dad had been out shooting grouse with some of his posh friends, the red feathers above the eyes of the grouse the only bright colours amidst the speckled brown of their feathers and the faded greens and browns of the fields and the heather. The clink of glasses always followed the boom of the shotguns and the beating paws of the gun dogs. Dad often got roaring drunk after a day out shooting, and would drive home then almost fall out of the car.

But this day he hadn't driven home; quite the opposite.

After his pronouncement and another couple of whiskies, Dad crashed his way up the curving staircase and went to bed. We four kids and Mum sat down to watch *The Two Ronnies*. Mum made a supper of mugs of hot chocolate and a plate of homemade biscuits and brought it through on a big tray. And we would never ever discuss this revelation of Dad's.

This incident joined many others in a library of secrets, never to be spoken of. The memory though is as bright and clear as a flawless cube of ice, its shock and upset, with some comfort at his wish, even now.

Sydney: 23 January

When I land, the weather in Sydney is scorching, bright and blue. I take a taxi over to see our oldest son, Jake, who is living on his own in a small flat near our old house. I talk on the phone to our second son, Ben, who lives south of Sydney and is about to start an apprenticeship. I stay a night and wake to another scorcher. Then I collect my car from just outside our old home, and drive west over the Blue Mountains and then further west over the dry plains of the Central West, which has been drought-ridden for a few years. After a four-hour drive, I arrive at our new home and the start of this new chapter for our family.

There is also my own new chapter: the death of any parent is a life punctuation, and now the death of Mum means my siblings and I are the oldest generation. The 'auld yins', as Papa used to say. But I feel I am grieving Mum as a child, as her child. How will this play out as I try to change things, in daily life and in my own mind? Does it mean freeing myself of the messy mixed emotions about my own childhood? Can I let go of the effects of all the bad bits while keeping the positives from the wonderful parts?

Orange

Paul had managed the removalists the week before so I arrive at our new house to find our beds in the bedrooms, our sofas in the sitting room and my desk in the sunroom. Alice and Tom have chosen their bedrooms and their new school uniforms hang in their cupboards. They are excited, chattering about their holiday with Paul in Tasmania. Alice shows me a video of the trip she has made. I melt back into my family.

Here we are in our new home, a much smaller one than the five-bedroom house with a backyard pool in Frenchs Forest. Paul has retired from his thirty-year career in oil and gas; he's only in his early fifties but he is ready for a change and so are we all. Paul spent years working twenty-eight days on, twenty-eight days off in Yemen and Kurdistan. This was exhausting for everyone. We could have moved over to Saudi Arabia, but decided to change our lives and have a 'tree change' to Orange instead. We are renting out the Sydney house to bring in an income and Paul will be studying editing and publishing this year, and caring for his children in a way he never has before.

Paul and I both grew up in the countryside in Scotland and we are ready to slow down, live a simpler life and, crucially, spend a lot less money than we did in Sydney – here's hoping anyway.

A few days later, the day after the twins start Year 7 at their new school, I brave the garage. Boxes are piled upon boxes, bikes lean here and there, the drum kit has been set up.

'There's never going to be space in there for an actual car, is there?' I say to Paul.

'Not for a while anyway.'

Close by the roller door is my old blue trunk.

'Can you help me carry the trunk into the sunroom, Paul?'

Dad bought me this trunk when I made my first marvellous escape from the peril that was my childhood. The trunk has been with Paul and me since we first left Scotland with Jake when he was only three months old. It was stored in a room in Karachi for a year then came with us to Sydney and was stored in garages in Neutral Bay, North Sydney, Willoughby and Frenchs Forest. In twenty years it has never been opened, not once.

Paul and I take a handle each and lift the trunk. It is heavy, very heavy, and we need to stop and start as we bear it through the house. My arms are sore when we place it by my desk in the sunroom.

Later I walk all the way around the kids' school, hoping they're getting on well in there. I feel the sunshine on my skin, and aim to be fully present, mindful. I pick lush dandelions for the rabbits, just as I did when I was a child walking our black Labrador, Bob. Close to the house I see the range of hills in the west, the phone towers on top of Mount Canobolas. At 1390 metres it is higher than Ben Nevis, Scotland's highest mountain, one I have never climbed. My family were from a long line of coast dwellers, sailors.

Wide views; so much less domestic work with only two children at home, not four; time to play. I remember being a child, the pull of the dog on the leash, the sound of the rabbits thumping their feet. I take the dandelions home and watch as our larger bunny Lola bites at the end of a dandelion leaf and then nibbles it all. The end of the leaf pops into her mouth and I remember seeing exactly that when I was a child in Scotland. Lola moves next to a dandelion flower, nibbling the stem until the yolk-yellow blossom disappears, just as dandelion flowers did with Snowy more than forty years before.

Happy memories of childhood; there are many, and now that both my parents have died, can I enjoy those happy memories? Can I let go of the bad ones? But then, there's that old blue trunk. I will need to work my way through all that it holds and all that is conjured forth when I lift its lid.

)ℰ

On the final day of January, the kids are safely at school and I'm walking down Summer Street in East Orange. I am heading towards the mug of sublime coffee at Bills Beans cafe which is calling my name, and also towards the old friend who called my phone earlier. I love this wide street with its old workers' cottages, some freshly done up and sparkling smart, with pot plants and wooden chairs on the bull-nosed verandahs, others scruffy and worn, with paint peeling off the doors, looking as if they've never been touched since they were built in the nineteenth century. I had longed to buy one of these houses but just could not find one large enough for us. Instead we bought a teenager of a house, low-ceilinged but very practical, with four bedrooms and two bathrooms. Our house is from the 1980s not the 1890s, a home without history and with a truly appalling letterbox.

I walk past hedges of rosemary and rose bushes gaudy with blooms, some tied up carefully, others straggly and sprawling drunkenly over fence posts. I am almost at Bills Beans when I notice a rather grand old house on the other side of the road. This house has a name on a peeling varnished sign by the front door: *Ormiston.*

I nearly trip into the gutter. Ormiston! The name of the village I was brought up in, an East Lothian village twelve miles from Edinburgh. And I had been in Ormiston only last week, perhaps for the final time. The house called Ormiston is exactly the sort of house I had hoped to live in here in Orange, a home with heart and history and character, with high ceilings, like my childhood home, the old farmhouse Marketgate in the village of Ormiston.

'A large flat white, thank you, thank you.' My kind friend Sarah walks inside to place our order while I sit down on one of the metal chairs at a table outside the cafe. I decide not to mention to Sarah that I am feeling swept away by the name of the house opposite. There are plenty of other matters to natter about. Too many.

'I really am thinking of swapping Paul for a dog,' I say.

'Well, you'd be wanting a greyhound then, won't you? A rangy hound that needs one big run a day and spends the rest of its time asleep. That's Paul, isn't it? I've seen him at parkrun.'

'Yes, he loves running. But look, if I thought that a greyhound was the right dog for me, I would just hang on to Paul. No, I'm thinking of a fluffy wee dog that would dote on me. A little lapdog who would be my best pal and would always, always be glad to see me. A wee beast who wakes up joyful every morning, full of daftness and nonsense and exuberance, ready to bound into the day.'

'So the twins are becoming teenagers, am I guessing?'

'Yes, they will be thirteen in May and I can feel that the shine is wearing off me as their mum. The grunting has started from Tom and the deep, long sighs from Alice. I really do not know if I can manage another set of teenagers. I'm too bloody old for it.'

I really am too old for it. I was forty-two when our gorgeous twins were born. We had been trying for a third child, so one of them was planned but we don't know which twin is the planned one and which the bonus extra. But anyway, here we are. I have just turned fifty-five, our older boys have left home and the twins have just started high school.

And my husband Paul really is a greyhound. Tall and rangy and ascetic, he is a fussy vegetarian who does not care about food. I am a Labrador myself and all our children reminded me of Lab puppies when they were young. For them, each day was a new beginning, which started with a lot of tail-wagging and romping around. And they ate everything. But now the teen years are upon us and their tails are not wagging as they used to.

In our twenty-five years of family life, Paul has always totally put his foot down about getting a dog. He would set off for the airport, heading for twenty-eight twelve-hour days of graft in the Middle East and would say before he left, 'If I come back home through that door and there is a dog in the house then I will walk straight through to the garden then out the gate into the bush and I will never come back.'

For all those years I did understand. Paul is cut out for a life of peace, quiet and serenity, but between myself and the four kids (and the two cats we did adopt when he was away) there is almost no peace to be found in our noisy home. I would have impulsively picked up a pooch, but Paul's firmness on the matter had restrained me, and I secretly knew that he was saving me from myself. As usual.

But things feel different now.

'I have always thought I would get a wee West Highland Terrier, you know the white furry ones. My mum named me after a Westie that she met when she was pregnant with me. Maybe that should be the dog for us? A Westie would be loyal and sensible and would lie on my feet and gaze lovingly up at me. No one else does.'

'You are definitely in need of attention, I can tell that. Look, I know it's hard when teenagers invade the house.'

'It feels like two giants have come along, stolen my wee twins and are now just pretending to be them.'

'I know, but take it easy, Seana. Think of all the changes you've just had. This is no time to make any more. So you cannot swap Paul for a dog of any description, or even beg him on bended knee to let you get one. You need to just stop for a bit, settle in, adapt to this new town, new life. Get used to the new reality of Paul not working, of your mum having gone. Easy does it.'

I do love a sensible friend, a loving, kind and sensible friend. I don't tell her just how bad I'm feeling, how desperate. That old sensation of needing to leave is upon me. I want to get away, to escape. I know it would sound crazy, this urgent urge to depart right now when we have only just moved here. We have upped and left Sydney after twenty years. I have started all over again. Again. And already I want to get away. Again.

'I'm going to have another coffee,' I say. 'Would you like one?'

'No, I'm good thanks.'

'I need another large one. Feeling a bit dusty this morning. I drank a bit too much of a lovely local Orange red last night.'

Don't tell her how you really feel, Seana, keep that well under your sun hat. Don't mention the things you said to yourself this morning, the internal swearing and lamenting about the sore head, the yellow tongue, the itchy eyes. Shh ... don't say it out loud and she'll never know. Keep chatting about Labradoodles and sausage dogs, keep it light.

TWO

February

Orange

It is the first full week of the new school term and the kids seem to be settling in well. Thank God for children who get up each morning and go to school happily. Late one afternoon, I pull my two favourite frying pans out of the cupboard, turn on the stove and pour the olive oil. Here I am in this somewhat dilapidated kitchen, cooking sausages. Again. Bloody sausages. How many sausages can one mother cook in her lifetime?

From when I was a little girl, I always thought I would have children. Giving birth was always in my life plan. Looking back, I think that I always wanted to know what it felt like to give birth. I hadn't computed that, once birthed, children stay around for a very long time indeed. And you have to look after them, feed them, every day. Maybe if I had known how many sausages were involved I would have given the whole parenting thing a much harder look.

In one frying pan, I've got short, fat, organic, grass-fed beef sausages and in the second I have long, slim, vegetarian sausages. This is my family's cooking life, since Paul is a long-time vegetarian but the children are not. For myself I prefer to eat vegetarian but I will eat anything. Anything! And if I'm in the joyful position of eating something that someone else has cooked for me (thought out, planned, shopped for, cooked) then I'll scoff it with gusto, tears of gratitude dripping onto the plate.

Thin beef sausages, fat lamb sausages, many varieties of vegetarian sausages, chicken sausages, barbecued, grilled, roasted or fried like today. The kids love them, but I look at these sausages sizzling in the pan and wonder when the day will come that I pick up a fork and instead of poking it into the sleek side of a sausage I just stab it into my eye and scream.

In Sydney I have driven miles across town to buy kangaroo sausages and even crocodile sausages just to relieve my sausage doldrums. The tedium of motherhood, the rancid repetitiveness of it, is all there in these two frying pans. So much of all this mothering malarkey was never for me.

'I'm not cut out for being a mum,' I would say in the early days. This self-defeating self-talk only made things worse. After my first son was born, I kept waiting for life to go back to normal and it took about three years and having a second baby before I realised that this was normality now and we were never going back. And this new normal involved a lot of sausages. Over the years I've found my peace with many of the more boring and repetitive tasks of motherhood. I have hung up the washing mindfully, peg after peg, slowly and carefully. I have folded the clothes, concentrating on just folding. At times, too, I have been able to pay other women to clean and iron – God bless them all.

But, today, here we are again, the sausages browning, a tray of roast spuds in the oven, a tray of beetroot and cauliflower, too. I open the oven to check they're nearly done, my glasses steam up and the earthy, sweet scents of the beetroot froth out.

'Honestly, I deserve a mother of the year award for this dinner,' I say to the cats. But instead of presenting myself with a bouquet of flowers, I pick up my stemless glass of red wine and let a large mouthful tumble down my throat. One large glass of wine on an empty stomach is my go-to at this time of day, taking the edge off my maternal resentment.

Cooking dinner for the family has been my job and, after two decades of it, the only thing that amuses me is following the #everyfuckingnight hashtag on social media. But let's not forget the excuse my boredom and dinner fatigue give me to pour that large glass of wine and numb my racing brain with it as I cook. And the second glass too. And maybe a cheeky third as we eat dinner.

In motherhood, as I tell every new mother, it's the first twenty years that are the hardest.

〉Ｆ

I close the blinds to stop the February sunlight slanting in and sit down at my desk in the messy sunroom to start sorting slides and photos into piles: print, copy or let go. There are hundreds and hundreds to look at and all my Scottish family are there, the *weel-kent* faces of aunts, uncles, grandparents, and great aunts and uncles.

There is Grandpa, Mum's dad, who was an electrical engineer, standing with Mum when she was a baby. The family lived in Ipswich while Grandpa worked to keep London's electricity supply going during the Blitz.

Mum used to say, 'I was born in the Blitz, no wonder I'm nervous.' She was actually born in 1939 just six weeks before war broke out, but we knew what she meant.

Grandpa came from a grand Edinburgh family of shoemakers and had studied at Cambridge in the early 1930s. He finished his career as chairman of the South of Scotland Electricity Board. I remember being in his chauffeur-driven car with him when I was a little girl.

And here's Papa, Dad's dad, a short, smiling figure. Papa was a cooper who made barrels for a beer company for all of his working life. He left school at fourteen, delighted to depart as he used to get the belt every day for not doing his homework, except when he had chilblains. There he stands with Gran, shorter than him and looking very smart in a flapper dress. Gran's family were all Highlanders, MacDonalds from Rannoch Moor, economic migrants to Edinburgh. Gran's mother had abandoned her husband and two tiny daughters; she ran away with a man to London.

'I never knew a mother,' Gran would say. She was brought up by her dad and her granny.

'Granny MacDonald had twelve bairns, twice twins, and then the two of us after that.'

Gran was a good-looking woman too, always slim and with fine, pretty features. She was youthful in heart, mind and body, wearing hot pants in the seventies while she was in her seventies and not letting herself down at all. She had great legs. Gran lived until she was ninety-nine and was active and healthy until just a few years before she died.

There's Dad as a little boy at Portobello Beach, aged around ten; he's wearing a tam-o'-shanter and riding one of the donkeys, a wide smile on his face, open and cheerful.

In another slide, he is a teenager standing on a Highland roadside, holding his bicycle. Dad was the youngest of three children, the baby of the family and the favourite. Gran, Papa and Dad used to go on cycling holidays all over Scotland. Gran and Papa rode a tandem and Dad cycled alongside. They would stay at youth hostels or camp as they went. Later Dad and Papa built canoes and paddled through the Hebrides. In these photos, they all look vital, rosy-cheeked from the wind, healthy and happy.

Here is Dad again, in his late teens, trim and handsome, playing his trombone with his jazz band at the Royal Mile Cafe. Dad's eyes are deep blue and his hair is thick and chestnut brown, always parted at the side and swept back from his face in a classic short back and sides.

I open a box of slides marked 1961, the first year of Mum and Dad's marriage, before any children came along. There's Dad standing on seaweed on the shore of a Scottish loch, holding the painter of the double canoe. He's looking right into the camera, smiling widely, and behind him are low craggy hills beyond the deep blue of the loch.

There's Mum standing on a rocky beach with the canoe alongside her; she's wearing shorts and a waterproof jacket, her brown hair blowing in the wind as she looks off to the side, a cheery smile on her face. In another, she is sitting behind the canoe which is on its trolley. There are small houses behind her, painted white, low and nestled into the hill at their rear. In the next slide she is in close-up, her head turned to look over her shoulder, gazing directly into the camera, hair tousled, looking half asleep.

Oh, and here's a photo of Mum that I haven't seen for many years. I have always thought it was the very image of Mum before she had us kids. She is sitting on the grass at Dalavich where she lived in the early 1960s, in front of the wooden house, with a black cat on her knee. The sun is high and the sky behind as deep a blue as Scotland can manage.

Mum is wearing a checked blouse and a plain skirt and she looks excited and amused.

Nineteen sixty-two, and along comes my older sister Kirsty, and in this first photo of motherhood, Mum, looking around fourteen years old, is seated on the doorstep of the house, holding her sleeping baby who is wrapped in a lacy woollen shawl. Mum wears a pale pink mohair jumper and a houndstooth checked skirt. She looks into the camera calmly, a half-smile on her lips, red lipstick on, her hair in a chignon. She really does look at ease and comfortable in her skin. And on her left hand is her engagement ring and wedding ring, the hand cupped softly around Kirsty's body.

And there's me. I've got to 1964 and this first photo shows me screaming in my cot. Flick past that and we're on holiday, camping at Arisaig, four tents on a grassy field. And there's one with me in a carrycot, my huge cheeks rosy and round. Mum is dressing me. She kneels beside me with a little cardigan, ready to put on next. She is wearing a stripy green and blue swimming costume, her hair is in a messy bun and she's squinting as she smiles in the sunshine. A wicker basket holds the picnic and my sister is climbing the rock behind wearing a sunhat and a bare behind.

In the next photo, Dad and Mum stand beside *A'chailleag*, the small sailing boat Dad built with a friend. *A'chailleag* means 'the girl'; Dad built her when Mum was expecting Kirsty. She's floating in shallow water and they're leaning against her. In all these photos, Mum and Dad look relaxed, enjoying the sunny day and the beautiful mountains and moving waters of the Hebrides.

⚘

I drag my old carcass out of our lovely comfy king-sized bed next day and it feels as if my thighs, tummy and bottom wobble along a few seconds behind my skeleton. I've never been a slim person and I kind of believe that a bit of comfort eating can be a good thing. It is comforting after all.

However, the comfort of shortbread, haggis, stovies and Scottish breakfasts with potato scones, square sausages and black pudding, plus many bags of Revels, while working well for the brain, has smeared itself like butter all over my body and this is butter which does not melt.

I call my body fat my 'internal wetsuit' and never need to wear a real wetsuit when swimming in winter in Sydney or in the chillier waters of Scotland in summer. However, this inner wetsuit is less sleek seal and more blubbery whale. Something must be done.

It's a skill to know when you've gone too far. Whenever my weight hovers close to the obesity range, I know it's time to get a grip.

Mens sana in corpore sano. The benefits of a Classical education!

It's time to work on both the healthy mind and the healthy body. I join Weightwatchers and start to steady myself food-wise. Lucky for me all I need to do is cut down on the most ridiculous overeating and I do lose weight. It's my active mind: the brain uses heaps of glucose so just think faster and you can eat almost as much as you like as long as it's healthy grub. So it's farewell to having five Anzac biscuits for breakfast, and hello yoghurt and fruit.

Whenever I trimmed off a few kilos in the past, I always managed to keep drinking alcohol. If you don't eat too much, a couple of glasses of wine at night has a much bigger impact and the swirly head feeling is significant. As usual, I plan to keep a few points for my nightly glasses of wine, and honestly, who measures how many millilitres are in that glass? The wine is my reward for eating more wisely, for looking after myself and for just getting through the dreary domesticity of each day.

Now about that *mens sana*. It's time to find a new psychologist in a new town and I know that whoever she is, she will be earning her hourly rate. My mum has just died, we've moved, Paul has stopped working and earning. As if that's not enough, the older boys have moved out and, much to my surprise, I feel a tugging in the chest when I think of them. They are too far away. I had always thought that jubilation would be my only sensation when my kids left home. There is a tiny bit of that, and fewer sausages to cook, but the pull is physical, like someone has fused a thick rope onto my ribcage and gives it a gentle tug many times every day. Also, the itch to get away, to escape, disappear, waft off into the sunset, is nibbling at my toes and whispering in my brain again.

I make an appointment with a GP. She tells me I am anxious and depressed and we talk about starting SSRIs again. She writes me out a Mental Health Care Plan and a referral to a psychologist. I make the call, book an appointment, and then cook the dinner. Not sausages tonight. Not sausages but three glasses of wine. They're small ones, I tell myself.

You're doing well, Seana, only drinking a few nights a week, mostly on weekends. You should be very proud of yourself. But wouldn't you like a bit more sometimes? It's been a while since you had a real bender.

Get lost! The hangovers in Scotland in January did my head in. I want to feel good, I want to wake up happy. You leave me alone, I'm doing all right at the moment. Leave me in peace.

)ᶠ

Next day I brave the old blue trunk again, looking at photos from 1967 when my brother Callum was born.

My first memory of Callum is of him surviving a life-threatening incident unscathed. If only that luck had continued throughout his life. I was just three when Callum was born. He slept in a room that had no windows, just a big skylight on the ceiling which could be opened and closed with a thick rope on a winder. There was a terrible thunderstorm one night and the skylight smashed; glass speared down onto the carpet but none hit Callum in the cot. A baby's escape from peril. I remember Mum's white face and the glass being brushed up.

There are no photos of that incident. But I do find one of Callum in the garden at West Brighton Crescent, our family's first home in Portobello, Edinburgh's seaside suburb. He is a knock-kneed little boy standing on the garden wall wearing a white anorak with blue elephants. Do I remember him like that? I think I do. Fifteen months after he was born, Morag came along and next is a photo of her, a fat baby looking up as the trains rolled by on the embankment.

I remember walking to school in my first term, Mum with Mo in the pram and Callum walking and being so slow, me knowing it was him making the journey take such a long time. I remember him toddling around, his little tummy just the size and shape of a plucked chicken. It was such a perfect chicken shape that I wondered whether there could be one hidden inside him.

And here's a photo of Dad sitting on a hillside holding baby Callum on his knee, a hand behind his back to prop him up. Dad's hair is wet; maybe he has just finished a swim. He's wearing a warm woolly knitted jumper and his legs are bare. He smiles tentatively into the camera and looks so bloody young. Callum has only a light amount of fluffy blond down on his head and he's dressed in a pale cardigan; his legs stick out from the towel and his toes are turned up and it's as if he's staring at them in wonder. A little loved boy, a cared-for boy.

The next photos show Callum sitting between Kirsty and me on *A'chailleag*. We all wear bright yellow life jackets tied with shoelace bows at the front and we are grinning. Kirsty has one arm around Callum and so do I. He has a big sister's arm on each shoulder and we are so much taller than him. We're wearing our beloved terry-towelling sailor caps, Kirsty's white and mine's blue.

In these photos, Callum seems a shy boy. Like Kirsty and Morag he takes after Mum with brown hair and dark brown eyes, and has a quieter disposition than mine.

I am a mother of three boys, and how I adored them when they were small like Callum is in these photos. How they were cared for too. I miss my own wee boys. I see these photos of Callum and remember him so well, gentle and young with his elder sisters, who tried to take care of him both when children and as adults, but failed.

And I am missing Callum too, feeling all the thousands of miles between my home in New South Wales and his home in Scotland. I remind myself that he is not unhappy there, he plays his guitar, he has friends. But a slimy feeling starts to slide around in my stomach. He lives far from all his family, his sisters scattered north and west and me the furthest, south and south and south some more and then east and east and east, to exactly the other side of the planet, as far away as it is possible to get. And when I first left and then left again later, Callum was one of the people I had to get away from. Far away now, and those days are long ago too, but here I still am. Maybe it is Scotland I am longing for, now that it would be safe to live there again. Perhaps my internal itch is an urge to return to Caledonia, wear tartan, tramp heather on the hills, hang my washing out on sunny windy days, rush out to take it in when the rain comes.

)É

Later that day I place the order of service for Mum's funeral into a plastic folder at the bottom of my inbox. I shuffle through other orders of service until I take out Dad's. It has lain there for almost ten years. I remember creating it in Word and photocopying it at Ormiston library. In it is the poem which Mum had found many years before. She had tucked that poem away in a safe place and pulled it out when Dad died. I read it out during his funeral service.

Gone From My Sight

I am standing upon the seashore.
A ship at my side spreads her white
sails to the morning breeze and starts
for the blue ocean.

She is an object of beauty and strength.
I stand and watch her until at length
she hangs like a speck of white cloud
just where the sea and sky come
to mingle with each other.

Then, someone at my side says;
'There, she is gone!'

'Gone where?'
Gone from my sight. That is all.
She is just as large in mast and hull
and spar as she was when she left my side
and she is just as able to bear her
load of living freight to her destined port.
Her diminished size is in me, not in her.

And just at the moment when someone
At my side says, 'There, she is gone!'
There are other eyes watching her coming, and other
voices ready to take up the glad shout;

'Here she comes!'
And that is dying.

This poem was written by Henry Van Dyke, a nineteenth-century clergyman.

Dad loved the sea, loved his yacht *Penelee* and his sailing adventures all around Scotland and Ireland and even across the North Sea to Norway and the Baltic. When he was fifty, he took a year off work and sailed around the Mediterranean. This poem was perfect for him.

Ormiston, Scotland: 1970s

'I am the last Victorian father,' Dad liked to say. Eyes a little bloodshot, puffy of face, he would pontificate on the evils of the modern world.

'Women not looking after their own children. Men are being weakened. You feminists are trying to turn us into Americans. Move with the times? You always say I should move with the times. I will not!'

He could go on like this for some time, sober or drunk, and he would often finish with a flourish.

'And I only want men at my graveside when I am buried!'

Ormiston, Scotland: August 2009

Dad did not quite get his wish on the day we buried him at West Byres cemetery, just a few miles from Ormiston, the village he had lived in for almost fifty years. The weather was suitably Scottish, and the Scots word *dreich* was apt: bleak, chill and dire. Gunmetal grey clouds scudded across the sky as a barrage of rain fell. There were women at the graveside, however only men lowered his heavy coffin into the grave that had been dug for him that morning.

'Look, there's the wee digger that dug the grave,' I whispered to my sister.

'He'd have much preferred it to have been dug with a shovel, don't you think?'

'Aye, more traditional.'

The grass underfoot was slippery and the coffin heavy; the men held cords which were more ceremonial than weight-bearing while the undertakers took the real strain. We women held umbrellas overhead.

Jim McRae, one of Dad's building and sailing friends, looked down at the water pooled in the grave and quipped as the coffin was lowered in, 'Ah well, I always knew he'd end up in a watery grave.'

If only Dad had been lost at sea! In fact, my father died from a sharp blow to the head caused by falling down the stairs. No, he wasn't sober; he was never sober at the end of his life. That fall down the stairs was certainly not his first, but had proved his last.

Dad's grave had space for two, and after the funeral I asked

Mum whether she had bought it with the plan of popping herself in there too when the time came.

'Definitely not,' she said. 'I'd like to be cremated and then can you have a woodland burial for me, maybe that place near North Berwick.'

'OK, Mum, that sounds pretty definite!'

'I am definite. Do not put me in that grave with your father. Callum can have the space above if he would like it. I don't want my ashes anywhere near Dad's body, thank you.'

Mum organised a granite gravestone for Dad. It tells the truth, but not the whole truth.

With love we remember
David McDonald Smith
Builder, musician and sailor
Born 19th April 1938
Died 3rd August 2009
Dear Dad of Kirsty, Seana, Callum and Morag
Loving husband of Alison

Mum left space on the gravestone for another inscription but for the next ten years she insisted that her name would not be the one added to it.

❧

Before Dad died and stayed dead he came close to meeting his demise with alarming regularity. His sailing adventures had always been erratic, even during the decades when he stuck to his own rules and did not drink alcohol underway. The good ship *Penelee*, which he bought in the 1980s, was known up and down the West Coast for running aground. Around the Hebridean islands and lochs, running aground is not difficult due to the huge tidal range. Many passages are easy to sail through at high tide but become impassable at low tide. Dad would often have a tilt at them and end up with the boat stuck, going down with the tide to lie on her side. As the tide rose the boat would float off, all would be well again and his swashbuckling could continue.

Dad would take his friends sailing with him and go hell for leather into howling gales and stormy seas. We called this 'bachelor sailing' as all the men forgot that if they drowned, between eight to twelve bairns would be rendered fatherless.

Being out at sea was perilous enough but at least Dad was sober. He had fallen overboard more than once when at anchor, and yes, drink was almost always involved.

'How did you get that bruise on your face?' Mum asked when he returned from taking the boat through the Crinan Canal one autumn day.

'Ah, just took a tumble,' Dad replied. 'Nothing too serious.'

Later we would hear more of the story from a friend who was on the boat that weekend with him.

'This time it nearly was very bad,' he said. 'We had been at the hotel, eaten dinner and then done more drinking. We had all had a few. David was the first to leave. He toddled off on his own, it wasn't a long walk to the boat. But he got a bit lost and we think he tried to get onto another boat and woke the people on it up.'

He took out a hanky and blew his nose. 'Then, it sounds like David found *Penelee* where she was tied up alongside the canal bank. He fell between the bank and the boat, and he was getting squashed in between them. He couldn't get himself up, the fenders were getting in the way and he couldn't work out how to swim out from between the boat and the bank.

Fortunately, some people heard the splashing and managed to get him out somehow.'

It was another marvellous escape. We knew cats had nine lives; we wondered whether Dad might have more.

He had once been walking home drunk along the Tranent Road, on the road itself not the footpath, in the early morning hours. The postie was driving along in his van and he clipped Dad as he went by. But a bruised and swollen hand was all the damage done on that occasion.

Then there was that time when he had been drink-driving after a shooting meet. He had driven his Range Rover straight into a tree, with the front passenger side taking the brunt of the crash. The windscreen popped out whole and Dad had crawled out. The Range Rover was written off but Dad was unscathed. He did get charged with drink-driving; however the courts went on strike soon afterwards and his was one of the cases that were cancelled due to the backlog. A rumour went around the village that David Smith had bribed the courts to go on strike or bribed the Procurator Fiscal. That was a miraculous escape from legal peril. Not his first. One more life down but Dad always felt he had many to go.

'Do you think that because you were drunk you don't actually remember that time you nearly drowned in the Crinan Canal, Dad?' I once asked.

'Now come on, Seana my dear,' he replied. 'You know I've made a pact with the devil. Nothing can kill me. I truly believe that if I had never drunk whisky, I would live to be one hundred and fifty.'

Dad's impervious bluster was as blowy and incessant as the weather most winter days in Scotland.

Dad was the sun in our family; Mum and we kids revolved around him like planets. Dad was vast, blazing and glorious, the source of our heat and light and life. Gazing towards him, we hovered in his magnetic pull, moving always and only in relation to him. Slowly we planets circled our sun, tied entirely to his desires and movements. His life force was ineluctable, our trajectories around him too. Dad was all powerful and we were all powerless, circling and circling and circling.

Dad was charismatic. I always sense a frisson of danger when I hear that word. I don't know about you, but I have met many charismatic people and most of them were not quite safe to be around. Ah, but Dad could be so full of life and joie de vivre. He told jokes and hilarious shaggy dog stories. He conjured daredevil tales from Scottish history, kept his audience enthralled as to what would happen next to Robert the Bruce, or Bonnie Prince Charlie. Might Edward, the Hammer of the Scots, invade again?

Dad's intelligence was clear as was his work ethic and organisational ability. He was captivating and capable, warm and loud and very successful. His building company, Campbell and Smith, employed almost 100 people at its busiest, all dependent on his leadership for the jobs that provided the wages that supported their families. There was a lot of responsibility and Dad did not cope well with some of the stresses. We used to make a joke that we would head for the hills when Dad had to sack one of his workers as he would definitely get falling-about drunk and potentially dangerous that night.

Some people only saw Dad when he was golden good company; others saw his dark side but could brush it off, what with it being the 1970s and '80s. Only the family at home truly saw the full range of Dad's Dr Jekyll and Mr Hyde personality.

Dr Jekyll and Mr Hyde make such a good analogy for the problem drinker who so desperately wants to drink sensibly but never can, and who allows himself to change into his worst self.

For us it was the lack of predictability that caused the damage. We never knew whether an exuberant Dr Henry Jekyll or a malicious Edward Hyde was going to walk through the back door. We had to adapt fast to whoever arrived, and these shifting sands we lived on swallowed us whole.

)(

I know that many children of problem drinkers decide to never drink, and stick to it. Scotland is a country with many problem drinkers, but also with a high rate of people who are completely teetotal. A reaction to the alcoholics, probably. Why didn't that work for me?

As soon as I could, I started drinking. As young teenagers we were given wine and Advocaat Snowballs. All the parties and all the music and all the good times had alcohol tightly knit into the fun, the social structures. Looking back, I equated booze with merrymaking and relaxation even though I knew that alcohol was often a trigger for Dad's aggression and violence. When I started going to parties and to the pub, not drinking was unthinkable – everyone drank. It would never have crossed my mind not to drink. From my mid-teens until I was thirty I drank like a fish, like a barracuda, like a great white shark. Never questioned it. It was normal, necessary.

And you are drinking like that again, Seana. Every single time you meet friends, often when home alone, too.

Look, I was really good when pregnant, wasn't I? I breastfed the kids and stayed off the bevvy. I behaved when they were little, didn't I?

Yes, but then look what happened. It grows and grows, it creeps, and then you stopped for that year. But since then, you are right back where you were. Be honest with yourself, Seana. You want to be healthy but how can you be when you drink as much as you do? Couldn't you just stop?

No, definitely not. I can't. I couldn't. It would kill me. I need to know I have alcohol when I really need it. A crutch, yes, for my emotional broken bones. Every human needs a crutch. Look, I'll try to keep it to within the safe drinking limits. Fourteen units a week, I think – is that right?

No, Seana, it's ten standard drinks a week and no more than four standard units in a day.

Shit, that's maximum half a bottle of wine. If only! And that twice a week, with two standard drinks another night, being one large glass of wine. That's not much.

No, it isn't. But look, it's up to you. Those are the recommended limits but your life is your own. Do what you fancy. And remember, you deserve it, you need to relax. And it's not like you're going wild the way you did in your twenties, is it? You don't lose days and nights, sleep with random strangers. You never have to run to the loo to vomit the day after a big night. Relax, be good to yourself.

THREE

March

Orange

The start of March means summer is over and autumn begins. Here in Orange the leaves curl to russet and flame, but the weather is still warm and getting to the pool early for a swim is not a hardship. The outdoor 50-metre pool is a regional Australian classic, with sloping lawns on one side, a small stadium on the other and a diving pool at the end with a tall diving tower.

Early in the month I arrive in the dark, wearing my hoodie towel and favourite blue and green stripy swimming costume. Steam glows pale as it lifts off the pool water, wafting up into the blue-black sky.

I join two other swimmers in the slow lane, using my fins to help push me through the water, slow steady kicks and long pulls, slow rolls from side to side as I ease myself into the rhythm of a pool swim. So different from swimming in the sea where there is always water movement, where there is vastness all around you. This pool is a mere puddle by comparison but it has to do. Really, it's already done its job perhaps; I did not drink anything last night because I planned this early start.

As dawn starts to paint the sky in cloudy streaks of pink and orange, the diving tower glows and the row of poplars behind turn golden green. I am here for an hour this morning, counting off my laps in groups of ten, changing strokes and taking off and putting on my fins to keep boredom at bay.

'Too far from the sea,' I repeat to myself in time to a lap of breaststroke.

'Take me back to the ocean,' I chant on the return lap of freestyle. The ocean holds us while we swim, while it shifts and slowly turns, tuned to the moon.

At Manly in Sydney I love to swim over the rocks, moving with the water in time to the sweeping tendrils of seaweed, the shifting fish, all of us moving in the back and forth of the waves, back and forth. I love to swim in Sydney's rock pools when waves break over the side, whooshing us swimmers along with them, across the pool, diving under breaking waves into a foaming whiteness, the water light and bright.

Here in the pool, I move through the water but it does not carry me along as the ocean does. I simply stitch my way up and down, up and down. It's wet, it's a swim, but it's not a real swim.

Near to the end of my hour in the pool on this early autumn morning, a rain cloud comes by, showering the pool even though there are sunbeams darting down too. It's a remarkably Scottish combination of sunshine and rain and I am thrilled to be in it. There's no ocean movement in the pool but water is falling down to meet me instead.

My time is nearly up but this is too beautiful to leave. I swim in the rain, watching raindrop shadows bloom in concentric circles on the bottom of the pool, overlapping into fields of shifting flowers, a Marimekko print spread out like a watery carpet.

ЭС

One day in early March I begin to tidy up our bedroom cupboard and on a shelf find a small cardboard box which I packed in Scotland in January and carried home in my suitcase. As I cut the sellotape and open the flaps of the box, I am hoping that the tiny sherry glasses and two of Dad's solid crystal whisky glasses will not be in pieces. They are whole, and I take them through to the lounge and put them in the cupboard of the bar area, currently full of all our games, recipe books and my cameras. When will we ever use crystal glasses? We keep no spirits in the house at all. This is Australia: I don't know anyone who regularly drinks whisky or who keeps a proper bar in the house. Here it's all eskies and slabs of beer and bottles of wine. Such a difference to my childhood home.

I do not even keep bottles of wine in the house usually, one of my many cunning ploys to keep my drinking down to a dull roar. Wine is generally bought just one bottle at a time. I drink that one bottle and then buy another. There have been times when I have bought a few bottles and I definitely drink a lot more when there's more to be had. I could say the same for peanut butter ice cream: the more you have the more you consume.

Paul keeps beer in the house; usually he buys six cans or bottles at a time. But beer has never been my drink and even when feeling pretty desperate, stressed, angry, hungry, lonely, tired or all of the above, I have never broken into his beer stash. Which I often pat myself on the back for.

I can't be that bad, can I?

)(

How many people say there is nothing worse than walking alone into a room full of people they don't know? And how many mums have written on Facebook that they loathe the school drop-off, the mums gathering, glancing at and chatting to each other? But I think to myself: What are they talking about?

On this March evening these two things are combining and I feel thrilled. I love entering a room where I know no one because experience has shown that I will walk out of that room having listened to some excellent stories and made some new pals.

Dad used to tell a story of how a little boy in a family we knew had said, 'I met a little girl and she was fat and jolly.' That little girl was I, myself, and I loved hearing the story. As a child, I saw myself that way: jolly, cheerful, a chatterbox. Even now, as a somewhat emotionally battered and domestically distracted and worn-down mother, I still see myself as a gabber, a chatterbox, a bletherer. When I worked in television and now, when running a website, communication is key. Chatting to people has always been both my work and my pleasure, my hobby.

So I am heading off to the school's Icebreaker Drinks on this Saturday evening feeling very jovial. It's being held in the upstairs bar of the Canobolas Hotel, a grand old dame of a country pub which dominates one end of Summer Street, the main shopping street and thoroughfare of Orange.

I puff up the wide staircase and fly like a bullet straight towards the waiter, who appears before me holding a large tray of drinks. A glass of fizzy local wine? Why thank you, I will.

I look around and see that there is a large silver balloon

with 'Year 7' written on it floating in the corner of the room. I waft over and introduce myself to the curly-haired woman who is holding it and ask her about her family. Who does she have in Year 7? How are they getting on? Yes, me too. I have one of the two sets of twins in our year. Yes, a boy and a girl, they are about to turn thirteen. And how long have you lived in Orange? Really? We are brand new to town, tree changers from Sydney and enjoying being here so far. Absolutely, Sydney is far too busy.

Excuse me, I'm just going to get another drink from that waiter. Would you like one?

A whole tray of full glasses, red wine, white wine, tall flutes with sparkling wine. What to have, white or fizzy? I take both and the glass of red for my new friend and go back to chattering. Talking, gabbing, windbagging, nattering. I am flying, can feel the whizz and the buzz of the booze in my chest and in my tummy, excitement, sparkle. The rush of the first couple of glasses of alcohol and the thrill of talking to new people.

And, at the start of the evening at least, I am good at conversation. I like asking questions and I am a good listener. I love hearing stories, sometimes teased out one query at a time, sometimes in bursts of hilarity from a fellow chatterbox.

Another waiter, another wine, and I restrain myself to one this time. I know I don't need another since my last glass is not yet empty, but tell myself not to be picky. It's free.

I meet a lovely nurse manager of the local Emergency Department, always handy, and her paramedic husband. I chatter with a teacher who is also new to Orange, to another teacher and to a single mum newly arrived in Orange too. Chatting and drinking and chatting and drinking.

I can't help it. I'm Scottish. If there are drinks going free then a mad urge to drink them all comes over me. They must not go to waste. I must get my money's worth. Someone is giving me something for nothing and it is my duty to consume.

)€

What shite was I talking last night?

Next morning, that's the question that winds itself into a tight turban clamped to my head, squeezing my skull while my horrible hangover scratches me with sharp claws, screams accusations. What did I say? There's a stage I get to when I'm drinking when I flip from being a good listener to a non-stop talker. Did I let anyone else talk? Did I go on and on? Was I talking about myself all the time? Did anyone get a word in edgeways?

While blethering, nattering and wittering on are proud Scottish traditions and I revel in doing them all, when drunk I fear I become a painful bore. Was I slurring? Did I slump across any tables last night? Was I talking rubbish to all and sundry? Was I embarrassing myself?

Can't you remember what you did last night, Seana?

Sore head, I need some coffee. But I don't want to get out of this bed just at the moment. If I try to stand up, the whole room might shift on its axis and throw me back into the bed again. Give me some time.

What do you think the kids are up to, Seana, are they awake?

They're nearly teenagers, they'll still be asleep for a while. And even if they wake up, they can look after themselves. They're not in danger if I just stay here a wee while.

What did you do last night? How did you get home?

Let me think, let me think slowly. Umm ... I remember jumping into a taxi to get home. Tapped my card to pay. Came inside, I don't think I brushed my teeth.

Regrets and self-recrimination are my Sunday morning

companions. Usually I aim to jump out of bed to get on with something else and ignore them. Today, my head is cramping and my tummy is heaving. It takes me a long time to rise. I empty the dishwasher slowly so the plates don't bang together. I put the washing machine on, drink more coffee.

Don't drive, Seana, you've run too many risks that way in the past. Don't drive until much, much later in the day.

Later that morning, I pour myself some ginger tea from the green spotty teapot that I keep in the fridge, add hot water and take it out to the garden to sit in the sunshine. The ginger tea is supposed to keep my immune system working like a wee Trojan but I know all the alcohol I have been drinking is battling against it.

But honestly, the amount I drink now is so much less than before I had the kids. And I haven't injured myself for a long time. I've only ended up in Emergency through drinking once. And that was years ago.

Edinburgh: 1991

It was a freezing night in Edinburgh and I was in my late twenties. I was out with the boys, a tight group of friends of an ex-boyfriend, Neil. Newly back in Scotland from Sydney, again, I was living in Glasgow but spending the weekend in Edinburgh. We ate at a Mexican restaurant owned by one of Neil's friends and many margaritas gave up their lives for us. Neil and I decided to dance the Gay Gordons on Waverley Bridge and that was going fine until I tripped over. It was a very frosty night. We had carried on regardless, heading to a club for more drinks. But my ankle had started to throb and burn, so when Neil asked if I would like to go back to his place I gave the best knockback line I have ever used.

'So sorry, I think I've broken my ankle and should probably

go to Emergency.'

I actually went back to my friend Jeannie's flat and next morning she dropped me off on the opposite side of the road from the Emergency Department of the Royal Infirmary of Edinburgh. I hopped over the road and inside where I sat with other quiet souls, all of us looking sorry for ourselves. The Sunday morning in Emergency after the Saturday night before.

One bloke was as white as milk, very pasty, even by Scottish standards. His leg was clearly broken. Who were those two men in blue with him? We got chatting and it turned out he was a prisoner at Saughton Jail, Edinburgh's finest. He'd broken his leg playing soccer.

I also met two brothers from Ormiston – one had been in Callum's year and their sister had been in my class at primary school. Once I was seen and given a temporary plaster, they gave me a lift and I hirpled up the three flights of stairs to Jeannie's flat where I stayed until I returned to hospital for an operation.

All right, that had been a low point. But I hadn't drunk a single margarita since, and to be honest I had loved, loved, loved being knocked out for that operation to put a plate on my ankle bone, and had loved even more the doses of morphine I was given over the next few days. My middle of the night hamming up the pain would have made an actor proud.

And it wasn't as if I had nearly killed myself; not like Dad had that time.

Ormiston: 1983

A spectacular example of Dad's many marvellous escapes from peril came the night he attempted to fly out of his bedroom window. All of the bedrooms were upstairs in Marketgate so this window was five metres or more above the ground. It had been just another drunken night with an argument. Dad had locked Mum out of the bedroom. The very solid old doors of this farmhouse had large locks with proper iron keys in them. Mum had quietly toddled off to sleep in another bedroom. This was not an unusual event.

She was woken by a very hard knocking on the back door.

'Do you know your husband is crawling down the yard dressed only in his underpants?' asked a neighbour.

Who knows what had actually happened? This much-discussed event was agreed by most to be a genuine attempt to fly. There was never any suspicion that Dad might have been trying to harm himself. He could never tell us what was in his mind as he opened the window and made his escape. Dad remembered nothing of the fall, either because he was in deep blackout at the time or through shock.

Not for the first time an ambulance was summoned to Marketgate. Dad was taken to the Royal Infirmary. What was significant was that Mum did not go with him in the ambulance. This event had happened when I was in my first year at university and Mum was early on in her emancipation. She sent him off alone and later drove to the hospital in her own car. This became part of the village gossip.

'And your mum sent him off to the hospital on his own, ye ken. She's a hard wummin your mum, hen.'

Not really. She hadn't pushed him out of that window even though many might have forgiven her if she had.

Dad's leg was badly broken but, as Mum reported to me by phone, the surgeons had to wait until he had sobered up before they could operate.

'He was claiming to see green fish climbing up the walls of the waiting room and they did not think that was the best time to get started on the leg.'

Dad eventually went to surgery and his shattered shinbone was pinned together. He wrote me a letter from the hospital hilariously signing off 'Love in infirmity from the Infirmary'. This was the only letter Dad ever sent me.

In Scotland a cast is called a 'stookie', from the Italian word 'stucco' meaning plaster. Getting his stookie in and out of his trousers was going to be difficult but a Scotsman has a national and natural sartorial advantage in these situations. Dad wore his kilt every day while his leg was in its stookie. He hirpled around on his crutches, still going down to his builder's yard at 6 am to send all his workers off to their daily jobs.

Dad appeared completely undaunted by this accident and there seemed to be no lessons learned, no self-reflection, no quarter given to any whispers of introspection.

Naturally, his heavy drinking continued apace. I came home for the Christmas holidays and I will never forget the sight of Dad slurring his words as he crawled on his hands and knees up the staircase. Wearing his kilt, he dragged his broken leg up, yelping slightly each time the stookie banged, step by step. It was a sight to behold, pathetic but practical, Dad's sheer bloody-mindedness.

These were the same stairs that killed him, of course, but that was decades later. Back to our tale. Weeks later the stookie was chipped off and Dad could walk again, his leg withered and scarred. The telling of this tale of Dad's audacious but doomed attempt to fly became one of his staple drunken stories. He lauded himself and he laughed at himself for years afterwards. Until the drink made him forget that story too.

For me, it has always been a tale that told of our family's madness. But also, that small act of marital defiance, of not going in the ambulance to hospital with Dad, was a step for Mum.

Orange

I make myself a coffee next and drink it in the garden. Am I worrying about my drinking? Is it time to stop for a while? Am I getting out of hand again? Surely not.

I had been pretty good up until those Icebreaker Drinks, just a regular tippling away in the evenings, buying one bottle of wine at a time. A bottle usually lasted two nights, sometimes even three now that I was eating less and so getting a bigger hit from each generous glass.

What about trying to drink only at weekends? And yes, Thursday could count as the weekend. But Sunday wouldn't. Or perhaps just drink at lunchtime on a Sunday, get a little lunchtime buzz which could fade away by dinner, and then there'd be no hangover on the Monday morning? None at all.

I am cultivating so many devious plans to keep my drinking in check.

Should I stop again? Not drinking had never been an issue when I was pregnant and feeding the kids, had it? I would have the very odd one, but not many. The shame of being absolutely pissed before I knew I was pregnant with Jake had given me a fright.

In the early days of Jake's autism diagnosis, when he was three, I worried that it was that bender that caused his autism, or perhaps the morning-after pill I had taken the morning after the morning after. On one level I knew that these things were not true, but they helped me keep a lid on my drinking when I was expecting, when the babies were little and while they were very young.

I learned early on that hyperactive toddlers and hangovers do not mix. On our first New Year's Day in Australia with Jake when he was eighteen months old, I suffered horribly in the playground, eating ice cream and lamenting my boozing the night before.

Maybe I should do a year off again like I did about five years ago. That was at a time when I felt super stressed, like now, when my drinking had escalated and escalated, and when I worried that I had been so busy trying not to end up like Mum that I was accidentally turning into Dad. I do not want to die like Dad did, that's for sure. So very young, and those awful last few years. I don't want to die like him but even more urgently, I do not want to live like him.

}𝑓

This March, it is almost ten years since Dad took his final tumble down the stairs at Marketgate. He probably had dementia, alcohol-induced; he definitely was having little falls, probably strokes. He toppled down the stairs, was taken to hospital and died with Mum and my sisters by his side next day. I flew back to Scotland for his funeral, to make sure he went into that watery grave, that he wasn't just kidding and about to arise from it.

Ormiston: 2009

On the day after Dad's funeral I cleaned out the booze cupboard. In its glory years it was the centre of the house, the drinks were poured and passed out from there. Dad and his friends drank whisky mixed with water.

'We don't drink whisky neat. Who do you think we are? Americans?'

Bottles of spirits were kept on the main shelf of the booze cupboard. There used to be all sorts, with the most frequently used sitting at the front: several whiskies, gin and Martini. There were heavy crystal decanters there too. On the shelf above were the sparkling crystal whisky glasses, above them the sherry glasses and the wine glasses, rarely used.

In the lower half of the cupboard there were cans of beer and the spare booze, to refill the top shelves. Because you couldn't run out, obviously.

Cigar smoke and the peaty scent of whisky being poured, Jelly Roll Morton and Fats Waller joyous and loud on the record player, funny stories told by deep voices, the chatter of the women.

By the time Dad died, the booze cupboard was filthy, neglected. As I opened the door I saw cobwebs on the bottles at the back and a thick layer of dust over most of the glasses and bottles. Only a tiny area was still in use: there was just one almost empty whisky bottle that was clean, one glass, used in the hours before Dad took his final tumble and down the stairs.

Marketgate, our family home, was a Victorian farmhouse built in the 1880s, its thick stone walls still covered with the original deep layer of horsehair plaster. In the sitting room, to the right of the fireplace, was a painted wooden door that opened to the booze cupboard recessed into the wall. Most of the rooms in the house had a large cupboard like this. The top half of the door had a smaller door set within it, and its own lock with a little key still inserted.

A drinks cabinet, a booze stash – every family needs one. Well, every Scottish family with the money to keep alcohol in the house did, back then.

It was the job of the kids to fill the water jug. This could be a terrifying journey, from the kitchen sink along the hall and past the stairs back to the lounge room. Woe betide us if we dropped the heavy, precious jug.

'Do not ever suggest ice! What are you, English?'

There was an open fireplace where a coal fire burned at night to bolster the central heating. A fireguard protected the kids, a wooden coal scuttle was to the right, fire tongs and a poker on the left. Above, a wooden mantelpiece was home to an old carriage clock, family photos and the little silver dish called a 'quaich' which Mum and Dad received as a wedding present.

During his final years Dad would buy one bottle of whisky at a time, shuffling across the road to the Co-op in his slippers. Occasionally he would be banned from that shop, if he had wet himself once too often or gone over there already drunk and belligerent. There were times he would get into his car and drive two miles to the next village to buy his booze, sometimes drunk. He was an accident waiting to happen, but luckily the accident that killed him did not happen on the road.

I peered into the cupboard and saw a dusty mausoleum to the rum, gin and beer bought years ago and left unopened for a decade or more. The bottles sat there, as drinkable as ever no doubt, while Dad rotted away in his chair beside them.

There had been no drinking socially and no parties in this room for many years. A dust archaeologist could have dated the last one. No friends had sat drinking with Dad in his later years; he was by himself in his chair watching the TV whose channels he could no longer remember how to change. Dust also covered the dozens of VHS tapes about World War II which he could no longer remember how to load into the machine and press 'play' to watch.

I did not tell Mum or my sisters what I was doing; the solitude and the time it would take was important. This was my job; my job to put an end to it.

Starting at the top shelf, I took out all the glasses, carrying them on trays into the kitchen and lining them up by the sink:

dusty sentinels. Then I brought out all the old bottles, blowing some cobwebs away, sneezing occasionally, hands grey and powdery, slippery.

I emptied most of the bottles and washed them. Like Dad they were long past saving, unwanted, neglected, left untouched for many years. It was a waste as I was sure the alcohol would not have gone off but there was something very satisfying about pouring alcohol down a sink, the smell and the final gargle as it went.

Gran would have said, 'I'd rather see a church crumble!'

But I was remembering all the years I had wanted to pour Dad's booze away. I had dreamed of smashing all these bloody bottles. And I remembered the teenage years of sneaking booze out to drink alone myself, the times in my twenties when I poured myself glass after glass and necked the lot.

With a dustpan and brush I swept out the dust from each of the shelves, leaving a fine layer and many ring marks on the painted wood: vodka, Advocaat, Martini, rum, gin, sherry, brandy. The ring marks from leaks were so old they were no longer sticky.

Then I brought a bucket of soapy hot water and several cloths into the sitting room and laid newspapers on the carpet in case of spills. I plunged the cloth into the bucket, happy that the water was scalding hot, and gave it a half squeeze. Slowly, slowly, I wiped away the years. I dipped a clean cloth into the water, wrung it out tight and wiped again. Rinse, squeeze and wipe again. There was all the time in the world for this cleaning, this removal.

Another bucket of water clean and bubbling with soap was next, another cloth and then a final wipe down with a dry cloth. The white painted inside of the cupboard was remarkably clean and bright; that must have been a really good paint job all those years ago.

Next, I went to the kitchen and gently washed each beautiful crystal glass. The bright, gleaming glasses sparkled in the summer sunshine that was spilling through the huge kitchen windows. I replaced the glasses, solid decanters and water jugs in the booze cupboard.

Then I closed the booze cupboard door, and it was over. Music, laughter, a hundred funny stories, cigar smoke and firelight, friends and dancing; solitude, neglect and decline. Dad and his drinking were done now, finally and forever.

And in this room, peace at last; his suffering was ended, ours too. And for myself that cleansing marked the end of it all and came with great relief. I was grateful, as I always knew I would be, when it was finally, finally over.

)€

A couple of days after Dad's funeral, my sisters and I were sorting through Dad's sock drawer. We planned to take out all the kilt socks and to take them home so that our eight children could use them on Christmas Eve just as we did as kids. Mum and Dad's bedroom had a big wooden wardrobe which Dad built. It was painted, like the pale creamy walls. Nothing in that room had changed in at least thirty years. The views from the huge windows were of the yard and fields beyond, the windows Dad had once plunged from.

'How good are all his socks though?' I said as I pulled out a pair of woollen ones, fine and knitted in an Argyll pattern. 'I think I'll take some of the non-kilt ones home to wear myself.'

I paused, then said, 'Do you remember when Dad kept the shotgun in this hanging cupboard above?'

'Yes,' Morag replied. 'It was just leaning against the corner, wasn't it? With a box of shells on the shelf above.'

Out came a pair of long cream kilt socks, knitted by hand and made to be worn right to the knee, held up by garters, with the *sgian dubh* tucked down the left side of one. Each Christmas Eve we laid one out on our beds and by Christmas morning Santa had filled them up like long fat sausages. An apple and an orange in the foot, then toys and sweeties, magazines and a pound coin. As we got older there would be make-up, face masks and hair conditioner, Terry's Chocolate Oranges and £10 notes.

'I know, but don't look now. Can you see the belt there at the back of the drawer?'

Morag pulled it out, held between her thumb and forefinger. Dad's heavy leather belt with the metal buckle, the one he beat our brother with in the old stables. This happened several times but the worst time was the beating Callum got for shoplifting when he was about thirteen. And I was back there, in the garden, hearing the whack of the belt and his shouts and screams. I froze just as I did that day. My body felt like it had dropped to the ground even though I was still sitting. I knew what was happening in the stables, I heard the thud after thud and scream after scream and not a word from Dad. He had done his shouting before he dragged Callum to the stables.

Later, Callum was in his bedroom, crying, humiliated. Bawling at me not to come in. I felt as if my body was lying out there in the garden, even though I was walking around. I saw Dad sitting in his chair, drinking whisky, and I did not enter the room. Then Mum and Dad were yelling at each other and I tried to melt away into the wallpaper, to slip down into the carpet. The threat of more fighting, violence, ever present.

My sisters and I shared glances as we looked at the belt

lying curled on the carpet. We shied away from it, leaned away. There was no talking among us, no more laughing. We took the kilt socks for our children to lay out on their beds for Christmas Eve. We took a few pairs of other socks for ourselves too. Feeling nauseous, I picked up the heavy leather belt, that big metal buckle, pushed it back into the rear of the drawer and then closed that drawer, closed it hard.

Coming to terms with a death means coming to terms with the life that was led. Nothing that happened could be changed, and those of us still alive could make of our lives what we wanted. Dad's life was his; he was not all terrible, but he did some terrible things. That was over and now it was up to us to live with memories, to choose what to focus on, and to choose how to live our lives in the aftermath.

Orange

On March 9th it is Jake's twenty-second birthday. He comes to Orange to celebrate with us. A grown man now, still my darling and still dependent on us for many things. I feel physically ill when he sets off to drive back to Sydney. Not so much that he might have an accident – he learned to drive at nineteen and twenty and his visual-spatial skills are strong. It's more that my body is telling me it is all wrong to live 250 kilometres away from him. Paul joins him in Sydney as usual that week. He is fine but I am not and one night I break all my new rules about only drinking at weekends and finish off the bottle of wine I had bought, meaning to use only a little of it in the spaghetti bolognaise I was making for dinner. Easily done.

Thump. I wake at seven next morning with a bastard hangover. *Thump.* I feel as if I have only slept for about two hours, not the six or seven that I did sleep. *Thump.* The insides of my skull are being pushed out every time my heart beats.

Thump. There's a pool of cold vomit in my stomach and it wants to hurl itself out.

I'm a mess, I know I'm a mess. But I have to get up to get the twins ready for school. Butter bread. Tease pieces of ham apart – this makes bile rise in my guts. Make sloppy berry smoothies for them. I can't eat anything at all myself. Shit, I need to stop drinking. But how could I ever manage it? How did I manage it for that year once before?

Sydney: 2013

My year off alcohol had come a few years after Dad's death. Those 365 days precisely off alcohol had happened when the twins were seven years old and the big boys were teenagers. I do not know whether my drinking had escalated because of Dad's death, whether there was some picking up of the baton he had dropped. Was it because Paul was away so much working in Yemen and Kurdistan? Never the world's most natural parent, I had such big responsibilities with the four children. Motherhood was pretty shattering in those days.

My drinking had got out of hand in the run-up to the year I stopped. Just like now. I often felt trapped at home, always restless, and alcohol was giving me the escape that I had craved always and forever. That glass of wine on an empty tummy while cooking dinner around 5 pm was my shot of instant relaxation. It could transport me and chill me out within the comfort of my own kitchen. I could be physically there but not all there mentally. Drinking is a simple way to check out briefly if you just have a glass or two or four over the course of a whole evening.

Sorry kids.

In the months before I gave up for that year, just like now, when I got the occasional chance to drink a lot, I would seize it. Sometimes when we had people visiting I would get falling-around drunk. A few times I went to blogging conferences and got embarrassingly wellied at parties where booze flowed free.

The tippling at home was consistent too, but I was not generally going wild. But then at Christmas I gave myself a fright. I had a mean go at Paul on 27th December after days and days of drinking more than usual. I was looking to have a fight with him, could feel myself trying to bait him. Wisely, he did not rise to my sarcasm and barbs but my own meanness gave me such a shock that I decided I had to stop drinking for a year. This had been coming for a while. That year the twins had started school and I had been going to a gym, getting fit and feeling much better. It had been dawning on me that my urges to feel healthy and bright and well were regularly being dashed by my drinking.

The whole year I had off alcohol was hard. I went to AA, read books, chatted to other women who had stopped and, most crucially, took up ocean swimming. That gave me an excitement in my life that had been lacking, a challenge, times when I was fearful, times I felt brave. Getting up early to swim meant I was happy not to have drunk the night before.

'I feel so very healthy, and to be honest, smug on Sunday mornings. I get up and do the seven am group swim from Manly to Shelly Beach and then go straight to the eight am AA meeting in my wet towel, with an essential coffee,' I told my mum.

She was happy for me. Not that she had seen me drinking a lot around those years. I kept all that from her.

'So will you start drinking again?' Paul asked as that year of sobriety drew to a close. There didn't seem to be an edge to his question.

'Oh yes, it was always just for a year,' I replied. 'And I do think I've learned a lot, there are all sorts of other ways to celebrate, commiserate, relax. I will drink again but I'm sure I've got a good handle on it now and will just have one or two glasses of wine occasionally.'

Haha!

On day 366, I poured a glass of red wine. And we were off! Slowly at first, but very surely.

Orange

And here I am again, thinking and thinking and thinking about drinking. Worrying and wondering. I remember that year off so well, how good I felt, especially on those early morning swims with friends. But I also remember all through that year that whenever a shy thought about maybe stopping forever popped into my mind it felt like a metal portcullis crashed down. I would immediately feel like bursting into tears and an ache would pulse between my heart and my lungs. Never drink again? Give up forever? I could never manage it.

*

The twins are getting along well at school. They swing off down the road with their heavy bags and don't even complain about the heat. Tom is playing cricket and we watch his matches on Saturday mornings, enjoying the different ovals, most with stunning views across vineyards to Mount Canobolas. Alice is playing a different sport each week. They both enjoy the sports training two days a week after classes finish.

One day late in March we all go for a walk to Borenore Caves, an area of karst limestone with significant Indigenous history. We stroll by the river and through bush to get to the soaring Verandah Cave where Wiradjuri families came to fish and sleep. On the way we foolishly enter a long cave with no torches and Paul almost falls into a deep hole. I show the kids how to hold a blade of grass between their two thumbs and blow through it to make the sound of a bird. We pick blackberries.

'There'll not be many walks like this again, will there?' I say to Paul as the twins charge ahead of us on the walk back to the car park.

'No, soon they'll tell us that they don't want to go anywhere with us, ever, just like the older boys did. They'll be thirteen soon.'

'And we won't force them to do things with us, will we?'

'Definitely not. They need to find out what they want to do themselves, get jobs, be with their friends.'

'There's so much fun stuff to do here. The adventure playground, the waterfalls and rivers, exploring the goldfields.'

'I know. But honestly, Seana, soon they'll refuse to do any of that with us.'

For the moment, the kids and I still get to the pool often. They climb and climb up the ladders on the diving boards. They leap from the top board, while I watch from below. They splash and play, they ask me to race against them in the pool and, for the first time, Tom beats me in a 50-metre race.

They are growing, leaving. Teenagers soon, sparks of anger already flying out now and again, sarcasm, contempt.

FOUR

April

Shellharbour, New South Wales

April arrives and with it two weeks of school holidays and the chocolate feast that is Easter. We book a holiday house for a few days in Shellharbour, just south of Wollongong where Ben, our second son, lives. When term ends, we drive east towards the ocean.

At Shellharbour stately pelicans turn their heads to watch us as we walk along the path from the house to the beach, their old man throats quivering below their long pink beaks. As one, the group of these huge sea birds stretch out their black wings and rise up.

Alice and Tom and I are walking along past the harbour towards the open-air saltwater pool. Shellharbour once was a busy fishing town, its harbour walls a safe anchorage in the easterlies. Now it is a tourist destination and we pass families spread out on the small beach, hear the yells of children playing in the playground behind.

We see the pool ahead, built into the rock shelf by the beach and looking much as it did when built in 1894. Free to the public and washed by the waves, this is one of the many ocean pools that dot the long coast of New South Wales. This pool is 50 metres long, and painted blue inside with lane markings, with a shallow children's splash pool under shade at one end. The kids run off for an ice cream but I head straight to the pool, step out of my clothes, pull on my cap and goggles and take a deep breath. It has been too long between sea swims and I am out of practice at this. Just get straight in, do not delay, do not think about it, just dive.

Arms fly up, legs push out and I stretch away, feel my body hang in the air for a brief moment then crash through the surface, that jolt of movement arrested, into clear cold blue water. The salty tang of ocean air flows deep into my lungs, then slow bubbles tickle my ear as I pull through the water, finding the rhythm, three pulls, one breath. The release of it, body horizontal, arms sweeping through the air, then pulling strong through the blue of the water. Moving forward, earth and gravity gone, liminal I lie between air and water, legs fluttering behind, released from their daily major efforts on the hard earth, working now only to balance the main effort of arms and shoulders.

Back in the sea, back in the sea. What the hell were we thinking when we moved four hours inland? Too, too far from salt water.

Much as I love actual ocean swimming, diving under the waves to get out the back into the swell, then swimming along parallel to the seashore, I only ever do that in a group of swimmers. A pod. Lots of people swim in the ocean alone but I am too chicken. I swim with groups of friends and with the largest swimming club in the world, the Bold and Beautiful at Manly.

In the ocean pools of the New South Wales coast I am washed by breaking waves, might see tiny fish darting, look at anemones and shells; I feel as if I am part of the ocean, the chill and the sting of it, the breathlessness and the wash and the movement, but I am also safe. Here at Shellharbour this bright blue sea pool is doing the job. I rest at one end, look around in awe then set off for my next lap.

Scotland: Late 1970s

As a young child I swam in gelid Scottish seas all summer. We dived off the boat or threw ourselves off the dinghy to make the biggest splash possible. On the boat we would rarely wash; there was no shower so our skin was salty for two weeks, our hair matted and salt-damp. Once when I was a young teenager we were anchored in Tobermory just off the rows of colourful houses that line the harbour.

'Ahoy me hearties,' came a cry, so we put down the ladder, and two bearded men climbed aboard with diving knives between their teeth, laughing as they said hello, wetsuits gleaming as the water rolled off. These were the Mellor brothers who had owned our boat *Penelee* before Dad bought it. They were on a scuba-diving holiday on Mull and told us tales of scallop-hunting and seeing the ethereal spreading tentacles of lion's mane jellyfish from below.

I was thrilled and decided I must try diving. When I was fifteen, I joined the Scottish Sub Aqua Club and through my late teens and twenties I dived at Scapa Flow, Cornwall, and on an underwater archaeological dig off the coast of Italy; I mapped coral reefs off Sabah in North Borneo and then explored Sydney Harbour with its shy seahorses. I flew north to scuba dive on the magnificent coral heads of the Great Barrier Reef.

My last scuba dive had been off the coast of Karachi when Jake was a baby. I had joined a boat trip to dive the wreck of a ship called the *Himalaya*, where huge fish hung above rusted decks, and a spear fisherman scared me half to death. Later, an ear condition required operations which meant I could no longer scuba dive, though having the four kids would have stopped me too.

Starting to ocean swim had made me feel like me again, made me feel real fear at times, mental and physical challenges. But most of all, I loved seeing all the fish, the rays and the jellyfish, the odd turtle. It was a release that had long been lacking, a freedom with a dash of fear that I had forgotten, which made me feel vital again, aware of being alive.

As a child our holidays were first at the seaside and then spent sailing on boats. And those were the best memories of my childhood, by the sea and free, no fighting between Mum and Dad, no fear. When I swim I am a child again, free, wild, adventurous.

Loch Etive: Late 1970s

For some years we stayed at a house called Kil Modan on the shores of Loch Etive for two weeks every summer. Granny and Grandpa, Mum's parents, owned Kil Modan as a holiday home before they retired there permanently. Our boat *A'chailleag* would be launched from the small stony beach in front of the house. Painted white, with one wooden mast, her stays rattling in the wind, she would bob on the little waves, safely tied to the mooring buoy Grandpa had laid.

We would all jump aboard and set sail on *A'chailleag*, taking the tent with us, and would go off for a day or two up Loch Etive or out through the Falls of Lora to the little islands of Loch Linnhe.

On one day we sailed up the loch and anchored beside a river.

'Let's walk up it,' said Dad. 'Put your swimming costumes on kids, we'll go exploring.'

So we four kids, Bob the dog and Mum and Dad rowed in to shore, pulled the dinghy above the high tide line, sauntered over the mossy green banks and started climbing up beside the river.

'It looks like there's a wider area above.'

'I can hear a waterfall, come on.'

Callum ran ahead around a corner and out of sight. When we caught up with him, he was standing staring at the river which was running down the hillside in a series of small waterfalls and slides. The water wasn't rushing fast and there was green algae on some of the rocks.

'It's a slalom course,' said Mum. 'Let's slide down it.'

A whole afternoon was spent sliding down the river's twists and bends, whooshing down into deeper pools where we could swim around. The sun was warm but not too hot. We had sandwiches and bottles of water and plenty of time.

'There's a fish!' My brother tried to grab a lithe brown trout but it darted away too fast.

Dad showed us how to hang motionless in the water, our hands stretched down waiting to tickle a trout's tummy then flick it on to the bank. This never worked but it kept us busy in between bouts of sliding.

We were there with clouds scudding about, far from any roads and with no other people around, some sheep wandering nearby and plenty more to be seen among the tangles of heather on the hillsides.

These were the golden times, captured by a camera, printed to a slide, never forgotten. Etched in our memories because we learned so much about life then: such valuable lessons on how to thrive. These holiday memories were a counterpoint to the lessons we learned too often at Marketgate: how to survive.

On another trip to the same spot we pitched one tent on a flat soft bank by the river and Mum slept there with we three girls, while Dad and Callum slept in *A'chailleag*'s small cabin.

The next morning, a huge thunderstorm was brewing and we packed up camp quickly, watching the low black clouds roil in from the west. Everyone was aboard when the rain started, hard raindrops whacking onto the deck and leaping straight back up. We sat below getting damp from our own breaths. Looking through the portholes we saw lightning hit the shore close to us, straight bright arrows of light crashing onto the mossy grass. We could smell burning and the thunder was monstrous all around us.

Mum smoked a cigarette, face white, eyes white too. Later she would tell us about the real fear of that time: that lightning would strike the mast, causing the jerrycans of diesel lashed to the mast outside on the deck to explode.

'And Dad said, "Don't be so silly, Ali, that won't happen." But I knew it could.'

Shellharbour

How lucky we were with our West Coast of Scotland holidays as kids. Meanwhile, Alice and Tom are leaping into the pool here at Shellharbour and scoring each other's style. I often feel that the holidays we take them on are too safe, boring. They need more adventure in their lives. Perhaps this is the year for it? Mum died at only seventy-nine; that's only twenty-four years older than I am now. *Carpe diem.* Maybe it is time to be bold, to seize life by the scruff of the neck like a puppy, lift it up and give it a great smacking kiss on its slobbery mouth.

My urge to get away and escape is ever-present. This drive down to the coast has been good for me, but I still long for more exotic escapes. In reality, it is too hard to take a break on my own. Perhaps an adventurous holiday with the family will do instead. Perhaps that will keep me going, stop this endless itch, the urge to get up and get going and not come back.

And perhaps my drinking is pulling me under at our new home in landlocked Orange because I'm not swimming in the sea anymore? Last year in Sydney, Sunday mornings had a healthy routine. I met with swimming friends at Bilgola, all year round. We swam in the pool and then often leapt into the sea for a splash too. We dried off and sat chatting at the cafe on the beach. The perfect combination of exercise and friendship, nourishment for the soul, great for the brain. And all with a dash of daring, a wee bit of bravery attached.

The lure of the Sunday morning, the massive adrenaline buzz that I knew was coming from the swim, plus the serotonin and oxytocin bath for the brain when we sat together, talked, listened, supported and laughed. All that was attractive enough to stop me drinking too much on Saturday nights. But now, no Sunday swims in Orange, and a lot more Saturday night bevvying.

What might stop me?

Couldn't I just stop myself?

※

On the day we are driving back from the coast west to Orange, I pop off before breakfast to fill up the car with petrol. As usual, I use the E10 pump. Paul worked for thirty years in oil and gas and has told me that the more expensive fuel is actually marginally better for the engine, but I always use the

E10 because it is cheaper and less damaging to the planet because of the ethanol that is added.

Ethanol! Hold on, that's the same substance that is in all alcoholic drinks, in fact, that *is* the alcohol. I hear the petrol whooshing into the tank, my hand feels the vibrations of the liquid moving through the pump handle, and I can smell the oily scent of petrol. Ethanol! I am pouring the same thing down my throat as I'm pumping into the car.

Hold on, that cannot be right.

E10 means 10% ethanol, and most of the white wine I drink is about 10% ethanol too. What?! Surely not.

Yes, Seana, come on, you knew that. Spirits are about 40% ethanol, red wine about 12–15% ethanol and beer is much less. You knew that!

Yes, but I didn't quite equate it with what I've been putting into the car for all these years. Seriously, that cannot be good for you.

Oh, come on, it's not as if the other 90% of wine is petrol. That would kill you. It's only 10% of the wine, and it's the ethanol that gives you the good sensations.

Yes, Seana, but it's the ethanol that causes all the bad sensations too. And it's exactly the same substance as I'm pouring into this car right now. How can it have taken me so long to realise this!

※

We drive the long road home, kids bickering in the back of the car, music playing. Up and up and up and over the mountains, down the steep bends at Mount Victoria onto the parched plains of the Central West. And all the way I am startled by the image of the petrol with 10% ethanol powering the car as we drive.

But nonetheless, we get home, and I drive down in my

ethanol-fuelled car to buy a bottle of white wine, return home and pour a glass of 10% ethanol and drink it up. And my stress is eased, an immediate hit, a burst of relaxation in the brain.

Well, it was a long drive and bickering kids are emotionally wearing. You deserve to relax before you start the washing, the shopping, the cooking. Mum's little helper does help.

Yes, that first glass ... even the second ... and just don't worry about tomorrow. Have another glass, swallow your ethanol, don't think about tomorrow until tomorrow.

Orange

Back in Orange, the twins start Term 2 and we settle into our school term routine. That same week, I set off for my first appointment with Anna, the psychologist recommended by my GP. I park just outside the old worker's cottage where she has her practice, then open the door with its intricate stained glass. I close the door and see that sunlight falls to the floor in shadows of emerald, sapphire and ruby red.

During my first session, I explain my family of origin story, my overwhelming confusion because so much of my childhood was idyllic yet so much was horrific; then our migration, the four children, our eldest son's autism diagnosis, Paul's retirement, Mum's death, and the move from Sydney.

'It's too much, it is all too much. And already, I am wanting to leave, move on, change everything. And I cannot stay still, and I don't know what I am doing.'

I could gush for Australia, or for Scotland. I am a master in letting the words pour out of me, in telling my story. I can generally get all the basics out in the first hour with a new psychologist, therapist, psychiatrist or counsellor. Practice.

My brother's schizophrenia, the house fire, his imprisonment, the constant uncertainty, the unbelievable reality that Mum stayed with Dad and never left, Dad's cognitive collapse by age sixty-five, that I love to travel, that my four kids make that very tricky. My guilt, oh my guilt. I am so privileged yet often I cannot cope with my life. My words froth out, splatter all over the carpet, stick to the walls. And those are just the words. My thoughts are there too, swirling and whirling round the edges of the room, then becoming muscular and spinning into the middle, my mental state made hurricane, tornado, willy-willy.

Anna is a comforting presence in her room of pale soft colours with its comfy sofa, no clutter. And I have a cup of tea made for me by the receptionist which I hold like a hostage before me. Anna turns her chair away from her desk, she sits still; occasionally she types into her laptop, quietly. She is tall, and, like me, she is physically sturdy, comfortingly so. She has soft edges, a gentle smile and an air of calm that I have felt in various people throughout life and longed to have myself.

I say, 'I had a counsellor in Glasgow who really helped me a lot. She said that old memories are like jack-in-the-boxes, they can leap up and give you a big fright. She said that what we were trying to do was to take out the springs. The jack-in-the-boxes are still there and they will appear in front of you, but they shouldn't leap up and give you a fright like before.'

'That's a good analogy,' Anna replies, 'but some of yours still have their springs. EMDR is the best tool I have to reduce the trauma. It works.'

I have heard of EMDR (eye movement desensitisation and reprocessing) but do not know much about it. I trust Anna and we decide to try it during my next session.

❧

Sitting again in Anna's room, as we start to use EMDR with one of my triggering memories, I feel a hard lump of reluctance lodge deep in my gut. But I know I can try, at least.

I get comfortable and then Anna says in her low, calm voice, 'Think of that memory, go right back there. How upset do you feel on a scale of zero to ten?'

'Definitely a nine, my heart has started thumping.'

I am a child again, standing just outside the kitchen at Marketgate. I open the heavy door and walk into the kitchen. Dad is standing in the middle of the room watching Mum at the kitchen sink, the place where she stands for much of the day. Mum's head is bent forward and her dark brown hair covers her face. I think she is crying although there is no noise. Her shoulders are shifting, hunching forward with each silent sob. Dad appears angry.

'What do you need?' Dad asks me, without looking at me.

'Nothing.'

He is so entirely focused on Mum that there is no space for me in that kitchen. I am a little girl looking up at my dad. The portable gas fire is on, and with its oily smell the room feels stuffy and moist.

)ế

I move my eyes left, right, left, right, following Anna's fingers as she sways them from side to side. I have tears streaking down my cheeks but I can talk.

)ế

Without taking his eyes off Mum, Dad says, 'Don't worry about your mother, she's only depressed.'

Depressed – that's a very long word. I wonder what it means? I can tell it isn't good and that Mum is sad. Dad doesn't care at all. Why isn't he helping Mum? How can he stand there and say that when she is clearly unhappy? Why is he so angry?

It is all there, the relentless, endless existence at the kitchen sink. All that washing up, all the potatoes Mum peeled. The fact that Dad is only very, very rarely at the kitchen sink himself. The window looks straight out to the yard and anyone passing can see right in. I wonder if anyone will go by and notice Mum crying. Maybe she will just dip her head down and pretend not to see them.

⅍

I stop talking. Anna stops moving her fingers in front of me. My eyes stop shifting side to side. We sit quietly for a while then Anna asks, 'How do you feel about what happened in that kitchen?'

'I was just a little girl. I was so upset and confused and I wanted to help Mum but I couldn't. And I didn't know that long word and I didn't know what was happening.'

'That's right, you couldn't help her then. What would you have liked to do?'

I reach over to the box of tissues and pull out a couple.

'I wish I could have taken Mum away. I wish I could have waved a magic wand and made Dad be kind to her.'

'OK,' Anna says. 'Let's start again.'

My eyes start to follow the rhythm of her hand as it moves left to right and right to left.

'What else is happening?'

The dinner is cooking and I can see that the pulley high up near the ceiling is full of clothes that need to be taken down

84

and folded. And Mum is still not looking at me. I know that Dad doesn't want me there. Why is he being so mean? Why can't he be kind? I leave the room.

〴

Anna asks, 'Why do you think he couldn't be kind back then?'

And sitting here, aged in my fifties now, not five years old, I know – so I tell her. Dad was overwhelmed by everything and he had no patience. Mum's job was to look after the house and the family and he just wasn't interested. If she could not cope, he would not be able to work, and work is what he did.

I can feel my adult, rational brain shifting gear; I hear a thunk within my skull. It was all too much for Dad. And he was so guilty. He had to stay in denial about the alcohol and the violence and his part in Mum's distress because his whole world would collapse if he let the truth in.

I understand why Mum was depressed and why she could not cope. I would have been so much worse if it was me in those circumstances. I would have drunk alongside Dad and I would have been violent to the children too. But it was still wrong and it wasn't fair.

'It's not fair. It isn't right,' I say.

I tip my head forward, let tears fall. We stop the EMDR and I settle myself down, think of the safe place Anna and I agreed before we started: deep, long pulls of breaststroke at North Curl Curl ocean pool on a still, sunny day. Fish flitting ahead, no sign of the blue-ringed octopus. Cool water holding me up, my eyes dipping above and below the water, slowly with each stroke.

'No, it wasn't fair,' Anna says and her voice is soft and calm and kind.

'It happened to you and you couldn't help your mum then, nor for many years. These things should not have happened to a little girl. But they did.'

I cry and cry and cry, for Mum, for me as a little girl and for Dad too because I can understand him. He was a man in the 1970s and men drank; they worked and were one hundred per cent responsible for everything, and all his employees relied upon him. I do not say that I forgive or forget, but I do understand, and I am pretty sure that I would have been very similar if I had been him.

'What would you like that little girl to know?' Anna asks.

'That she is right to feel upset and confused,' I reply. 'That she needs to soothe herself. That her mum cannot help her and that her dad is out of control. She needs to cry and she needs to know it will not last forever. They are obsessed with each other and there is no space for her. I wish I could tell her that there will be space for her in the world, but not in that house, not ever.'

Towards the end of our precious hour Anna asks if I can think about that memory again.

I'm up high now. I am as high as the washing on the pulley up near the ceiling and I am looking down. I see a very little girl who is sad and upset and confused and I can sense my dad's anger. I can still feel Mum's distress but it feels more obscure. There is a light grey smoky haze over the scene now. The image is hazy, blurry.

'How upset do you feel now, on that scale of zero to ten?' she asks.

'It's down to a three now.'

I stay up high there in the kitchen for a few minutes more, feeling sad for that little girl who learned the word 'depressed' too young, and who knew that she would need to leave her family home if she was ever to feel safe.

Ormiston: 1970s

It was a normal Sunday morning at Ormiston. I might have been nine or ten years old. Mum and Dad were still in bed when I walked downstairs in my pyjamas. On the kitchen table lay leftovers from a late-night snack the night before, some cheese and ham on a plate, some dark rye bread just starting to curl at the edges, the butter dish. I took a plate from the cupboard and sat down to make myself a wee feast. Lashings of butter on the rye bread, a topping of ham and a slice of cheddar. I bit down, felt the cheese split under my teeth, the ham part, then the rye bread crumble into my mouth. The butter melted as I smelt its rich scent, cut through with the sharpness of the cheese, the meaty tang of the ham.

Next, I fed the rabbits, pulling hay out of the bags kept in the wee room beside the bathroom where the huge chest freezer lived, the freezer that fed us fruit and veggies from the garden through the winter. I scooped some rabbit pellets into a dish. When I opened the door, a stiff breeze forced itself in and I pushed against it to get outside. Snowy saw me and I heard the thump of her foot as I approached.

'Don't be a daft rabbit, it's just me,' I told her. 'No need to be scared.'

The hutch door was stiff but I heaved it open with one hand, then placed the food in the cage. There was plenty of water in the bottle that hung on the outside of the mesh of the cage door.

'I'll be back to clean the cage later on,' I told Snowy as I headed indoors to put the kettle on, planning to take a cup of Nescafé to Mum as a treat. I heard Callum and Morag playing upstairs and I knew Mum would be starting to get up now.

With the coffee swishing in the cup, I walked slowly up the stairs to the landing and saw that Mum was getting dressed in her bedroom. She was already wearing her bra and a large white bandage was wound around her ribs; it looked tight. When she stood up, I saw that she had a black eye, and the right side of her face was bruised.

'What is it Mum, what happened?'

She didn't look at me as she bent over slowly to pull out a drawer and take out a pale blue soft wool jersey. She flinched as she lifted it over her head and smoothed it down over that white bandage, over her slim bare tummy.

'I tripped and fell against that door handle, and I've given myself a nasty bump and some bruises.'

Mum walked over to her wardrobe, took out a pair of brown corduroy trousers and tugged them on. Still, she hadn't looked at me.

I wanted to believe her but I was not sure how a person could bump against a door handle and cause damage in two different places.

I watched Mum as she sat down on the bed to put on her socks. Pain crossed her face as she bent. I could see her expression through the curtain of her hair. I knew something was very wrong but I could not ask for the truth. I could not say the words out loud. I knew she wanted me to not ask any more.

My scalp itched and I felt pins and needles in my legs and arms. I didn't know what to say or do.

Mum picked up the coffee from where I had placed it on the bedside table. She drank it down slowly.

'Thank you, dear.'

She stood and started to walk out of the room past me, still not looking at me at all.

'Mum, where's Dad?' I asked.

'Oh, don't worry about him,' she said and walked down the stairs, slower than usual, one hand on the bannister.

}€

I must have heard that fight. I must have known about it. But it is completely eradicated from my conscious memory. How does that happen? When my sisters and I have talked about this incident over the years, my younger sister Morag has the clearest memories of the actual fight.

'I was sitting at the top of the stairs and I saw it from up there. They were fighting in the hall at the bottom of the staircase. Mum was on her hands and knees screaming for Kirsty to help her. Dad was sitting on her back, thumping her really hard.'

And Kirsty told me that she gathered up myself, Morag and Callum and hid us in bed with her while they kept fighting. She heard Mum screaming to her for help but she did not go. No wonder Kirsty's urge to help, influence, save others has been so strong for all of her life. She tried so hard to help us and save us back then, but she was just a little girl and she could not. She tried her hardest; she did her best.

Orange

On a warm day towards the end of April I sit in the sunroom, looking at a box beside my desk. What to do with Mum's old diaries? That is the question swirling through the sunbeams today, along with the dust puffed up from the box where twenty-five volumes were stored.

TUESDAY 23RD FEBRUARY 1988
Jim and Cath bought six wee fish. My fish appears to be growing a new tail!

SUNDAY 23RD JULY 1995
David and I went for a run to Melrose and got jerseys and saw Abbey.

THURSDAY 2ND JANUARY 1997
Showers of sleet and rain, but went for a walk along Portobello Prom.
Even though not at freezing point, cold wind off sea made it very cold.

'I really do not want to keep them,' Morag told me on the phone a few months ago. Kirsty WhatsApped to say that she too did not want to read them, nor look after them in her house. So a cardboard box was shipped all the way from the shores of the Moray Firth to me here in the Central West of New South Wales.

THURSDAY 22ND JANUARY 2009
Police came in the afternoon as someone had reported David drunk
when he had been down at the garage buying booze. He didn't fail a
breathalyser! Find that hard to believe, he is indignant and said police
apologised. Grrrr.

TUESDAY 30TH JUNE 2009
Made elderflower cordial and elderflower and gooseberry jelly.

MONDAY 28TH FEBRUARY 2011
Dentist – bad news, my only real front tooth needs to come out. Top
denture loose, not enough teeth to keep it tight so will have to get a new
pink one.

SUNDAY 6TH MARCH 2011
Bonsai Blether. Repotted cedar. Can't make up mind which side of that
wee tree should go at the front.

I pull out one of the Australian Conservation Foundation diaries that Mum used for most of the 1990s. Mum had a pen pal in Melbourne; they started corresponding in 1947 and for many years Mum's pen pal sent her an Australian diary as a Christmas present.

TUESDAY 12TH OCTOBER 1993
Got my back cracked – painful. Dr B said when he was finished, 'Good, both your legs are the same length now.'

SATURDAY 23RD OCTOBER 1993
Everything white. Walked Tosh along to the pond, beautiful, trees all covered with snow, but hazy and very cold.

I am loving reading the banalities of our family life and of Mum's life after I left home. She died just over three months ago, but Mum's spirit is with me here. These diaries are bringing her back to me.

Next, I hunt for the diary recording the days around my eldest son's birth.

MONDAY 10TH MARCH 1997
Went to see Seana and baby in afternoon. We held him when he woke up. He feels quite solid being 9 lbs. Seana was full of beans and so happy. It's so amazing that he was inside and then quite quickly outside, a complete new person. He has a chubby face and chin, huge feet and hands.

If family life had been all like that then I am sure that my sisters might have been more keen to keep some of these diaries. But among the dog walks and horse rides and plum-picking, Mum worries away about Dad's drinking. Until these diaries arrived I had no idea that Mum wrote so much about it.

From a page-a-week diary in 1992:

David went to Mike's then phoned Billy Orr! What a fool – he slept in Callum's room.

Don't know what David said but Kate is upset and Mike is angry with him.

David drunk and I went home before him and moved beds when he came in about 2.30 am. What a fool. He gave me a Valentine card and wanted to go to the pictures, but failed.

David stayed up late, came to bed at 3 am.

David has been pretty good this week.

David out at a building 'do', sat up late again, wasn't too bad but probably shouldn't have driven.

David came to bed at 5 am, had been asleep downstairs I think.

Is it wrong for me to place these personal diaries in year-by-year order, from the tiny Collins Gems with space only to jot in appointments, to the page-a-day and page-a-week diaries filled with tiny writing; that so-familiar, tiny handwriting?

Should I be sending Mum's words into a fiery oblivion out in the garden rather than opening random years and reading bits and pieces? Would Mum have wanted me to read them? Would she be angry with me? I am far too curious, nosey, not to read them. Who wouldn't want to? Wouldn't you?

Some of the daily activities she records are so familiar – picking blackcurrants, making jam – and I feel I am sitting at the kitchen table with her again.

Surely Mum would have destroyed these diaries herself if she truly did not want her daughters to read them? When Mum moved out of Marketgate and into the Stables after Dad died, she sorted and discarded many things. But she took the diaries with her to the little cottage she built for herself.

Cruel dementia moved into that cottage with Mum, but as she began to find computers and cameras and microwaves impossible to manage, she was still quite comfortable talking with us. Perhaps she wanted to read these diaries herself again. Perhaps she intended for us to read them one day.

I pull out a piece of lined A4 paper and start to read about one terrible night when Dad was wild, drunk and furious with Mum and my younger brother.

> *As I dodged behind the hall chair, he hit me and said, 'Go on, phone the police,' which I tried to do while he hit me. Got two nines but he yanked the phone off the wall. I still held the receiver. He hit me with the phone on the head and I felt blood dripping down over my eye. He picked up the chair and tried to hit me with it. I fended it off with my left hand. Struggling and screaming at him to stop. Said he was going to kill me and then shoot himself. He stumbled, I got away and ran to Mike's house.*

Mum got four stitches and Dad was charged. Did Mum write this to bear witness to the violence? Did she not want her story to die with her? Was she trying to work out whether to stay or go? She never left. What is the right thing to do with all the words she left behind?

THURSDAY 30TH JULY 2009
10.20 am. David to doctor. She spoke to him quite directly about drinking.

Three days later Dad fell downstairs, sustained a massive brain bleed and died in hospital aged only seventy-one.

WEDNESDAY 3RD AUGUST 2011
David died two years ago today. Didn't go to graveyard.

Just for today, these diaries will not be cast away, not burned, not even recycled. Not now. I will read them all, and I will keep sections of them, keep them safe, a mixture of the mundane and the truly dreadful. That's how life was. I shall make a scrapbook of sorts, talk to my own children about it, pass it down to them. Mum's diaries can be curated; the essence of them will remain, the truth of it all, much to remember with fondness, much to recall with sadness. A life to be remembered, in her own words.

SATURDAY 15TH JULY 1989
Hot 80°F. Went for a ride at 9 am. Beautiful – barley fields pale gold and rippling in the wind. Picked Morag up at 6.30 pm. Nattered most of the evening.

FIVE

May

Orange

May is a riot of russet and red, orange and yellow and glossy chestnut brown. Drifts of fallen leaves lie deep in the parks and along roadsides. I love to lace up my walking boots and go hunting for piles of leaves to walk through, shush shush shush as I move, boots completely covered by leaves. In Sydney there are few deciduous trees and no autumn leaves to walk through. That noise, the leaves moving under my feet, pushing my ankles through the piles, that's pure childhood to me. The colours too, and also the chill. Orange is high above sea level, high altitude wine country, and the coming winter will be dry and cold, frosty and bright. We live almost 1000 metres up; the beaches and blueness of Sydney are far, far away, and far, far down.

The twins turn thirteen in a flurry of cakes and presents. Their two big brothers come to visit, and we all walk around Lake Canobolas. I cook and cook, shop and shop, surprised by how quickly food disappears when these young men are with us. I used to joke that parents with just two children were complete part-timers. How easy would that be, I thought, when I had the four of them under my feet, in my car, climbing over walls, jumping in the pool. Funny how when life gets easier it doesn't always feel easier. You adapt to the demands. I do miss the older boys. Tug tug tug goes that invisible rope when they get into cars and drive east back to Sydney and Wollongong.

In the middle of May, another drinking event comes up. This time it is the Year 7 Parents Drinks at a winery just outside Orange, one of around thirty wineries around town.

'With thirty of them, I should be fine so long as the droughts don't destroy any vintages,' I joke with a friend. I am always laying out my wares: look at me, I am a person who knows how to have fun. Meet me, and I will be the life and soul of the party. Just add wine.

When the tickets for this Parent Drinks were offered, I snapped them up super fast, my fear of missing out on full view even to myself. Paul is not so keen to go.

'Too noisy, too many people, too much small talk,' he says as he reluctantly gets ready.

'I'll drive,' I counter. 'You can have a drink.'

My hangovers and early morning self-recrimination have been building. Driving is an excuse that should keep me safe from over-indulging. And there are always taxis should things go awry.

We park at the vineyard and walk down to the outdoor area where a wood fire is blazing and people are chatting. We pick up tickets to take to the bar for drinks and I get straight in there, asking for my two drinks at once so that I can feel the hit and then, hopefully, sober up before I have to drive home. It's one of my clever little tricks; I do it all the time when I'm the driver.

Food comes around, little bowls of curry and soup and arancini balls, but I decline at first as I really need to feel that warm hit in my stomach and the first rush of relaxation in my brain. Which indeed I do.

I leave Paul outside and wiggle though bodies to find my friends, chatter away and then edge off to chat to someone else. My heart is beating fast, really fast, and that fizzy feeling is bubbling at the top of my skull and I could just jump on a table and yell: 'This is living!'

This feeling lasts about an hour and after that the evening feels tough. I see people taking sips of red wine from their glasses and my mirror neurones kick in so that I can feel the taste of that wine on my tongue, heavy-bodied, dense and rich, can feel it slip down my throat, hit my tummy. I am craving that person's glass of wine, wishing they could drink it faster so that I could feel that feeling again. So many people hold on to their glasses and sip slowly. I notice, yes, I am always alert to what and how other people are drinking. I see a woman stagger slightly but she manages not to drop her glass. I see her look up at her companion, clearly not quite understanding what has been said. I know that person is a drinker, one of us. But I can't be one of us tonight and I've lost my early buzz.

So I start to eat plate after plate of the food that is being served. I almost snatch it as the waiters come around. I'm ashamed of myself as I do this, but I need to fill the gap that stopping drinking has left. I try a glass of sparkling water too, and it feels good to hold in my hand but it doesn't fill the hole left by my faded buzz. Food does though, the richer the better. The desserts come out and I eat and eat and hope that if I just flit from group to group no one will notice how many I'm throwing down my throat.

When I'm drinking I rarely want to leave a social gathering.

When I cannot drink as much as my body and brain want to, I am glad to go home. We leave. Paul has had a couple of beers and a glass of wine and is more chatty than usual. The roads are quiet as we drive back into town and there are no random alcohol breath-testing policemen at their usual spot. And that's a relief because I sank those two large glasses of wine very fast and although I ate a huge amount afterwards, you can never be sure.

When I wake in the morning, I think of the number of times I did drink and drive when I was young. And then of the times I know I have probably been over the limit more recently, not actually vomiting out of the window as in the 1980s but almost definitely over the limit. And then, a thought. Maybe it would actually be good to be caught and charged with drink-driving one day. Maybe that would make me change and stop all this obsessing. Maybe Paul would start to notice that I am struggling inwardly and am often more drunk than I appear. Maybe I should tell him about the self-abuse of the morning after.

But he'd never understand, would he? Maybe he would if I really got into trouble one day. Surely I would take that seriously? Wouldn't I?

Seana, if you are caught drink-driving then you actually will be banned from driving. Did you think of that?

Oh buzz off, it might be good not to be able to drive. I couldn't do the shopping or drive the kids around or always be the one who takes the cat to the vet.

But people would know. You'd writhe in shame whenever you had to explain why you couldn't drive.

Maybe I would do something about it. Could a judge send me to rehab?

Do you need to go to rehab? Do you want to?

Yes, no. Yes, because my brain is spinning too fast, and my knuckles are white with all this holding myself back and I worry they will finally crack and my fingers will all fall off with the stress of the clenching. But no, because rehab means having to stop and I just don't think I could survive, could live, without drinking.

※

The week after the twins' birthday, I open up my old blue trunk again and pull out some of my diaries. I wrote daily, more or less, from when I was sixteen until motherhood and autism wore me out when I was thirty-six. Since then I have only written diaries of each of the children's first years, little books just for them. The twins have a diary each for their first year, pretty similar entries, mind you.

I don't know whether it's a good idea to re-read my teen traumas or not but I am exercised by the thought that Mum died leaving lots of diaries behind. I'm not at all sure that I'd like my kids to read these old diaries, so perhaps I will read through them, destroy what I need to and keep some pages that the children can have once I am dead and buried. That's the plan anyway, but like most plans it has a fatal flaw, and that fatal flaw is that it won't work.

I end up flicking through page after page, day after day, totally absorbed by what I'm reading, unable to stop, even though I feel tossed about emotionally by the words.

SATURDAY 23RD FEBRUARY 1980
Dad had got in last night extremely drunk. Mum and I discussed him for a long time before lunch. She says that he has always been in the habit of getting absolutely stoned so it's not just a way of escaping pressures. I do not know how Mum stands it. I do know that it makes her very unhappy.

SATURDAY 12TH APRIL 1980

Mum was in a real stinker of a mood but no wonder. Does Dad realise
he makes her and us so sad? Last night I think he got pissed again
when he was getting his stitches out at Ogy's – he's lucky to have a
friend who's a doctor. (He was pissed last Friday before the Campbell
and Smith dance and fell downstairs. He grabbed at a picture which
broke and he cut himself and Ogy stitched him up.) Mum stayed in bed
most of today but what I saw of her didn't inspire me to look again.

)€

I recall often feeling sorry for Mum, so very sad for her. Which
is not to say that she was not also difficult and violent herself on
occasion. Mum lost her temper many times and she shouted
and yelled at us a lot. She was victimised by Dad and then, to
some extent, she victimised us. Luckily we were all pretty kind
to Bob the dog.

I remember Mum whacking me with a wooden spoon, or
giving me and my brother and sisters wallops with her Scholl
sandals, the solid wooden sole thumping onto our bottoms.

But when I think about it, and now having had four of my
own children, I would have been so much worse.

Mum had we four children by the time she was twenty-nine.
Only one of us was planned, Kirsty, who was born in 1962. Mum
and Dad didn't have much time alone together: one year only
and then the nine months before Kirsty was born.

I was conceived just six months after Kirsty was born,
when Mum stopped breastfeeding. Crucial error, Mum! I
only understood just how unplanned I was when my own first
son, Jake, was six months old. I realised that Mum had got
pregnant at this point. It was like a stone dropping in water,
that realisation. Mum stopped feeding Kirsty and immediately

got pregnant with me. Oh dear. Poor Mum. Poor Dad. Poor Kirsty.

Dad told us more than once that Morag and Callum were not planned. I remember him saying, 'Callum was a mistake, Morag was a disaster.' The story went that Mum had gone to the doctor when she found out she was expecting Morag and asked whether she could have an abortion but the doctor was Catholic and said no. Of course, Morag turned out to be the child who was kindest and spent most time with Mum at the end of her life.

As I sit, surrounded by these diaries which I bought with my annual Christmas present of a Boots token, I think of how Mum's life was and how I might have behaved under the same circumstances. I have no doubt that she did better than I ever would have.

The crucial element was that Mum did not join Dad in his drinking. How she managed to resist the temptation to drown out her own pain and worries I do not know. Did booze just make her too ill, or did her sense of duty, her care for her children, her love for us, ensure that she only drank moderately?

I have felt terrible violence towards my own children and three times I have walloped them. Sometimes I have lost my temper and shouted, ranted and raved and foamed at the mouth. I once kicked a door wearing heavy clogs and made a hole in it, a flimsy door, mind you. I kicked my daughter as she lay tantrumming on the floor. Just once. These were not my finest hours; actually, let's not be over-dramatic – these were not my finest minutes.

But imagine if I had been with a violent husband, and drinking along with an alcoholic husband.

Mum shouted and yelled at us a lot. Torrents of vitriol and

abuse, temper lost. She was so tired and so stressed for so much of her life and she let fly at us. It was safer than losing her temper at Dad.

I make myself a strong cup of tea and return to look at the diaries, to be catapulted back into the past. I find it easy to forgive Mum for the yelling, the nastiness, the sarcasm, the whacks with her Scholls and with the wooden spoon.

And yet Dad's violence, the fear of that, the consequences of it, are still there, deep within me, engraved in my brain and in my behaviour, that jack-in-the-box.

THURSDAY 24TH APRIL 1980
Got up a bit later than yesterday. There were screams and yells because Dad hadn't got home until God-knows-when this morning. They both went back to bed. Dad until lunchtime, Mum until 3.30 pm.

WEDNESDAY 20TH AUGUST 1980
Mo and Callum start the new school term. Mum and I went shopping. Bad night though. Dad never arrived home and the Range Rover was outside the Hopetoun pub, so we put two and two together. He came home quite early for him. Poor Mum didn't want to see him and she came up to my room where I was. She was literally shaking and very jumpy. Dad cornered Callum in the kitchen, then followed him up to his room where he sat for ages talking to Callum in the same 'fatherly' way he used to talk to Kirsty and I. Mum and I hovered expecting bashes and thumps but these never happened. He was in there for about 30–40 minutes, and not being nice to Callum. 'Giving you three seconds to leave the house' and 'I don't give a damn where you go.' Eventually he fell asleep on the floor and I got Callum out. He was very upset about what Dad had been saying and a bit shocked. I gave him coffee and now he is sleeping on my floor.

The actual violence launched against us is painful to remember but comprehensible. The isolation of it and the fear it caused; the acute trauma to the brain that happened – everyone can understand that, and the dissociation that occurs, which must be protective in the short term or we humans would not do it.

You cannot actually leave a dangerous place when you are a child. You need to get up in the morning and go to school; you still need to function on a daily level. Ideally you would be running for the hills or at least to your granny's, or you would be calling the police or the social work department. But you can't. You stay and you get on with it. Day after day, month after month, year after year.

It is the shifting sands that do the greatest damage though, the never knowing what is coming next. We ricocheted between privilege and terror, between adventure and fear. There was a constant underlying threat: no true comfort and relaxation. I have always needed big jolts of joy, very intense experiences, in order to feel real pleasure. Happiness and excitement had to get through a deep layer of numbness to get to the pleasure centres of my brain. Day after day, month after month, year after year, you are still there. You stay and you get on with it. You steal a shilling from your mum's purse and buy two sticky buns to eat as you walk to school.

*

The urge to get away, run, escape, disappear had been with me for as long as there was violence and aggression in the house. I took myself off to a Scottish Youth Hostel Association pony-trekking weekend camp when I was only twelve. Staying over with friends from school was always good, a relief, respite.

Leaving home, getting away – running away, really – was

sensible at the time; departing Marketgate was adaptive behaviour. It did leave me with a constant urge to disappear when times get tough though, and that restless feeling is upon me now, as May brings some lashing rain and windy days, some chilly nights too.

This wintery weather is ideal for baking Anzac biscuits and for reading my old diaries, with a cup of tea constantly to hand. I find my brown Boots page-a-day diary from 1977. Flicking through it, I read all sorts of Valentine's verses that we young teens used to collect.

> I may not have a figure,
> But what I have is ample,
> If you'll be my Valentine,
> I might give you a sample.

FEBRUARY DIARY ENTRIES

Nothing special happened, but I'm completely happy. I have such great pals. Me 'n' Alison were talking about when we grow up.

Molly the dog from the Wee House died of rat poisoning. I got an electric shock in Biology and the belt in Maths. Went skating with the Guides. It was great.

JULY DIARY ENTRIES (AWAY ON THE BOAT)

Had some good sailing. At night, we kids went to Seagull Island. There were seals, they all swam away except for a little black baby. It was asleep. We woke it and it was not frightened. Its mother (who was going mental) called it and it swam away. Kirsty is fishing in the dinghy now.

Sailed to Sanna Bay, stopped at Tobermory. High tide at Sanna, Kirsty and me swam in bra and knickers. Very cold. I dived off a rock.

August diary entries

Augabed my way through the day.

Eight bunnies born, I think. Covered in fur, eyes closed. Beautiful!

One bunny died, think it was squished. Went to Portobello outdoor pool with my pals.

There was a disco in Ormiston, we danced a lot.

Yes, I remember all those days, can almost feel the salt on the stiff winds that we sailed in. Feel the snap of the cold sea, smell the smoked mackerel. That diary from 1977 does not mention any fights at home. Maybe there were none. Or I didn't hear them. Or I didn't write about them, was fully inside our cone of silence?

What I do know is that I was happy at school, and had good friends there. We were only thirteen in 1977, enjoyed mucking around together and going in and out of each other's houses. Whether we lived in our own houses or in council houses did not matter. Yes, I knew our family was better off than almost all of my friends' families, but we young teenagers all laughed and played and danced at discos together very cheerfully.

Ormiston: 1980

I did not write diaries in 1978 or in 1979. I find the dark-red 1980 diary again; it bulges with extra pieces of paper sellotaped in, looks a bit battered. I turned sixteen years old in the January of 1980 and, reading the entries, I can see that I was miserable, depressed and struggling. Where had the cheerful teenager gone? Why did I feel cut off from the close friends of my younger years?

January 1980 diary entry

The need to get away, fly off, be free comes over me time and time again.

I don't care if I'm running away. I want to, I want to run and be free.

I feel really left out. God I want to leave so much. So yet another early tearful night whilst all the family are downstairs and I've gone to bed.

I definitely want to leave, scoot, run, go, escape from this choking place. Every day I realise that the Ross High School is not the place for me.

My 1980 diary tells the story of my escape. Some kids start drinking and taking drugs to escape a troublesome, confusing family life. Not me. I was always on the up and up, using my noodle to get the hell out of Dodge. Reading these diaries today, I can see that I put all the emphasis on wanting to get out of the school I was at. I was scathing in my diary.

It's really a hell of a strain being a swot in an ecosystem designed for apathetic idiots.

Cringing with embarrassment all these decades later, I wonder at the loyalty dysfunctional families show to each other. I had to get out because of what was happening in the house, not because of school. Yet, at the time, I blamed it entirely on wanting to change schools. We were all living in a world of denial, of course, and I was the hero child. It was my duty to succeed.

When I tell people about the school I was at from age twelve to sixteen years, I often say that I was frequently scared there, certainly far too scared to go into the toilets.

'There were tough girls in there smoking. We just had to hang on.'

There were fights in the playground and I can remember kids having legs and arms broken. But there were some excellent teachers at that school. These were the days when teachers used the belt, or tawse, a leather strap often carried over the shoulder under the jacket. I only had the belt a couple of times, being a studious if chatty child.

There were 200 pupils in my year group at the Ross, and in our second year thirty of us were sent off to do Latin while the remaining 170 did social studies. I think they studied sex education, but we smarter ones were thought to be such swots that no one would ever want to have sex with us. Or perhaps we were smart enough to find contraception for ourselves and to work out what to do if we found ourselves in extremis, with the bonus that we would know what *in extremis* meant if we were in it.

At the end of that year I asked our bearded and dandruff-shouldered Latin teacher, Mr Howie, a question.

'I'm going to keep on with Latin next year. Could I do Greek next year too, sir?'

'I don't think we have a class for Greek. No one has done it at this school. You need to talk to the headmaster.'

So I did: I went off to make an appointment with Mr Eunson, tall, dark and forbidding in his academic robes, his jet-black hair cut severely around his square head. When I saw Darth Vader in Star Wars, I knew exactly whom he'd been modelled on.

'Greek?' he said.

'Yes, sir, I'd like to learn Ancient Greek.' I was trying not to stare at the licks of spittle that always hung around the corners of his mouth.

'Well, I'll see if I can make that work for you.'

So the next year, my third at high school, I started learning Greek, with some one-to-one lessons and a book to work through on my own. Big thanks to the Ross High School for allowing me to set up my own extension program.

After that school year, in the summer holidays, I went to a Greek Summer School at the University of Edinburgh and met some other state school pupils who were studying Greek. Well, there were only two of them, making three of us among many more private school kids. I was put into the beginners' group and loved reinforcing what I had learnt and also sitting in the beautiful gardens of George Square surrounded by the historic and new buildings of the university. I loved getting the bus in to Queen Street Station and then walking up through the streets of Edinburgh, knowing these streets and these walks were the start of me getting far, far away from Marketgate and Ormiston.

I read my 1980 diaries now and feel sad for the teenager I was. What a sorry tale of woe. I was crying many nights, spending many hours alone in my bedroom in my lamentations.

⅟

Ormiston: 1979, 1980

The Scotsman newspaper was where I found my escape one winter's day. I don't need to read the diary. I can remember that day very well.

The sky was grey, no surprise since it was early winter and was grey for almost all of the short daylight hours. I was fifteen and my mood was as grimy as the weather. I had been unhappy and grumpy for months. Some days the sky and I wore a light grey blanket of fine wool, draped high above, still giving some light. On others there was a dark grey blanket of rough, thick wool, coarsely crocheted, darker where stitches were missing, drooping in places, wet wool sagging low, waterlogged and about to unload in torrential rain.

Sometimes the greys were all around us: near the ground there was fog with fine rain, or dark-grey sheeting rain slashing, below a moaning grey-black sky gushing its lament.

On this day, I splashed my way from the school bus to the back door, yanked off my coat and shoes and hung them to dry. Then I made a mug of tea, pulled the biscuit tin from the cupboard, sat down and opened *The Scotsman*. I read the whole paper daily in those days, but the classified adverts at the back were my favourite section. Donkeys for sale, horses, dogs, cars. Funeral notices: old people, teenagers, young men and the occasional baby or toddler. Meetings were called, long-lost relatives sought, a forty-year school reunion announced. The jobs section told me all that I could be when I grew up: lift operator, head of chemistry, mechanical engineer, head of operations; a vet was needed on the Isle of Skye, a journalist for Forfar (that was appealing – journalism was a licence to ask questions and the chance to see my name in print).

On that day, I saw two adverts for scholarships to private schools. One was for Lomond School in Helensburgh and the other for Gordonstoun near Inverness. I knew Helensburgh as my grandparents had lived there for a few years, and my youngest aunt had gone to the girls' school there which had merged with a boys' school to become Lomond. And Gordonstoun was where Prince Charles had gone. It was famous for its hearty outdoor activities.

I went to the dining room and found Mum's writing paper, then wrote to the schools as each advert advised. I didn't think about it, I just did it; I applied for both scholarships just like that. I had read plenty of boarding-school books when I was younger, so I was all up to date with tuckboxes and midnight adventures. I had no further concept, only that a boarding school meant going away and, poor me, I didn't even know all the reasons why 'away' was such an attractive and alluring destination.

I took the letters, put on my coat and hopped over the puddles to the post office, bought stamps and gave the envelopes a kiss before I posted them in the big red postbox. I looked for a sign, a ray of golden sunlight beaming down to illuminate the top of the postbox through a ragged hole in the sodden blanket of grey sky maybe; but no, the rain fell and fell and I splashed my way home.

And I told no one about those two letters. I just knew that I had thrown two dice and I couldn't see where they had spun or what numbers might turn up.

About a week later, two letters fell through the letterbox. Gordonstoun asked me to sit a test which they would send to my current school. Lomond asked me to go over to the west to sit exams there. It was at that point I had to tell Mum and Dad what I had done.

⁑

Mum and Dad did not believe in private schools at all; I knew that. But they did agree to take me to sit the exams at Lomond School. No one, not one person, ever left the Ross High to go to a private school in those days. Private schools were for Edinburgh folk, not us here in East Lothian. So I only told one friend about it.

'I think you are mad to go so far away just because you want to do more schoolwork,' she told me. 'Couldn't the teachers here give you more homework?'

'I am hating it here. But I feel so nervous about the interview tomorrow, and Mum says I wouldn't like it at boarding school.'

'Well, hopefully they'll be nice to you.'

'I wish I didn't have so many pimples at the moment. It's not even the spots, my face doesn't feel confident. I will try to be very smart and give a firm handshake.'

I must have given a very firm handshake as a letter came offering me a scholarship place. This would cover half the tuition fees but not the boarding fees.

'Look, Seana,' Dad said, 'if you really want to go then I'll pay the rest of the fees for you. You've done well to get the scholarship.'

You can say what you like about Dad (and I frequently did) but he was very generous to pay these fees. Spending two years at Lomond School was to alter everything for me.

⁂

The Guidance Department at the Ross High had offices off the main hall. Guidance was usually frequented by children in trouble of some kind, either at home or at school, in trouble or causing trouble. I had never been there.

The big hall was used for sport and for assemblies with the headmaster. I had received prizes up on the stage, had been a member of the chorus in *Annie Get Your Gun*. Most recently I had sat the scholarship test for Gordonstoun in the hall. I had not got in there but I had the place at Lomond.

I knew Mrs Mitchell, as she was the teacher taking a group of school children, including me, in the school minivan for a three-week visit to Greece via many other countries. We had been to her house to chat about the Greece trip but I'd never seen her in her own Guidance office. I wondered why I'd been called in. Was I pregnant? Was my dad going to jail? Had I got into trouble with a teacher or some other kids without even realising it?

'Come in, Seana. Here, take a seat. No need to look so worried,' she said.

I sat down on the chair across the desk from Mrs Mitchell and she finished shuffling some paper into a neat pile.

'So I must congratulate you on getting the place at the new school. Are you keen to go?'

'Yes, it seems a good school and I think I'll like boarding.'

'Can I ask you, Seana, are there any particular reasons why you want to go to boarding school?'

What did she mean? Was there a right answer to this?

'I think I'll like being with other girls and I think I'll get more work and study done there.'

'Is there anything you'd like to talk about?' Mrs Mitchell's face was full of kind concern.

What was she going on about?

'How are things at home? Are there any problems there?'

'No, it's all just the same. Callum is getting into trouble but it's all just the same.'

'You know you can tell me anything and it will be confidential.'

Why was she asking this? I had no idea.

'Don't think so,' I said. 'I've been pretty miserable at school this year. I think I will be better off at Lomond.'

'Well, if there is anything you ever want to talk to me about, if there are problems at home, you know you can come to me any time.'

I walked out of that meeting and went back to class with no idea why I'd been asked in and feeling quite confused about what she had been asking me. I wondered why she was asking about home.

Today, sitting here with my 1980 diary, with the hindsight of many years, I can see that she felt or knew that all was not well in our family and she knew, when I didn't, that it was home I needed to leave, not school. In fact, it took me decades to realise that she was probably gently asking me if there was any sexual or physical abuse going on.

For me, there was no sexual abuse at home but there was certainly unhappiness, aggression, fighting. I was able to write about it in my 1980 diary, but I was unable to speak about it. Around the kitchen table we did obsess about Dad, talk about his drinking, but Mum never, ever would discuss his aggression and violence, nor her own towards us.

But I wrote it down.

Mum and Kirsty did not mince their words about their disapproval of me going away to a private school.

'You are such a snob, Seana. You think you are better than everyone else at Ross High,' Kirsty told me.

'You're right, maybe. Maybe I do feel I'm better – for sure I know I want to work harder at my schoolwork. Leave me alone,' I said. 'I've had a terrible day at school, hardly anyone spoke to me. Could you give me some never-known-before sympathy for once?'

Mum was at the cooker and turned round to say, 'Your problems are all your own. You are being stuck up, a snob. There are perfectly nice people at school.'

I felt my face go scarlet and start to throb. 'You are just calling me the same thing they call me at school. It really hurts me. Leave me alone.'

I pushed the chair back and stood up. 'You really hate me, don't you, Kirsty? I don't care.'

'Well, you might be even more unhappy than you are here.'

'I don't expect a bed of roses but I don't think I could be unhappier than I am now.'

And I wasn't unhappier at Lomond. Far from it.

⅊

Decades later my gratitude flows golden and strong to the two girls whom I shared a room with. A farmer's daughter and the daughter of expats in Korea, they had been boarding since they were ten. Both home-loving and kind girls, they welcomed me and made me feel comfortable and accepted.

Our boarding house was called Ashmount, a grand Victorian building on the street behind the school itself. Huge trees and thick garden walls and rhododendrons, grand and imposing. We girls were all sixteen to eighteen years old and we had a fair bit of autonomy under the care of Deputy Principal Mr Higgs and his wife. We made our own breakfasts and cooked dinners for ourselves at the weekend. We could have our friends in for coffee-and-toast festivals. There was endless chattering, laughing and gossiping.

I thrived in that first term, loved the challenge of having more work to do, studied hard. I could tell I was one of the brighter students at the school even though my English teacher had not introduced me to the class that way.

'And here's Seana,' she said, 'who has started to board here today. And she has never studied a Shakespeare play in her life. Imagine that.'

Yes, imagine that. The teachers at the Ross High had said they were sick of Shakespeare so they never taught it. Now we were straight into *Hamlet* and each line was meticulously explained and discussed.

I was studying English, French, Latin, Greek and History, and each involved a lot of explanation and a lot of learning things off by heart and a lot of homework. I was again the only person doing Greek in the school. My doddery and delightful teacher gave me work to do and supervised me one-to-one a few periods a week. I loved the attention.

I was surprised to be summoned downstairs to talk to Mr Higgs one evening. Had I done something wrong? Had someone reported me for the odd smoking session at the back door?

'Now, this is a real cup of English tea,' said Mr Higgs, his smiley face and balding head so familiar already. So sensible. So stable. 'One spoonful of tea per person and one for the pot, into a warmed teapot of course, and leave for at least three minutes.'

'Shall I pour the milk first?'

'No, milk in afterwards; this is a proper cup of tea, Seana.'

We sat down on the chairs in front of the gas fire.

'So, I think we should talk about your Highers and about after that.'

'Yes, it is still a way off but I will study over Christmas.'

'Good,' Mr Higgs poured out the amber tea, stirred in the milk.

'The thing is, we think that you should try for Oxford, the Scottish scheme. You would go there for interviews at the start of Sixth Year. But you would need to do really well in the Highers.'

'Five As?'

'Yes, that would be ideal. Do you think you could do that?'

'Yes, or at least try. I'm working hard and I can keep going. The teachers are good here. But I never expected this.'

'Well, keep working hard, and then why don't you come down and watch *Brideshead Revisited* with us? We'll give you a preview; well, a bit of one.'

Opportunity, grasped straight away. I made the decision fast and never let go of it. I would always have studied but that got me excited and even more motivated.

When I said to Mum that I was going to try for a place at Oxford if my Highers were good enough, she wasn't too impressed.

'Well,' she sniffed. 'What's wrong with a Scottish university?'

Orange

The end of May approaches and an ocean-swimming friend from Sydney is in Orange for the weekend so we have arranged to meet for dinner. Kate and I have ducked under foaming waves, met out beyond them to swim to further beaches. Still, we don't really know each other very well and we have never been out together before.

I arrive at Kate's hotel room and see that she's one glass of wine into a bottle already and a gentle fizzing starts deep in my brain.

Great, she's a drinker. Thank God I got a lift into town and will walk home. We are on.

There are so many Scottish euphemisms.

'Does he take a drink?'

'Does she like a drink?'

This is code for 'Does this person go for it with alcohol?' and very often those of us who do go for it don't even need to ask. We can see the drinker in the person standing in front of us. And this evening I can see that Kate is up for a few drinks, to coin another euphemism. This means that I can drink as much as I like and she won't be judging; in fact she might be grateful that she can drink as much as she likes and I will not be showing her up by just having one or two. All this with no words spoken.

We sink the bottle and wend our way through the windy streets to Sweet Sour Salt, one of Orange's best restaurants and one with an excellent wine list. I let Kate choose as I have never got beyond going for the cheapest or second cheapest on any wine list. If I'm trying to mask my ignorance I go for a local wine and hope for the best.

There is plenty to talk about: the last swimming season in Sydney, the conditions on the day of the Big Swim and the day of the Bondi Roughwater.

The wine flows and we match each other glass for glass. I am feeling so very jolly and exuberant, happy to be with a friend who can chat as much as I do. Like me, Kate drinks fast, so we order another bottle and I do not have that sinking feeling that occurs when my dining companions are sipping slowly while I'm glugging. Ah, the sweet relief of drinking with another drinker.

We part ways on Summer Street, the main street of Orange, and I waltz home to our house in East Orange, feeling high and delightfully dizzy-headed, and I may stumble a couple of times but I don't fall over and I get home, brush my teeth and collapse into bed and sweet immediate sleep.

But the morning is a very different story. I wake slowly and know this will be another lost day. One more disappearing morning, fading into the itch to drink more that tends to start about 3 pm. When I close my eyes the sun shines through and I see bright red, then pink; the colour changes each time my heart beats, red, pink, red, pink. And I am wondering what rubbish I talked last night, but not with the same intensity as I often do. Because last night I was with another drinker and I am hoping that my gratitude to her for drinking a lot with me will be matched by her unspoken relief to have gone out with me, another drinker like her.

My heartbeats are strong and relentless, thumping against my ribcage. My heart feels stiff in my chest; it is shoving the blood through, pushing it out hard. My heart is saying, 'Hear me, hear me. I am not breaking but all your stress and anxiety is being pumped through me like a gas dissolved in your blood and I need to keep pumping hard and pumping hard or the whole mixture will explode.'

Go for a swim today, Seana, try to undo some of the damage. Let the pool calm and soothe you.

Yes, be healthy, do the right thing. I work so hard to be healthy, I want to live a long life – I need to for the late-in-life kids. And I do want to feel good in the day, too. But man, I feel shit right now.

Why are you leading these two lives? Why do one thing that destroys the other?

Don't ask me that! I don't know, but I just seem to be stuck deep in it, and this urge to drink is getting worse and I've got my nails digging into my palms as I clench my fists right now. Leave me alone.

SIX

June

Orange

June is the start of winter and the nights are cold here in Orange. This is a shock, as we're ex-Sydney softies who have not seen frost on the ground for twenty years nor scraped ice off a car windscreen since we left Scotland.

Paul wears a woolly hat and wraps a blanket around himself as he sits reading a book in the garden just after sunrise. He is a fresh-air fiend, oblivious to the chill. In the mornings I work on my writing jobs then walk around the streets of East Orange, as in love with the pretty workers' cottages as I ever was, even as their gardens wilt and settle to wait out winter.

One day, I tackle the last of the cardboard boxes in our bedroom, and find the soft velvet bags in which I placed Mum's jewellery when I was in Scotland in January. In her will Mum left me her engagement ring, the band worn thin by daily wear, one emerald and some tiny diamonds around it. I pull out her heart-shaped crystal pendant with three pearls on a gold chain, her opal and garnet pendant and her Chinese-style jade and silver bracelet. We also shared out Mum's other jewellery and from a velvet drawstring bag I take out the jewellery that Dad had commissioned for her using a large piece of amber which he had bought during his ill-fated sailing voyage around the Baltic. The Celtic style of the necklace, earrings and ring suits the warm tones of the amber. I replace them in their bag and pull the drawstring closed.

I wonder where Mum's own jewellery box is. Made of white leather, it sat on her sideboard for all the years she lived at Marketgate. I used to love seeing Mum dressing up to go out, lifting the top and drawing out the two small trays to choose which necklace and bracelet to wear.

I place all of Mum's jewellery in a wicker basket with a lid and put it in the Pakistani tallboy in our bedroom, where it can live alongside my other favourite bits and pieces. It has been a long time since I regularly wore different earrings every day or the necklaces I collected in my twenties.

In that same cardboard box are the last of the books I took from Scotland, mostly history books. I carry the full series of *The Fortified House in Scotland* into the sitting room and tuck them into our bookshelf.

Robert the Bruce, William Wallace, John Knox, Lord Robert Dudley, Mary, Queen of Scots, Edward Longshanks, the Hammer of the Scots, the Battles of Prestonpans, of Killiecrankie, of Bannockburn, then of Flodden and the disaster of Culloden. These stories of Scotland were my oral history and stay with me here on Wiradjuri country where I live now. Dad was a keen historian; as kids we believed he knew everything about Scottish history. That's because he would often tell us so, both when sober and when drunk, at what we called 'The Great I Am Stage'.

'I am the only person in this family who knows all about

the family of Flora MacDonald.'

'I am the greatest reader Scotland has ever known.'

'I am the only person here who can tell you about every battle of the Second World War.'

But Dad wasn't always bombastic – he really did know at least 1001 tales of Scottish derring-do and he was an ebullient storyteller.

Ormiston: 1970s

Dad had been out for lunch and rolled home one afternoon very merry, jolly and affectionate. He went through to the sitting room and put on a record. Fats Waller sang out through the house as Dad came toddling through to the kitchen.

'Come on, you two, come and sit and talk to me. Tell me what you've been up to.'

Morag and I went to the sitting room and sat down on the sofa. The rich smell of cigar smoke had quickly filled the room; a fat Havana lay smouldering on the ashtray.

'Can I have a puff, Dad?'

'Oh, most certainly, young lady. Help yourself, but do not inhale it. Just puff it a little bit.'

I picked up the cigar, put the damp end between my lips and tried to puff but, not used to it, I did inhale some smoke and then coughed and coughed, feeling as if my lungs had been scorched.

'Well, it does take a bit of practice after all,' said Dad. 'But that's an expensive cigar to waste so let me take that from you. Now then young ladies, who's going to pour me a whisky?'

Morag jumped up and took the water jug to the kitchen to fill up, then she poured whisky into one of the solid crystal tumblers and added water. We were all well trained and knew just the right proportions to pour.

'Now then girls, this amber ambrosia you see before you, this peaty, sweetish golden nectar is truly a drink made by the gods, and maybe for the gods, too.'

Dad took a big swallow and smacked his lips together.

We stayed still, knowing that a chat with Dad usually involved him chatting and us listening; nonetheless, this felt like a real treat. We craved attention from Dad and to have the full flood of his summer sunshine, his good humour, his wit and verbal dexterity beamed upon us was intoxicating.

'Now let me tell you another story about the reign of James the Fourth of Scotland. Can you tell me what you remember that I've told you so far?'

And then Dad would give us a history lesson, with another couple of whiskies to help him along. His stories were lengthy, genuinely factual and told with vim and vigour.

By the time King James was on his deathbed, Dad was slurring his speech but still full of life and passion.

'By Jove, those kings and queens had hard lives, they really lived, you know, girls. Those were the days of battles and raids and fighting hand-to-hand. I would have got on fine in one of those battles too.'

He jumped up and pulled the bugle down from above the fireplace and gave it an almighty toot.

'Another whisky, Morag.'

He turned the glass in his hand, the firelight sparkling red and orange alongside the tawny liquid.

※

But for all the fun times, there were as many disasters. At one stage, even Dad realised that the amount of whisky he was drinking was excessive. Whisky definitely did make him madder than other drinks, more angry and erratic, and, at a certain point, he decided that the thing to do was to drink pink gin instead. Because clearly that's practically being teetotal.

So Dad drank pink gin for a few years – rather a bold choice for a Scottish man. I loved the Angostura Bitters he used, the pink colour. Dad would get one of us to pour it down the side of the glass and then add the gin and tonic and give it a stir. No ice! This was Scotland; who needs ice?

Dad had drunk beer as a young man, and as a young father he had brewed beer at home in barrels. A spoonful of malt for us kids was rich and tongue-tingling, sticky, sweet and delicious. On the boat he would drink Valpolicella; in fact, when he had the shipwrights make the cupboards for the new fit-out of *Penelee*, he asked them to shape spaces within the cupboards that would exactly fit a 1.5-litre bottle of Valpolicella so that they wouldn't fall around in the cupboard when the ship was under sail.

Orange

Early in the month I have another appointment with Anna. I hold my cup of tea and settle into the sofa, about to start an EMDR session. The tissue box is on the table to my right. Sunshine washes in through the windows in one strong slant, revealing dust in the air. We are ready but I can feel my resistance, this time a small heavy black stone sitting deep in my chest.

'I would absolutely prefer not to be here doing this,' I say to Anna, who sits on a chair across the room from me.

'I am sure, but in all my years of working as a psychologist I've seen nothing as good as EMDR for helping trauma. Be brave.'

I sit quietly for a moment and relax. I am about to talk through a memory of being physically trapped in my bedroom when I was a child.

It is night-time and I am reading in bed. I am around eight or ten years old. I can see the table by the bed and the bedside lamp; the base is a heavy ceramic bottle with a swirly green and yellow pattern painted on. Very 1970s.

Dad is sitting on the bed shouting at me. I am trapped by him, I cannot get away. I know that Mum is out on the landing but she isn't coming in to help me. Dad is yelling.

'You're a bloody leech. You and the rest of them. And you can all fuck off. I don't care about any of you.'

The weight of Dad on the bed, his whisky breath, sweet and sour, my blankets tucked in tight, the feeling of being stuck under the sheets, trapped in the bed, trapped in the room.

Dad says, 'This is my house and you will obey me in it. Stay in this room. You're useless, stupid. And don't you dare say a word back to me.'

Anna stops moving her fingers and asks me what else is happening. I pull a tissue out of the box and dab my eyes, half annoyed with myself as I don't believe tears always need to be wiped. Often they just need to be wept, felt as they fall from the eyes, slide down the cheeks.

The most vivid part of the memory is of looking at that heavy lamp and wondering whether I should pick it up and whack Dad over the head. Would I manage to knock him out? Would it be dangerous? He might grab it and hit me. But I just want this to stop, I need to get away. I imagine the weight of the lamp in my hand, how high I would need to lift it before smashing it down on his head. Maybe I could kill him? Or maybe he would kill me? I want Mum to rescue me.

Left to right then right to left, my eyes move as I sob the

words out. I am back there within his fury and my numbing fear.

Anna asks, 'Could you have got out?'

'I don't think so, I think I was genuinely trapped.'

Anna talks slowly and pauses between her thoughts. She peers down at her laptop and types something in.

She asks, 'What would you have liked to have happened?'

'I wanted Mum to come in and make him stop. I'm sure she would've come straight in if she'd thought it would help. She was probably waiting outside for a safe moment to intervene.'

I remember my tea and pick up the cup, take a long swig. The temperature is just right; the scent of Earl Grey and the tea's warmth are soothing as I swallow.

'Do you know what happened in the end?' Anna asks.

'Mum did come in and he went away. It probably only lasted ten or fifteen minutes, but who knows?'

Anna types again then looks up at me.

'So what do you think now? About not being safe in your own bedroom, the place you should have felt safe.'

'It was terrible. I was so young. How could I have left the room or the house? But when I could leave home, I did and that was a really good thing to do because I was safe then. But this should never have happened. I was not safe in my home. It wasn't fair. It was scary.'

'Yes,' says Anna. 'That time, and all the other times you were trapped by your dad, none of them should have happened to you. But they did, and they were traumatic. You got out when you could.'

'I know, escaping when I did saved me, I know that.'

She types again, and I glance at my watch and wonder how forty-five minutes could have passed already.

'With trauma, people either feel fight, flight or freeze.

Flight was your way out and it worked. But you always leave things behind. What's your situation like now?'

'Nothing like that, nothing!' I cry. 'Yes, there are disagreements and very occasionally shouting and yelling, but there's no actual danger.' I sigh. 'The desire to get out is still strong at times though.'

'That's right, but it's coming to you from the 1970s and that was a long time ago. Live in the present, here and now.'

'That's easy for you to say!' I reply. 'But yes, I see what you mean. Although it was right to leave home as soon as possible, and also to come to Australia with all the loss and grief of that, the flight option is now surplus to requirements, right?'

'Yes, so if you deal with conflict by leaving home now, you might have less conflict but you might also lose your partner and your children. Do you want that?'

'Yes! At the time I do, but only in the heat of the distress. I can see now that it does go back to those terrible times of being trapped.'

Our session ends and we walk back together to the front of the building. I always feel shaken after an EMDR session; who wouldn't? And I feel that it will take days to let all the words percolate through my brain. But the past also seems more distant, less tangible than it did when I walked in for my session.

※

There was so much emotion in me describing that one brief night of being trapped by Dad. It stood for all the other times when he bailed me up and I could not physically get away. But more than those times, and more damaging, were the years and years and years of being in distress and not being able to

126

leave the situation because I was a kid. And the huge swings between terror and anguish, and joy and excitement. Our life was all bright blinding sunshine and deep dark shadows and it's hard to see a clear way ahead in both.

Later I ask my sister Morag if she remembers this incident of me being trapped in the bedroom.

'Oh yes – was that the time when he smashed the big Coke glass you had in your bedroom?'

'I can't remember a glass being smashed. Just that feeling of being trapped, and of being so close to smashing the lamp right on his head. I wanted to kill him but wasn't brave enough to try.'

'Ah, I'm thinking about the time when you were a teenager, and Mum was in the bedroom with you and Dad threw your huge Coke glass at you.'

'Coke glass? When I was a teenager? No, I can't remember that at all.'

'Well, I do!'

Morag had been in her bedroom beside mine, a little girl staying put in her bed, hidden under her covers and not daring to move, hoping the shouting and crashing would end soon.

So many memories, so many things we don't remember, so many we are glad not to. Dad's habit of bailing us up, sometimes to tell us drunken stories, sometimes to abuse us, remains in me as a feeling more than anything else. I didn't smash the lamp on his head, though. Dad lived for another thirty-five years.

Ormiston: 1975–1976

I was never sexually abused as a child. That was lucky, wasn't it? Well, not apart from that sleazy primary school headmaster who used to tap his hand gently on our bottoms as we played the recorder in one-to-one lessons. He was keeping us in time. Did he say that? Did I think that at the time? Could he possibly have believed that that was acceptable? Surely not? Not even in the 1970s.

Mr Watson, as our new headmaster, brought a lot of energy to our village school. There was a ten-mile sponsored walk to raise funds. He organised concerts where we kids sang cute little love songs to each other.

'Don't sit under the apple tree with anyone else but me.'

In retrospect, the sleaze was obvious and we school children absolutely knew that something was up. I remember my groovy young teacher being off sick one day and our class being sent to join the older class next door. We were all getting changed for gym and two kids knotted their ties around the radiator and the door handle so that when the headmaster tried to come in to supervise the changing, he could not. We saw him look in at us and then walk away. And we knew.

A very little girl told her mum that Mr Watson had been helping her to take her tights off even though she could do it herself. The police investigated and the headmaster was charged with twelve counts of sexual abuse. I was one of the twelve cases. Mum took me to the court in Haddington to give evidence. We had to wait a long time and were given vouchers to go out and buy some lunch which was very exciting for me.

Then it was time to take the stand. A small but deep room, dark wooden panelling, men in wigs and black capes.

'Can you see the man who you say touched you?'

I pointed over at Mr Watson, not looking directly at him.

'And what do you say he did?'

'He patted my bottom. He did it when I played the notes on my recorder.'

And then another man stood up and stared straight at me.
'And why did you never tell your mother about this?'
'I don't know. I didn't know if she would believe me.'
'Why would she not believe you? Are you a liar? Do you tell lies to your mother?'

I burst into tears and sobbed through my next answers. I remember being let out of the room and running along a corridor and down some steps. It was horrible. That man was so rude and mean.

The truth was, and I should have said, that I wasn't sure that what he was doing was wrong. It felt weird and secretive, but he was the headmaster, so was he really doing something bad?

I later heard that the judge had instructed the jury to find Mr Watson not guilty. However, good citizens, they found him guilty on eleven of twelve counts. He was struck off the teaching register, that was all.

In the scheme of things, that was nothing too serious. In fact, it was a positive outcome. A child spoke up and was believed. The rule of law prevailed. Mr Watson never taught again. I think of him now as sleazy, very 1970s, slimy as rotting seaweed.

So overall, my sexual abuse did not start until years later and it was all very much self-inflicted. I had been very successfully groomed: groomed by the times, by the low value of women and children and the high status of men. I was groomed by the osmotic and insidious knowledge that being sexual with men will get a girl a lot of attention, and that, above all, was what I craved.

I had learned at home that sex was important to Dad and that he related sexually to Mum very strongly and to other women too. Through his words and actions and through overheard conversations with his friends, I knew that men were interested in sex with women and keen to get as much as they could. The dolly birds on TV shows, *Benny Hill* and many others, just reinforced all this.

Clearly the memo about not being inappropriate about sex with your teenage daughters had not been drafted in the 1970s and '80s. Dad said some terrible things to Kirsty and me when we were around sixteen and seventeen.

Here he was, drunk at home when she and I got in late from a party.

'Have you girls been having sex with your boyfriends?'

'No, Dad, we've been at a party and we're going to bed now,' I replied.

'Those boys are pathetic ... They're just boys not men. Look at you, dressed like that and staying out late. Are you still virgins, girls?'

We were walking up the stairs by this time, hoping he wouldn't demand we come down and trap us in the room with him as he drank.

'Stop it, leave us alone, and yes, we both are,' said my sister.

'That's ridiculous. If I was a young man now, you wouldn't be virgins. You stay out late and you can come and go as you want. You would definitely have been having sex with your boyfriends in my day. What are these boys of yours doing?'

There were many messages in conversations like that, and I think I picked up on most of them.

I had not seen a loving and respectful sexual relationship between my parents. Plenty of passion, perhaps, but not loving kindness and no respect for Mum, or for any women.

No one ever mentioned in the late 1970s and early 1980s that women could enjoy sex. I knew men did, but women's experiences were never mentioned. I am sure I read heaps of magazines like *Jackie* and *Cosmopolitan* and I talked all the time to friends. But no instructions or even tips and hints were imparted, certainly not by my own mum.

Ormiston: Early 1980s

My older sister moved into a flat in Edinburgh when she was a student. As a schoolgirl, I used to stay with her and her flatmates in town in the school holidays, going out to parties with them and drinking cider, beer, wine. I loved accompanying them to Edinburgh's old pubs. I was following my big sister and copying her just as I had done since I was a baby. Life is so much easier as the secondborn – you just copy what you see in front of you.

Bannerman's Bar, the Jolly Judge, Bennets Bar, the Canny Man's, the Preservation Hall: I loved the smoky, beery atmosphere, the chatter and the joke telling, the smell of hops from Edinburgh's breweries as we walked from one to another. In those days, it was easy to be served alcohol in pubs when underage.

Remember that time we were walking home across Holyrood Park and were desperate for a toilet and couldn't wait, when I wet my pants and my friend Jane peed in her left boot? Remember how we always had to hold Kirsty's hair back when she puked into toilets and then we would all carry her out of the party because she never wanted to go home?

Those were innocent days; the early drinking did not involve any sexual shenanigans. I was lucky, in fact, and cared very deeply for the young man who was my teenage boyfriend. The first time we slept together was at Marketgate when Mum and Dad were away. We arrived there late at night and I went straight to the booze cupboard and drank vodka and whisky, straight from the bottle. I cannot remember a blind thing more about that night.

I do know that every time I first slept with a man for the next thirteen years I was drunk. Often blind drunk. But at least I did adore that first boyfriend: he was kind, a gentle soul. I knew him well. It didn't take long before I was sleeping with men whose names I never did find out.

The first man that I first slept with sober is the same fella who I share my bed with today. In my late teens and twenties did I ever have a sexual experience sober? Surely I must have? Or maybe I would still have been hungover if we had sex in the mornings?

From this distance, these thoughts feel searing and sad, something I would never ever wish on my own teenage daughter. At the time I thought it was normal, edgy, exciting, and being a willing sexual partner to almost anyone certainly worked as an attention-grabber.

Genova, Italy: 1982–1983

After I left school, my drinking and my sexual self-abuse really ramped up. I worked for the summer in a pub, saved up money, bought traveller's cheques and hopped on a train to suburban Munich and then another to sublime Venice and finally a ferry from Piombino to Portoferraio on the island of Elba. The Baraldi family were on their summer break at their country estate and I was to be their au pair for little Francesco. I had seen an advert on our school notice board and Carla Baraldi and I had been writing to each other.

Still, talk about a culture shock. Looking down over vineyards and olive groves, the house was enormous. An elderly retainer cooked our meals and served them as we sat at the dinner table. On day two the family took me down the hill 'to meet the peasants'. Staying at the house were three sisters with their six children and matriarch mother. I spoke no Italian but the Italian adults spoke English. My daily retreat was a fig tree which I sat underneath breaking apart the sweet black fruit that had fallen and scoffing the soft warm pink insides. I had never eaten fresh figs before and they came as a sensual revelation.

After the summer holiday, we drove up to Genova. My year there was like waltzing through a fairy tale. We lived in the oldest part of the old city, the *centro storico*, in Piazza San Matteo, on the top floors of a narrow building which had once been a palace of the Doria family. The San Matteo church, with its stripes of white marble and black slate, was just across the piazza. It had first been built in the twelfth century and then updated in the fifteenth and sixteenth centuries, like our building. I hung washing up on the roof and watched the port lights flash, saw ballet dancers through the windows of the building across the narrow street.

The little boy I looked after knew the prostitutes who worked the corner of our building and blew kisses to them as we passed by. They were middle-aged ladies in fur coats and high heels, beautifully made up and very glamourous. I went to Greek lectures at the university. The Britannia Pub was just a few minutes from our building and I would walk fast through the narrow streets to meet friends there.

With British and Italian friends, I would get into the steep funicular railway and ascend to the heights of Genova, walk across the square, buy wine and sit on a rickety stool at the little wine bar called I Tre Merli. We played hilarious drinking games such as '*Il Capitano Bliff beve per la prima volta!*'

Coming down on the funicular was much more wobbly than the ascent.

This was the year when my drinking became deeply embedded in daily life. All socialising revolved around it and I couldn't help but notice that my Italian friends drank far less than my British ones. I got myself into situations when drunk that I might never have sober. But sober wasn't something I was aspiring to; quite the opposite.

⅓

A sharp rap on the door of the hotel room. I was lying on the carpet with my bra still on, knickers gone forever and a terrible case of the whirligigs. I'd almost vomited when the pilot I was with had been manfully making love, or something like it, to me. My efforts to move my hips to try to get into some rhythm of pleasure only made me feel more nauseous so I hoped it would be over quick. Which it was, but the night wasn't.

The pilot answered the door and came back to ask, 'Do you have your passport on you?'

My bag, where was it?

The room listed as I scrabbled around for my bag and shoved it towards him. He found the passport and prattled away in Italian. My brain could not unscramble what they were saying, apart from the word '*prostituta*'.

'What a cheek! I'm not a prostitute,' I mumbled as the pilot helped me off the floor and onto a chair.

'No, but that's what they thought and prostitutes are strictly not allowed in this hotel.'

He was tall, taut, dark, his beard a sheer glittery black. I knew he had a ballerina girlfriend in South Africa. Who cares?

'Home,' I managed to mutter.

'Yes, and I have to get up really early to fly tomorrow. So I'll see you downstairs.'

He helped me pull on my shirt, skirt and coat and walked me to the front of the hotel. I was weaving, staggering around.

He kissed me goodbye at the door and said he'd see me when he got back from this series of long-haul flights.

It took me hours to get home that night. I was completely legless and so very vulnerable. I did get back, though, and fell into the stupor that sleep had become.

When I woke up the next morning, I realised that the pilot would already be airborne. How could he be sober? He definitely would not be. Or had he never been as drunk as I was?

'Fuck me,' I said to a friend at the Britannia Pub that night. 'Never fly Air Botswana.'

⚘

Rome to Majorca: 1983

I left Italy in June, travelling down to the suburbs of Rome to stay with Helen, the daughter of a friend of my gran. She had been brought up in Portobello in Edinburgh and had married her Italian husband in her twenties. I had stayed with Helen at Easter, seen the Pope lead the procession of the Stations of the Cross around the Colosseum. All had seemed well between herself and her husband then, but on this night I heard them arguing and then shouting and fighting. And I did nothing. Nothing.

Next morning as we sat and had breakfast I did not mention the blue-black bruise under her eye nor the scratches on her forehead. Her husband had already gone off to work. We said nothing of the night before. Nothing. Never mentioned. We were very well-trained Scottish women, were we not? Just pretend it is not happening.

My train journey from Rome to Barcelona was an epic of sleeping in crowded corridors, drinking wine hidden in paper bags and eating panini. I was tipsy when I got on the boat to Palma de Majorca, and meeting two young Irish guys in the bar saw my boozing gauge swinging wildly upwards into wobbly, weird and barely awake territory.

The Irish boys, slim stringy fellas with wispy beards, great talkers, had a cabin and I think that we all slept there but am pretty sure I only had sex with one of them. Hopefully the other was asleep. This was one of those absolutely blind-drunk shags. I can only remember wriggling my jeans down. The guy was so pissed, how could he even keep a stiffy and ejaculate? Maybe he didn't. This was all before real notions of consent were invented, of course, and both of us were too blind to have been anywhere near able to consent to whatever sticky messes we were making. Oh dear.

It was the early hours of the morning when the ship docked in Palma, the port city of Majorca. Some friends from Genova were working on a superyacht that was in the harbour somewhere but in my hazy stupor I decided to go across the island to Porto Cristo where my family was staying. I did have quite a bit of cash and I must have negotiated a price with the taxi driver before we set off on the seventy-kilometre journey. Surely.

My pants were damp, my crotch must have been stinking. In fact, I probably smelled pretty bad all over after that journey from Rome, but the taxi driver let me in anyway.

As we drove fast across the island, the taxi driver would occasionally put his hand on my thigh. I was smoking and, speaking Italian, I would threaten to burn his hand with my cigarette if he kept doing it. I may have been pretty lax about who I had sex with but I did have an upper age limit. My head was spinning and several times I was sick out of the window.

This middle-aged man dropped me right outside the

building where my family was staying, sometime in the early hours of the morning. If he had persisted or taken me to a hotel, I would probably have let him have sex with me, but he didn't. He didn't charge me for the trip either and he said to take care as he left. Perhaps he had a daughter my age.

I tried to wake up my family in their flat but no one heard me so I ended up rolling my sleeping bag out and snoozing in a flower bed. It was soft at least.

Orange

Mid-June in my mid-fifties. I often feel like the world's oldest mother of teens, the world's most tired mother. My friends here whom I meet most Friday mornings for coffee are all between five and ten years younger than me. They are lovely women, supportive, kind, loving, interesting, funny. I am so lucky to always be able to meet wonderful women wherever I find myself.

So why do I still often feel that I need to leave, escape, disappear for a while? Most days I have that sensation, that I'm in the wrong place, that we should not have moved, that I need to get away. And some days, some mornings, are worse than others. Some weeks are worse than others.

꽃

I'm awake, it's morning, I keep my eyes closed. Pink light. What day is it? Is it Thursday? Can I have a drink tonight? No, no, it's Tuesday. No drinking until Thursday at the earliest, but you know Friday would be better. It's Tuesday, wake up. Get up.

꽃

I wake up, what day is it today? It's Friday. Friday! Thank God for Friday. I can have a glass of wine today. I'll buy a bottle this afternoon, and can crack it open while I'm cooking dinner. Friday. Hooray for Friday.

⚘

Morning, eyes still closed. I'm awake. I hear Paul rustling beside me in the bed, still sleeping. What time is it? Five am. I close my eyes. What day is it? Monday, it's Monday. Shit, it's Monday. And I feel shit. Should not have finished that bottle of wine last night. Should not have stayed up so late. Now I need to get to the toilet, don't want to disturb Paul. Maybe I will be able to get back to sleep. But my heart thumps and my brain rattles with each heartbeat. I'm so stupid, I did it again. I didn't need to finish that bottle. I finished it last night as I'm not supposed to drink on Mondays. I could have poured it away. No, I couldn't. Shit, it's 5 am and it's Monday. Can't have another drink until Friday. Faaark.

⚘

How to self-soothe amid such self-loathing? How to calm myself and ease off on the relentless self-abuse? I tell myself that I'm nothing like as bad as Dad was, nowhere near it. I never fall around, just the odd stagger. Yes, I am probably pretty short-tempered at times, but nothing like Dad, not even close.

Perhaps what I need to do is emancipate from myself, the way Mum freed herself from Dad after I had left home for school and university. Mum stayed living with him but she carved out her own life. Could I detach from my own drinking, so that I am not so affected by it?

If only I could be as Mum was with alcohol, never attached, never addicted and able to have one glass or two and no more.

Mum, how I miss Mum. How grateful I am to her. Watching her change her relationship with Dad helped me in many relationships in my life. She taught me so much about dealing with difficult people, difficult drunks.

Ormiston: Mid-1980s

Monday nights, every Monday night, Mum drove along the eight miles of road between Ormiston and the hall in Haddington where women – mainly women – shared their experience, strength and hope. Mum listened. The solar-planetary axis started to shift.

Mum learned to stop jumping on Dad's out-of-control drunken bandwagon. She learned to avoid conflict; she learned that it had always taken two people to have the kind of fights they had, and that she was one of those two people. She learned that no one, no one, can reason with a person who is drunk. There was nothing really special about their marriage, their family and their fights. Not that the violence stopped quickly though; in fact, it got worse for a while.

One Monday evening, Mum was getting ready to leave the house to go to Al-Anon. Morag and Callum had eaten their dinner and Dad's was staying warm in the oven. He'd gone out for lunch in Edinburgh and had not been heard of since.

Mum was getting into the car when Dad walked into the yard, shouted at her.

'I know where you're going!'

Mum looked down, closed the door and started the car, saying nothing.

Dad stepped to the window, whacked it hard with his clenched fist.

'I forbid it. Get out of this car.' Loud, aggressive – people could hear, people would know.

'Get out,' he yelled. 'How dare you talk about me to other people! How dare you say I'm an alcoholic! Get out.'

Mum began to move the car slowly, but she was not sure if she would be able to go. The kids were safely with friends; surely she could go.

Dad ran to the front of the car and, standing still, he banged on the bonnet, screaming at her to get out. He clambered onto the bonnet and thumped the windscreen with his fists, pounding. He pulled out his Swiss army knife and his keys and smashed them into the windscreen.

Frozen, Mum said nothing. Wondered whether to bolt from the car. She wasn't sure if her legs would move. She wasn't sure where to run to.

The windscreen shattered, glass flew. Mum ducked her face too late, felt glass, then blood seeping. Dad stopped himself from falling in. He fell sideways off the car.

Next day Morag saw a friend in the street and told her that when she saw our mum next she wasn't to worry.

'Worry about what?'

'Her face, she's got lots of cuts on it. But she's fine, it's not a big deal.'

*

On a sunny summer day Mum was watering her plants in the conservatory at Marketgate. She lifted the small watering can high and tipped it sharply to reach the plants at the back of the planter boxes. I was home from university for the holidays and we needed to talk about the night before, when Dad had bailed me up in the sitting room when he was drunk. He'd ranted at me and I felt trapped there, stuck.

'It's half funny, Mum. He called me a "female swine person" at one stage. And he wasn't going to hurt me, but I just don't want to be stuck like that ever again.'

'Let me make a cup of coffee and bring it through. Would you like tea? Can you do some more watering for me?'

I filled the watering can from the tap outside. The wooden windows of the conservatory were open and a whisper of breeze came in, just enough to feel on my face as I poured thin streams of water into various plants, Mum's little loves. Dozens of houseplants lived in this conservatory, on small tables and stands. There were spiky cactuses and pink flowering begonias; spider plants tipped voluptuously out of hanging baskets.

Outside the garden was awash with colour and movement, butterflies and roses, lilac and sweet peas. Fish swished in the pond and the tiny fountain tinkled.

Mum brought through the tray and we sat on the soft cushions of the old Lloyd Loom wicker chairs. I picked up a piece of shortbread, made to my Granny Smith's recipe with rice flour and lots of butter. It was very short shortbread. I lifted it to my lips and a piece broke off and almost melted on my tongue.

'The thing that really helps me is something I learned from another lady in an Al-Anon meeting,' Mum said. 'When he's ranting at me, I pretend there's a mirror between him and myself. He is looking at his own reflection in the mirror and he is raving at himself. When he says that you are a bloody idiot and he wishes you had never been born, he really is talking about himself.'

I kept nibbling on the shortbread, waiting for my tea to cool down.

'He knows he is wrong and he will admit to that when he's sober. He does see his own bad behaviour, Seana. But at the time, when he is drunk, he directs his fury right at us. Just slide that mirror between you and him. Let him abuse himself in the mirror whilst you stay safe behind it.'

The sweet scent of Earl Grey rose as I sipped my cup of tea, placed it gently back on the saucer.

'Let me think, Mum.'

I picked up another piece of shortbread, looked at the rows of prick marks, the pale golden colour. I snapped it in half. It crumbled and I licked my finger to collect small pieces from my skirt.

'Yes, Mum, all right. I can understand that. The things he says are not really about me. Even when he calls me a leech and says we all just stay with him for his money, he's really talking about himself being trapped by his own greed. He does say a lot of things that sound exactly like he is talking to himself.'

'Well, give this idea of visualising a mirror a try. It has really helped me. Also, I don't feel the need to defend myself when I slide a mirror between us. He's not really saying things about me so there's no need to tell him he's wrong.'

'Not that defending yourself ever works with him,' I said.

'No dear, you cannot argue with a drunk. Well, you can, but it is a complete waste of your precious breath. He cannot hear you.'

'OK, I'll use that mirror the next time, and let's see if I can manage to keep schtum myself and not make him worse. Why is he so argumentative when he's drunk?'

'I don't know, Seana. Some people, most people, are

not like that. But his personality changes when he drinks. Maybe we wouldn't mind if he just fell asleep in his chair like other blokes do, or just slurred and was silly. But when he's rampaging drunk, that's when trouble happens. That's his very own variety of a drinking problem.'

Mum took another biscuit, dipped it delicately, swiftly, in her own cup.

'But if we can all learn not to argue with your father, then lots of things will change. In Al-Anon I heard someone say: "When you stop playing the game, the whole game stops."'

'Oh yes, that's an idea that might work. But how easy is it to stop playing the game?'

'We can but try, Seana. The game has been going on a long, long time.'

ว๊

I see Anna the psychologist every three to four weeks and am never short of things to talk about with her. In my visit at the end of the month, I explain that the twins are now teenagers and can be grumpy at times. I tell her about how much I reverted to a scared child when my older boys were angry teenagers. Occasionally Jake would lash out in frustration and punch the paper-thin walls. He could talk but he still had a significant language disorder and so expressing himself verbally was hard at times.

'We learned that we needed to go into the garden when we had to discuss things that might make Jake annoyed or frustrated. That really helped. But honestly, I would get so upset, and would often pour myself a very solid glass of wine to calm down.'

'And did that help?'

'Yes, but only briefly. The thing is that I'd felt safe in my own home for all the years since I had left Marketgate, then suddenly I felt unsafe again. It was hideous, even though I was never genuinely in danger.'

'We will keep working on that: being present here and now and not flying back into the past.'

I tell Anna about how I already feel too busy and over-committed and about how familiar this is to me.

'I feel constantly harassed by myself, by my own thoughts. There's too much going on; I've said "yes" too impulsively to too many things.'

'How's the drinking?'

'Well, I'm both drinking more than I want to but also not drinking nearly as much as I would truly like. I can stop myself going the whole hog, but it's an effort. It's exhausting.'

Anna talks to me about my family of origin, what I saw and learned, and we chat about genetics a bit. She tells me that she sometimes has a glass of wine after dinner, but just one and that's plenty for her.

Whenever I meet people who literally can 'just have one' it's not so much my mind that boggles as my whole body. The entire notion is so astounding that I feel as if my eyes bounce out on springs and my legs and arms go loose and sloppy, as if a puppeteer is taking all the strain.

Just the one. Imagine having just the one, or even just the two and then, and then, and then, simply not having any more. Imagine that. I can't.

Why can't I have just the one?

At least we have an adventure coming up, at last. Mum's death has inspired me and we are off to Darwin and East Timor at the end of the month. That will distract me from my many woes, which I know are actually all in my own head. They're

144

just so busy in there. Honestly, my blooming brain. One good thing about a hangover is that it slows down the thinking and shuts up my inner chattering.

⁂

The school term finishes right at the end of June, bringing the winter school holidays for us here in Australia. As I pack for our trip to East Timor, I am overjoyed to be pulling my sarongs and light shirts and pants out of storage. Anticipation is such a delicious part of travelling and holidays; the packing is another. I love to pack last minute and very fast.

Into my soft wheeled suitcase goes my beloved Sony A7 camera and a notebook, toothbrush and toothpaste. I put on my travelling earrings, simple gold studs that won't tarnish, and take no other jewellery nor any make-up. This trip is an adventure and it's been far too long since the last one.

Well, Seana, off we go.

Yes, at last! The past couple of weeks have been good because of the excitement about going. My urge to get away was eased by knowing we were about to get away.

You've still been drinking a lot, though. Trying to only drink at the weekends hasn't been going too well. Your hands are shaky as you pack today.

Oh, buzz off. Leave me alone. Give me a break. The ends of terms are always stressful. Silence! Get me on that plane and get a glass of wine in my hands!

SEVEN

July

Orange

The July holiday to East Timor goes well. Interesting, beautiful and with fantastic snorkelling. It really is an escape, and the bonus is that I manage to find the one place that sells wine on Atauro Island. Bonus!

We arrive back home to Orange and the twins return to school for Term 3. Refreshed, I am ready to lift up the lid of my old blue trunk again. The photos have all been sorted out, and now it is time for me look again at my old diaries which span 1980–2000. I'm keen to start reading about the years at Oxford, the most privileged of my life. As I turn the pages, I read my daily notes on the socialising and the studying and the sheer astounding difference to any place or people I had experienced before. Twilight walks on Port Meadow, church bells, bicycles and being among the brainiest people I had ever met – those golden years.

Oxford: 1983

Mum and I walked through the arched doorway in the massive decorated wooden gate of Wadham College. It felt like walking into a castle, a fortified home of some sort. Very solid. We turned left into the lodge and met two porters, who welcomed me to Wadham in their burring West Country accents and gave me a key for my room.

We bumped my suitcase out of the entrance and into the main quad. It is a plain but perfectly symmetrical quad, unusual among Oxford colleges which are often decorated with colonnaded cloisters or trailing ivy. A square of pristine lawn lies in the middle, surrounded on three sides by solid four-storey-high Gothic buildings where students live.

On the opposite side is the main hall, with wide stone steps leading up to the doors. Above, two statues stand guard in their alcoves in the sandstone walls: Dorothy and Nicholas Wadham keeping watch over the college Dorothy founded in 1610 after the death of her husband. Wadham is a parvenu in Oxford, the oldest university in the English-speaking world. Teaching began in the eleventh century, the first chancellor was appointed in 1214, and University, Balliol and Merton Colleges vie for the title of the oldest, all built between 1249 and 1264.

Not the oldest, nor the newest, Wadham was and is one of the most progressive Oxford colleges. It was one of five all-male colleges that admitted women in 1974, just nine years before I arrived. Wadham has a much higher proportion of state school pupils than most other colleges.

Mum and I walked through a passage over ancient flagstones into the more modern second quad with a variety of buildings and many trees and garden beds. We found Staircase 12 and I unlocked my door and pushed it open to see two huge windows overlooking Longwall Street. There was a single bed, a small desk and a mantelpiece. On the mantelpiece was a bunch of flowers, a bottle of gin and a pyramid made from six packets of Silk Cut. A friend from Edinburgh had set up this welcome for me. Let the fun begin.

'I hope that's not a sign of things to come, Seana,' said Mum. 'You are here to study.'

Mum said goodbye and left to visit her friend Anna whom she had met at typing college in Eastbourne before she married Dad.

I opened my case and unpacked, strolled around the College, checked out the modern library then put on my black Commoners gown and walked to the main hall for dinner, saying hello to other black-garbed students. One of the largest dining halls in Oxford, ours was long and wide and tall, the roof vaulted above curving hammer beams of oak. Dark wooden panelling covered the lower walls, above were oil portraits in heavy wooden frames. Three vast stained-glass windows were set in the walls; on the fourth rear wall a minstrels' gallery hung above the Jacobean wood panelling. Three sets of long wooden tables with benches ran the length of the hall and on a dais at the end was the high table where sat the dons in full academic robes. Only a few women were among them.

I sat beside a girl with flame-hennaed hair.

'I'm Seana, First Year. Here to study Classics.'

'Oh luv, me too. I'm Ellen.' She gave a big smile. She was from Clapham in London and was chatty and friendly.

'This is very different to my old school canteen,' she said, and I knew I'd found a friend.

Waiting staff delivered venison, roast potatoes and vegetables to us, fresh from the college farms.

'I don't think we're in Kansas anymore, Toto,' I said to Ellen and we shared a laugh.

Next morning, I met my fellow Classics students. There were eight of us in our tutor's room. All the walls were lined with bookshelves, and there were piles of books on his desk and on the floor. I was intimidated. Yes, just a little. I had got As in my Latin and Greek Highers and for the two A Levels I did in my final school year, too. But here I already felt way out of my depth. Some of my fellow Classicists explained that they started Latin at age ten and Greek at twelve. Eek. We were paired up for tutorial groups of two. An essay was to be ready for the next week and we were to translate great chunks of *The Odyssey* from Greek and *The Aeneid* from Latin.

I was a workaday student at Oxford. I always finished my essays on time, ready to read aloud in our tutorials. I worked steadily on my translations, though our first set of exams were not due until two-thirds of the way through second year. I would listen to other students in a flap, hear how they had to pull all-nighters to get their essays done. This always smacked of self-indulgence to me, attention-seeking. I completed my essays and still had time to go to the pub. I was never going to set my tutor's heart fluttering with my incisive arguments, was never going to get a First. And I was an attention-seeker too, but those needs were met outside our tutors' rooms.

During my first year I joined the Oxford Union, the playground and training camp for so many British politicians. I studied in the Old Library there, its walls colourful with pre-Raphaelite paintings by William Morris and Dante Gabriel Rossetti above the bookcases.

One week I had been cleaning the men's toilets in Dad's joiner shop in Ormiston and pulling pints behind a bar in Haddington; the next I was listening to Old Etonians debating in the chamber with its dais where the president sat like a king. No wonder I kept quiet in that building.

I would take my books to the bar, sit at one of the tables beside the tall bay windows overlooking the gardens, read my book and sip my cider, watching the blokes at the bar, so confident, so well dressed and so sleek.

There was Toby Young: a noticeable figure even in his first year, he seemed to be everywhere all the time. In pubs, clubs, bars, libraries, in Blackwell's bookshop and all around the town, Toby was leaning against the wall observing, peering around rooms as he chatted to someone, seeing who else was around. Toby was honing his skills, ready to skewer in print.

Another notable character I saw at the Union was a bloke from Balliol with a mess of white blond hair. He too was notable and noticed around town. Handsome then, smooth-faced, tousled as he cycled around, he took notes in Classics lectures and rose to speak at the Union. Boris Johnson was my exact contemporary at Oxford, there from 1983–1987 and, like me, he left with a 2:1 degree, though, unlike me, he was reported to be upset not to get a First.

I listened to a debate one night, sitting in this version of the British parliament, though one where jokes and wit often seemed to trump the facts or boring statistics. It was debating, not seeking answers to problems. It seemed all about winning or losing. This was so different to Scotland, where people spoke their minds more plainly and would lay down their lives or pick up a claymore to defend whatever opinion they had at the time.

The speakers here were confident and articulate, but I felt they could argue the opposite side equally well, that they could argue from any angle. They did not mean what they said. They were skilful but not passionate. They did not care about what they argued for and against. It seemed a game to them all.

❧

In the UK your accent tells everyone all about you – if you're English, that is. Class lines are very real and your life story can be understood very swiftly once you start chatting. There was a fair amount of diversity at Wadham: many Northerners, students from Devon, Cornwall, Wales, many from London and the Home Counties, the odd Cockney.

I liked that people, in general, could not listen to me and know exactly who I was and where I came from. My east-coast Scottish accent reflected the mixture of humble beginnings and upper middle-class families that I came from.

In my first year I met a fellow with a very pukka English accent, who said to me, 'I'm from Perthshire, you know. We're Mackenzies. How about you?'

Stunned, I could not utter a word. My brain was wrestling with the notion that a person could be Scottish but have an English accent. I had never ever, not once, met a person in Scotland who claimed to be Scottish but had an English accent. This was just weird, and it took me a fair while to integrate the fact that some Scots are so incredibly posh that they speak with English accents. I mean, who knew?

❧

Pigeon post was the internal postal system between the colleges. Each student had a pigeonhole within their college porter's lodge. You scribbled your note, wrote the name and college of the recipient on the envelope and it would be delivered very quickly.

In my second year, I wandered into the lodge one sunny day to collect my post and saw a note in handwriting I did not recognise. Opening it, I saw it was from Allegra Mostyn-Owen who I knew from the university magazine *Isis*. I often saw Allegra at the magazine meetings, knew her also as the girlfriend of Boris Johnson. She had golden-blond hair, deep blue eyes, wide cheekbones. Allegra's beauty was delicate, a true English rose. David Bailey's photograph of her had graced the cover of the society magazine *Tatler* the year before. Allegra was posh but friendly too.

'Are you free to come to tea on Wednesday afternoon at 3 pm?' the note read.

I was, and I sent a note back by pigeon post to let her know I'd be there.

Allegra was reading PPE at Trinity College, just around the corner from Wadham. The back gates of Trinity were across the road from Wadham's front, tall metal gates set in a high wall looking into the enormous gardens at Trinity's rear, swathes of lawn, swaggering garden beds.

The entrance to Trinity is on Broad Street, close to Blackwell's bookshop, and is much less grand than Wadham's. The buildings within are vast though and it took me a while to find Allegra's room. I knocked on the door and she opened it, her face lighting up as she let me in and asked how I liked my tea. Tall ceilings, a large sitting room, comfortable chairs and a coffee table for the tea and biscuits. This room was much grander than my share house above the beer shop in Bullingdon Road off the Cowley Road. (Wadham College could only house its students in their first and final years.)

'I'm thinking of running as editor of *Isis*,' Allegra said. She gestured to the milk and I nodded, and she made another cup of tea for me in one of her china cups.

'You'd be good at that,' I said. 'You are definitely experienced enough.'

'The thing is, I'm wondering if you would run with me. We'd make a good team.'

Surprise! Being asked to work alongside this glamorous young woman was not at all what I expected. Why was she asking me? Would my Scottish accent and humbler beginnings balance her upper-class accent and background?

'Oh, that's kind of you. I had thought about running.'

'Do you have any exams in the next year?' Allegra asked.

'No, none, and you don't either, do you?'

'No, and I'm keen to run for the editorship. It might be tough to win if others stand too, but I think we'd work well together.'

'Yes, well.' I really was not sure what to say. My life as a student was so different to hers. I didn't need to make a decision, though.

'The thing is, Allegra, I'm going to be the diving officer of the diving club. That starts next term. I just couldn't manage both.'

'That's such a shame.'

'Well, it's exciting for me. There has never been a female diving officer before, so that's a step forward. And I love that club.'

'I hope it goes well.'

'And I hope you find someone else and do that editor job at *Isis*.'

Allegra did become editor of *Isis*, a role she did well. She went on to work in newspapers in London. She and Boris Johnson married the year they left Oxford, both aged just twenty-three. Later she was quoted as saying, 'He is a better ex than he was a husband.'

A sliding doors moment for me there. I wanted to work as a writer or in television and I had no contacts in London, which was where the jobs were. Having contacts is invaluable in those professions and so many of the students I met at *Isis* had parents who worked in media. I had none; my dad could introduce me to many bricklayers and stonemasons, but I had no entrée to the London media scene.

Never mind. The diving club, which, this being Oxford, was actually named the Oxford University Underwater Exploration Group (OUUEG), was where I found my people. Outdoorsy, funny, capable and handy, the divers could change sparkplugs, use compressors to fill air bottles, clean engines and read tide tables and charts. They were practical people, adventurous, many being zoology students. Underwater we were all classless and we used gestures and eye contact. We put our lives in each other's hands, helped each other with our wetsuits and tanks, masks, snorkels and flippers.

We did some excellent explorations: to Scapa Flow in the Orkneys to dive on the First World War German fleet at great depths; to Devon for shipwrecks; to Ireland for two weeks diving around Cork; to Cornwall for magnificent underwater scenery. I took part in an archaeological diving expedition to Giglio in Italy, helping excavate an Etruscan wreck at dangerous depths. The privilege of it all, the adventure.

OUUEG also provided me with two stable boyfriends in my Oxford years, which calmed down the ridiculous promiscuity of my first year. Getting drunk and then going to bed with a bloke was my attention-seeking behaviour of choice, and it worked like a charm. In my first year at Oxford it was all adrenaline, excitement, flattery, and wine, beer, cider and Pernod by the bucketful. Staggering walks up staircases, fumbling, trying to not to vomit in a stranger's bed. An emotional messy mess.

The two boyfriends that I had over the next three years at Oxford were kind to me. If only I had been kind to them. As with all boyfriends in my terrible twenties, I punished these two young men for the drinking that had attracted me to them in the first place. All the while I was drinking heavily myself. I dumped both of them horribly, with panic, some regret, but an urgent urge to get away, escape, escape.

}ϵ

By the time I did Classics Mods – my first set of exams – two-thirds of the way through second year, I was annoying my Classics tutor who was very old and had painful gout. He once threw a book at me when I mispronounced 'Dionysius' then told me to leave and come back in thirty minutes. Imagine that. I am sure I aggravated him in many more ways. He was annoying me too, to be frank.

Not being afraid of escape, departing, getting away, I changed course to Old and Medieval English and really enjoyed subjects like Making Anglo-Saxon Cemeteries Talk and Scottish Literature before 1600. I continued to work hard, never handing in anything late nor anything dazzling or independent.

The tutor who kindly took me on was a quiet and shy man, Alan Ward. For two years I had a 5 pm Friday night tutorial with him, often conducted in the corridor of the King's Arms pub which was on the corner of Wadham. Alan was agoraphobic and needed to see the route to the doorway. I could relate to that. He drank tall glasses of sherry and I drank pints of cider as we discussed *Beowulf*, the orthography of English and the intricate details of the language of *Sir Gawain and the Green Knight*.

Finals exams were ten three-hour papers covering everything we had studied in the past two years. No continuous assessment in Oxford. A few days later we had a farewell dinner for the English students in a room in college, speeches were made, and then we ate in hall and went for a walk around the Fellows' Private Garden, hoping to catch a glimpse of the elusive college pet tortoises who lived in scholarly seclusion there. With the scent of roses on the evening air, we saw the monkey puzzle trees, redwoods, oaks, limes, yews and cedars. Bells chimed the hour from Magdalen College and St Giles' Church, and a very special and beautiful part of life was ending.

Many of my friends were heading to London to work or for further study. Graduate jobs did not appeal to me, nor did living in London. I was to spend the summer on a scuba diving expedition in Sabah, the Malaysian state on the north side of the island of Borneo, and had organised a working holiday visa to Australia.

So I shipped some belongings north to Scotland and packed my diving kit into my biggest rucksack. On the morning before I jumped on a bus from Oxford to Heathrow, I filled my beloved tutor's room with flowers and wrote him a note saying that he had taught me a great deal, but above all that I knew very little and had a lot more to learn.

I flew to Kota Kinabalu via Singapore, my first trip beyond Europe. When I arrived at the house that was our coral reef survey's expedition base the scent of frangipanis made me wilt with pleasure.

I had taken some metal piping in my diving bag as we were literally going to plumb the depths. Well, we were making metre-square quadrants with which we would map coral cover and genera in the first quantitative study of the coral reefs in the Tunku Abdul Rahman National Park off the coast of Kota Kinabalu. I spent four months in Sabah, Singapore and Malaysia, met sharks and rays, turtles and lots of coral, and then departed again, further south and further east.

Sydney: 1987

I woke as the sun was rising and saw land below; then came ocean and beaches and I thought we must be miles from Sydney. Abruptly, the plane banked and sped over the coast and straight down onto the runway at Sydney Airport. I was confused as I waited for my backpack to spin around the luggage belt. How could there be beaches within a big city?

Bumming around the beaches of the Algarve before I went to Oxford, I had met loads of Aussies and saw that they seemed to be having the most fun out of all the nationalities. I had kept in touch with a couple and one of these friends picked me up in his Holden and whisked me back to drop my bags at his house. His parents were welcoming and actually said 'G'day' the first time they met me. How cool! And they were cooking a barbie for dinner. A what?

My mind was spinning with all that and very shortly my whole body was spinning around in the surf at Cronulla. We walked from the car park onto searing sand, running to dive into the sea to swim between the flags. I was looking around wondering where the palm trees were, confident that four months of scuba and swimming had made me sea-strong. But this was Sydney surf and I was quickly jumbled and tumbled around, held down and then thrown up. I ended up crawling out of the water on my hands and knees wondering where I had landed.

Cold lager at the pub had never, ever tasted so good; a few mouthfuls of saltwater set me up for the dry, fizzing cold of it. It was the exact opposite of a warming whisky after a freezing hill walk in Scotland. But culturally similar and equally necessary. Cheers!

Australia and Sydney were very good to me. I was offered a job as a barmaid at the Glasgow Arms in Ultimo on my second day in town.

'Are you offering me the job because I have a Scottish accent?'

'Well, that's part of it. But you have experience, too. Now let me show you how we pour our middies and schooners.'

'What are middies and schooners?'

I was foaming at the mouth to get a job in the media, though, and my youthful vigour must have been obvious one evening when I was drinking at the Evening Star pub in Surry Hills with the cousin of a friend of a friend who worked for the *Daily Mirror.* I was in the right pub at the right time. I met a TV producer from *60 Minutes* and after rabbiting on to him for ages, he asked me, 'Do you have a CV on you?'

'Funny you should ask that,' I replied, whisking one out of my leather satchel. What? Don't you always have a CV in your handbag when at the pub?

60 Minutes didn't give me a job but that producer passed my CV around and I ended up working on *The Midday Show with Ray Martin*, probably the best job I ever had. I worked super hard, truly grateful to have been given the chance.

'Well, you're the cheapest worker I have,' the executive producer did say to me at the end of the year. 'We got our money's worth.'

Ray Martin was a terrific boss, engaged and intelligent. He taught me a heap about punchy writing as he rewrote my introductions for the daily guest I was looking after. He didn't even mind when I organised an animal trainer to come in and her wombat widdled on his lap as he held it. Sylvester Stallone was equally understanding when I spilled coffee on his ostrich skin boots.

I had no idea that this first TV job was so good until I impulsively chucked it in after eighteen months and scooted off elsewhere. Later I would realise that I had started at the top, and even though I did enjoy many of the TV jobs I had over the next years, that first one was the best. And I threw it away, went skiting off around the world, then returned to work at Channel 10 and to freelance. In those mad years I went to Ghana, to Zanzibar, to Kenya, to Thailand, to San Francisco, to New York and to many other places. I was whirling around the planet itself now as it whirled around the sun.

When a family disaster happened at the same time as a boyfriend in Sydney left me, I even returned to the UK, working in London and then in Glasgow for the BBC.

And all the while, in those manic years of my twenties, I drank and drank and drank, drank and drove, drank and dived, drank and worked and drank. Television was a fairly boozy environment and I was a hard worker. I never ever lost a job because of my drinking, but I never stayed in one place for too long either. TV jobs tended to be short contracts and that suited me fine. I could work then go travelling for a while, work and then scuba dive, work and then jump on a train, and everywhere I worked or went, I was drinking and drinking and drinking. But that was normal, wasn't it? Wasn't everyone?

Orange

On 19th July, Mum's birthday, I call my brother Callum at his care home.

'Mum would have been eighty today,' I say to him.

'Aye,' says Callum.

'Have you been thinking about her today?'

'Aye, I miss her.'

'Me too, and I feel so sad for her. She should be still living in her wee house, busy in the garden, picking strawberries and raspberries at this time of year.'

'I miss going out to Ormie to see her.'

'Me too, Callum, me too.'

Talking to Callum on the phone can be quite tricky as he mumbles a lot. We tend to have pretty short conversations. He asks about the kids and he loves to hear what heavy metal music Jake has been listening to.

Time really has been the great healer when it comes to Callum. After all the turmoil when he was younger, and all the worries I had about Mum's safety before he moved into the care home, things are pretty settled now. I feel sad for him sometimes, for the man he could have been and the life he never lived but, overall, he seems pretty happy in himself these days. And he is safe where he is, much safer than he ever was before he was sent to live there.

Scotland: Late 1980s

I was safely far away in sunny Sydney during the years Callum developed schizophrenia. My sister Morag had lived with me in Oxford during my last year at university and she stayed on after I left. Callum moved south to live with her at the house in Juxon Street. He found a job washing up at the famous Browns restaurant.

Morag has always been sure that he was never the same after a weekend in London.

'He went down to a party. Someone gave or sold him some acid and he had a really bad trip. A really, really bad trip.'

'But didn't you say that he was pretty paranoid before that?'

'Yes, he was a bit, and he had left the job and the study in Edinburgh before then. He was changing things all the time, flailing around.'

'So what was different?' I asked.

'Well,' Morag stopped for a minute, looked away. 'It was just the amount of drugs he started using afterwards. He was taking loads of acid to try to get back to where he'd been before he took that acid.'

'How did he behave?'

'He thought people were following him, talking about him.'

'Did he say that he could hear people talking, or just thought they were?'

'I can't remember, and I wasn't thinking about that then. There's a big difference though, isn't there, between actually hearing voices and thinking people are talking about you.'

'I know. It's between paranoia and delusion, but we just had no idea about all that then.'

*

While Callum's brain was tearing itself apart, I was in Sydney and often to be found at Tamarama Beach being tossed around in the surf. Life was so different in Sydney. It was summer, frying hot. Cigarettes came in packets of fifty, there were prawns bigger than my fingers, jugs of cold beer glinted amber through the condensation. The midday sun bleached out all the colour, but during the early mornings and late afternoons Sydney's golden hour glowed with molten oranges, reds, deep blues and soft pinks.

I was full of all this and paying no attention, just getting the odd warning bell in letters from home.

'Why do you think it took so long to find out what was going on with Callum?' I asked Morag years later.

'It was the drugs and the drinking, the addictions were so clear and causing so much chaos. And we were all so aware of addictions, weren't we? Alcoholism and drug addiction we knew all about, we were expecting that. No one was looking for anything else. Maybe the addictions were also doing a great job of masking the psychosis.'

Callum's schizophrenia has often been florid. He hears voices in his head and for many years the voices were abusing him, saying awful things. When he describes the voices they sound like Dad talking, saying the sorts of things he said to Callum. Perhaps they aren't random voices in his head but are Dad's voice, echoing on and on, all those awful, hurtful, hateful, mean and vicious things he said, on and on and on and on.

Edinburgh: Late 1980s, early 1990s

Callum had done a piano tuning course at college after school. At one stage he had also started a stonemasonry apprenticeship in Dad's firm, but left. After becoming very paranoid and unwell in Oxford he moved back to live with Mum and Dad at Marketgate. Chaos ensued. Finally, Callum agreed to go to a drug and alcohol rehab called Castle Craig, a private facility in the Scottish Borders. The staff there felt that he had issues beyond alcohol and drug addiction and they sent him to the Royal Edinburgh psychiatric hospital. It was the first of many stays, mostly as a voluntary patient, though Callum knew that if he did not attend voluntarily then being sectioned was never far away.

There followed years and years of heavy drug use, hospital stays, a prison sentence, halfway houses, church homes, and stays in grotty flats in Edinburgh and a council flat in Muirhouse, not an area you'll find in Edinburgh's many tourism brochures. And then, finally, Callum was given a council house in Ormiston with 'care in the community' which didn't really work, neither for him nor certainly for Mum.

Callum received a disability payment every fortnight and would spend almost all of it at the pub that night and the next, helped by friends who only turned up fortnightly.

Did it all start that night at that party in London? Perhaps that was one trigger, perhaps not. Callum's trauma had started years before, and it had never stopped. And we will never know exactly what combination of genes and environment caused Callum's schizophrenia.

*

Before I had my own family, my visits from Sydney to Scotland often revolved around Callum. I would go to see him, wherever he was, in halfway houses, flats, homeless hostels. And then there were the times we had to go searching for him.

Callum was missing again; he had not been seen for days. The halfway house he was staying in had notified the police and they had been over to Marketgate to chat to Mum and me.

'We'll go out again and look for him. There are all sorts of places he might be,' Mum said to the policewoman, whom she had not invited inside.

'You must be very worried about him, Mrs Smith, if he's living alone out there in the woods.'

No, officer, I wanted to snap back. We're not worried about him living in the woods. We're worried we'll find him dead in the woods, you fool.

Callum had some favourite places to hide, places he stayed when he was sniffing a lot of lighter fuel, places where he and his pals spent hours building dens when they were kids.

That day was blustery and autumnal. We called the dog, took down his leather lead from the hook and slipped it around his neck. His wagging tail whacked our legs in excitement as we tugged on our boots, wrapped ourselves in our coats and opened the back door.

The wind caught my hair and I pulled it back in a bunch and then drew up the hood of my coat.

'Let's go down to the railway track. We can start at the bridge and then try the Puddle Woods.'

Mum nodded, her lips tight and white, as if she was biting them on the inside.

'Come on, doggy, let's go. You're happy to be going out, aren't you, even if we're not?'

We walked quietly along the main street of Ormiston. The huge chestnut trees were losing their leaves; piles of them lay on the pavement, the green turning brown, trampled and wet, their skeletons starting to show through.

As we passed the last house on the street, a very tall and solid three-storey building, we regarded the statue opposite. John Moffat was a missionary in Africa who was from Ormiston: a very serious-looking man, guarding the village.

There were tall beech hedgerows alongside the road that led down to the railway bridge, full of birds in summer, but quiet in autumn with the leaves thinning out.

'You can see a little nest in there, Mum. Look at that.'

'Yes, I see it, but the birds have all left now. The babies have flown away.'

Mum and I were both hurrying along, not talking much as we walked over the hump of the bridge and then down the side and under the bridge. There is a spot over a little stream where Callum sometimes set up camp, slept out for a few days. We pushed aside tree branches and snagging blackberry bushes as we clambered through to the small clearing in the wood.

The sound of the running stream and calls of pigeons were all around us, the rustling of the trees and the sound of our boots squashing and sucking as we stepped through mud and damp leaves underfoot.

If we said nothing then we could pretend neither of us was actually concerned he might be there, dead. If we stayed quiet and moved slowly then time could stand still for us, just for a short while, for some small reprieve.

The sound of the branches rustling high above surrounded us, but there was no wind in this little peaceful dell. There was no Callum either.

'But look, he has been here recently.'

Mum was an archaeologist of detritus, dating her only son's movements and presence from what he left behind. Here she found cigarette butts and also some lighter fuel cans; most were old and already rusty but there was one new one. She picked it up and shook it.

'Empty. I wonder if he was here and we disturbed him?'

'Hmm, I don't think so. If he'd been sniffing a lot, I doubt he'd have moved very quietly. We'd have heard him.'

The dog was having a marvellous time, chasing water voles in the river and then crashing through the undergrowth, sniffing around Callum's camp. He took off back towards the stream we'd crossed.

'Let's go on into the Puddle Woods.'

'Yes, and then we can have a look around that old coal bing near East Mains where we used to go for the Brownies and Cubs and Guides and Scouts sausage sizzles.'

Quick on our feet but slow in heart and mind, reluctantly we walked and searched and shouted his name into the woods.

'Callum, are you here?'

'Are you hungry? Just come home and we'll get you

something to eat.'

The twilight came creeping as we left the woods and walked round the last section of the railway track. The wind was chilling.

I tripped over a branch, fell on my hand and stayed there, awkward, clutching the air with my other hand. Pain was all through me, my hand but also my stomach and my heart, beating in shock, adrenaline released after hours of tension and searching. I could feel my walnut of anger deep under my ribs, hot and hard with fury for Dad, for Callum too. There were tears but they seemed pathetically inadequate. I walked ahead of Mum.

We did not speak at all on the route back to the house, except to say to the dog, 'Well, did you enjoy your walk, doggy? Ready for dinner now?'

I thought ruefully of my Sydney flatmate's parting words as I left on this trip home to Scotland.

'Enjoy your holidays. You're so lucky to be able to spend time in Scotland.'

When friends in Sydney said this to me as I prepared to head to Scotland for visits, I winced.

Oh yes, it's joyful. Mean thoughts gnashed the inside of my skull. *There's nothing better than a country ramble looking for a dead body or a lost soul. Just so scenic, positively Caledonian.*

Callum was found the next day and went back to his halfway house. He never did tell us exactly where he had been.

I flew back to Australia full of relief and heartache. Once again I drank my way through the flights, swallowing glasses of red wine and mild sleeping pills, then sunrise over the desert and the plane took me back into a bright Sydney morning.

Late July and I am reading through sections of my old diaries and come to the day when Mum told me about the fire. Suddenly, I'm right back there.

Sydney: 1993

There was an echo on the line, so I heard it twice.

'Sit down, Seana … Sit down, Seana … Something bad has happened, bad has happened.'

Granny, Mum's mum, had died just a couple of weeks before. Her death had been sudden although not entirely unexpected. Mum had called to tell me about it and about the funeral arrangements and I could not fly back to attend. Surely nobody else had died? Grandpa? Gran?

'There's been a fire at the house. There's a lot of damage.'

'Oh Mum, I'm sorry to hear that.'

My worry echoed back at me.

'Were you hurt? Is Dad okay?'

Mum's voice came down the line more slowly now. 'No, no we were not inside. Everyone is fine, even the dog and the cats. The dog, the cats.'

'What happened, Mum? Was it old wiring?'

Mum started to speak. I could just hear the echo of … surely not?

'It was Callum …' And then I could tell she was struggling to talk, her voice sounded gnarled, her throat too full to get the words out.

Startled, I stepped backwards in surprise as I realised that Mum was almost crying. Almost – she was stopping herself.

I wish I could go back and say to her, 'Mum, it's all right to cry. Your mother has just died and your son has set fire to your house. If there was ever a time to grab a few Kleenex and have a weep, now is that time.'

But those weren't the words I said. Instead I rescued her. 'Would you like to call back another time, Mum, and tell me what happened? I'm just so glad that no one is hurt.'

How did I learn the whole story? Maybe Mum rang me back later and told me how Callum had come to the house that day, furious and frustrated, wanting money. He and Dad shouted and yelled at each other. Callum picked up the heavy, blackened poker from the fireside, threatening. Mum and Dad went down to their neighbour Mike's house to let him cool off.

Callum did the opposite of cool off. He went out to the old stables and picked up a can of petrol meant for the lawnmower. He took it into the sitting room and poured it on the furniture, with the greatest amount on Dad's chair. Then he threw down a match and left.

The firemen arrived fast; they did not know if Callum was still in the house. The fire gutted the sitting room and burnt through the ceiling into the room above. The whole house was dark with smoke and the firemen groped their way from room to room looking for Callum, or his body. In the aftermath the whole house was smoke damaged, every piece of wallpaper, every carpet, every book, every piece of clothing, every curtain. A fire scorches everything, even what it does not touch.

Mum and Dad could not stay in the house so they borrowed a caravan and parked it in the yard. They ran electricity out and lived there while the huge task of cleaning up and rebuilding went on.

Mum didn't cry on that day and nor did she ever cry properly. When Dad hit her, when she was locked out of the house, when we kids were mean to her, when cats and dogs died, when people died. I remember her angry face, her sad face, bitter looks, sarcastic comments, meanness as she lashed us with her words, concentration when she whacked us with her wooden Scholl sandals. But I cannot remember seeing tears roll down her cheeks. I don't know why; there was plenty to weep about.

And I do not know how she stopped herself from crying. Maybe Mum compacted it all, her grief, her woes, her sorrows. Maybe she crushed the hurt as cars are crushed into tight, hard squares. Maybe they stayed deep inside her, later to seep out. Compacted metal and rubbish corrupts the earth that surrounds it as it leeches. Maybe Mum's emotional debris decayed and leaked out to corrode her brain. But that came later.

Callum was apprehended by the police, charged and sent to prison on remand. Dad's building firm got to work on repairing the damage. Each room was remade exactly the way it was before. Specialist cleaners removed all the soot they could. Then the carpet was replaced and all the wallpaper was changed. Dad bought himself an exact replica of the easy chair he had had before. That chair was the ignition point of the whole fire; it was where Callum had dropped the match.

'Do you think your brother is angry with your parents?' my counsellor asked.

'Well, I'd say so.'

When I heard about the fire, and Callum being in prison, I decided it was time to bolt back to Scotland. Again. Over a few years I went from Sydney to London then to Glasgow and then back to Sydney again. TV work tends to come in fixed-term contracts and I picked up jobs as I came and went, and kept writing for newspapers and magazines too. There was a messy blur of men along the way.

When Callum's court case for the fire came up, I was living in Glasgow and I went to the same court I had been a witness in years before. It seemed much smaller, and the Legal Aid defence lawyer was a great deal less intimidating. Callum pleaded guilty and was sentenced to some months in jail. He had been on remand so went back to the same prison, Saughton in Edinburgh. I waved him goodbye and went back to work. I had started seeing a counsellor in Glasgow and one day told her, 'I dreamed that I was falling through the sky with Callum. I needed to catch hold of him so we could fall together. It was my job to look after him. But I couldn't catch him and then I landed on a cloud. Honestly, a completely soft and fluffy cloud. What a cliché. But Callum kept falling.'

'Well, you don't need to be a psychologist to work out what that means. He's an adult, you are not in charge of him.'

'But I'm the big sister, I was supposed to look after him.'

'Maybe you weren't,' said my counsellor, looking at me kindly. 'Maybe you were only able to look after yourself, and how well have you really been caring for yourself? Even now?'

}ϵ

Edinburgh: 1993

I was reading *The Guardian* in the waiting room at Saughton Prison. Dad had dropped me off in the car park on that coal-black, cold, late afternoon, rain scudding down and wind swirling around.

Nobody else in the prison waiting room was reading any newspaper, far less *The Guardian*. I was hiding behind it really, finding it hard to concentrate on reading. The waiting room reminded me of scary walks down the High Street in Tranent, of walking alone in the East End of Glasgow.

It's not that I hadn't visited a prison before. I had been filming at Long Bay in Sydney just weeks before. That was work, though, and I had my own prison guard minder, not that I needed him at all. We were filming prisoners putting together care packages for a charity. This was part of their work program, the disadvantaged helping the disadvantaged. It was a nice story which we filmed quickly and we were back in the office by lunchtime. On that day I felt compassionate, professional and organised. Entirely different to how I felt on this day visiting Callum.

Here at the legendary Saughton, this felt like neither work nor play. Most of the people waiting were skinny women, with messy-haired kids. They wore the Scottish uniform of poverty, hoodies and baggy track pants. Many smoked, gamely ignoring the regular tannoy messages.

'This is a no-smoking zone, please extinguish your cigarettes. There is a smoking area outside.'

I was a smoker too and was enjoying sniffing in some calming second-hand smoke as I sat there. It was incredible that very recently I had been slurping cappuccinos at the Blues Point Cafe in McMahons Point, feeling totally at home. Here, I was a fish out of water, a kangaroo jumping through the heather, a wild haggis trying to survive in the desert.

Eventually, the tannoy called us in for the visit.

Callum was sitting at a low table. The chair scraped on the concrete floor as I pulled it out and sat down, tucking my handbag between my feet.

'How are you going, Seana?' said Callum, his head tilted down but lifting his eyes to mine. His hair was cut in a number one, very short all over. He looked so thin, his baggy colourless prison clothes hanging from his shoulders.

'OK. A bit freaked out by being here.'

'It's not too bad.'

'How are you getting on? Are you safe?'

'The guy I share a cell with is nice. He reads *The Scotsman* every day. Tell Mum that, she'll be pleased to hear it.'

There was an empty space where my brain should be. The heat was too much in this room and I shuffled off a few layers.

'What sort of things do you do in here? Is it really boring?'

'Not too bad. We can walk around, go outside for a short time. And I've met my pals.'

'New friends?'

'It's guys from the Ross High, you know, Shug, Jimmy, Deeks. They've been good to me. It's great to see people you know.'

It turned out that there's an Old Boys' Club at every school you go to, but pick your school well if you're looking for help and support in Saughton. Callum's friends from the Ross High in Tranent did look out for him. He definitely did not seem to mind his few months in jail, and it was the only time he went.

Dad had gone shopping and he picked me up again from the car park. I told him that Callum looked well and that he'd met some old pals in there.

'When will you go for a visit yourself, Dad?'

'I don't know, maybe I won't. I just don't know what I would say to him.'

Dad couldn't cope. He could not handle Callum's problems, his psychotic behaviour, his addictions.

Callum's diagnosis of schizophrenia did not seem to be known to the prison, and I made an appointment to speak to one of the social workers.

'Why do you think he's in a prison not a hospital?' I asked.

'I'm not sure. Can you tell me a bit about him?'

Being a person with no filter, I gave her the whole story. I told her about Dad and his violence towards Callum and how he and Mum fought a lot, about the drug taking and weird behaviour and then his time in the psychiatric hospital and how he had set the fire for which he was imprisoned because he was so furious with Dad and Mum. Once I started talking on these topics, which I did a fair bit, I really could not stop. My talking was compulsive and impulsive and I did not mind telling anyone about all the gory details.

The social worker, whose ears and head were ringing, I am sure, with the relentless torrent of Smith family history that was being regurgitated her way, said something which made me sit up and think.

'How do you think Callum feels being born to two parents who did not mean to have him and who were fighting a lot?'

'But we were conceived in love,' I said to her immediately, totally from the gut and without any thought. And I do think that was true. In the 1960s, as Mum and Dad made love, I am sure they truly cared for each other and that their lovemaking did signify love between them, the connectedness sex brings.

And that does matter to me, that when we were all conceived there was passion between them and there was love in action to create these new lives. Saying it that day to the social worker at Saughton Prison did cement a little something in my mind: that we came from love. Perhaps the existence of their four children was the best expression of Mum and Dad's love, of their youth and their passion for each other.

Orange

I speak to Callum on the phone again on July 31st, which is Morag's birthday.

'Can you remember the day Morag was born?' I ask.

'No, don't be daft, Shoshi. I was too young.'

As I chat more to Callum, I feel so grateful to the social worker in Ormiston who had finally called time on his attempts to live in the community. She learned that he had hit

Mum a few times, furious that she would not give him money for alcohol. We all hoped that this would be a turnaround for Callum. He would not be able to drink at all at the care home; perhaps that would help?

In fact, the opposite occurred. Alcohol might have been helping dampen the voices that plagued Callum. His psychosis seemed to grow worse and he had a few stays at the psychiatric ward of the local hospital. Callum also made a couple of game attempts to escape. The front door was locked but there were fire escapes so, at times, he was in and out of these like a yo-yo. He was once found walking over the Forth Bridge, trying to get back to Ormiston.

Mum's life was much easier with him away. No more early morning wake-ups when he banged on the door at 6 am. No more being shouted at and threatened. She would visit him fortnightly and he would be brought over to visit her, too. She still had times sitting quietly with him out by the pond in the garden. He would drink his sweet coffee, smoking and chatting, while she looked for the sturdy goldfish, survivors of the winter freeze.

Then Mum had to leave to live at St Olaf in Nairn, and Callum only saw her once more in the eighteen months before she passed away.

꙳

'Do you think there's a heaven, Callum?' I ask towards the end of our phone call.

'Hope so.'

'Maybe Mum's up there weeding her vegetable patch.'

'I've got to go, Seana, it's time for a fag.'

I hang up the phone and make myself a cup of chamomile

tea. The guilt I used to feel about Callum has gone now, that old guilt that Callum was the child who was sacrificed to save the rest of us.

I often felt that he was holding a mirror up to Dad, to show Dad his true self without the armour of money, privilege and normality that Dad had built like castle fortifications around himself and his alcohol addiction. Callum was drug and alcohol dependent, went to jail, was homeless, but he was honest about it all and never pretended to be someone he wasn't. Not like Dad.

Today as I start to check through the fridge, write a family meal plan and work out what shopping I need to get for it, I am feeling that Callum is also more honest than me. Alcohol cravings are weaving their smoky presence all around me every day. They invade my body, curl around my guts and my brain. I am resisting; some weeks I manage not to drink from Sunday to Thursday but it's hard. I know I have a problem. I have my very own drink problem. I have built my bulwark of home, family, wise husband, two cats and two bunny rabbits in the garden, so that I can keep up my denial.

I know what denial is, I know how it operates, and to know that I am in denial myself is searing. Yet still, the thought of stopping, of losing my anchor, my crutch, my pal, my instant relax, my thing just for me, my quick easy buzz, my completely letting go, is too much. I cannot do it.

Is it real denial if I know very well that I have my very own version of a drinking problem? I'm just not willing to do anything about it. Or not able. Denial, or despair?

EIGHT

August

Orange

August 3rd marks the tenth anniversary of Dad's death. Ten years. And Mum has been dead for eight months now. We have been living here in Orange for more than seven months. It's winter in Australia and the last month of summer in Scotland. I am definitely not going over for a visit this year and that feels like a relief. I visited twice a year for the past three years, for weeks at a time and with great disruption to our family life. And yet I never felt I was there for long enough, always wanted to stay longer with Mum, to be there for her when her need was greatest.

In Sydney we used to say that the Sydney winter was very close to the Scottish summer, but sunnier. Now, here in Orange, this winter is so chilly it almost feels like a Scottish winter, though still sunnier.

On this anniversary of Dad's final tumble down the stairs, I walk to the highest lookout in town from where I can see snow dusting the top of Mount Canobolas. Far, far away, the ridge of hills hovers against the blue sky. Far, far away, my mind shifts to Scotland, the huge mountains rearing out of the lochs of the West Coast, the splash and rush of the sea as *Penelee*'s bow cut through, the slapping of painters, the booming of the sails and the scent of heather and salt. Far, far away in time now, as well as halfway across the planet. Dad has lain in his watery grave for ten years.

I feel lonely as I walk home, down the steps and over the playing fields. I love to wander around this pretty area with its small streets and wide views. I need a dog, I really do. The teens do not want to walk with me, and Paul is a runner not a walker. I remember our family dog, Bob, when I was a child, how we walked for miles with him, alongside rivers, through fields, along the disused railway tracks. That dog's enthusiasm, his joie de vivre, the way his ears blew in the wind and the thumping of his tail.

I swish my boots through piles of leaves as I head home, in tune with the child I once was as I shift the leaves, but a mother again as I walk inside and do an instinctive mental tally: put dishes away, write the shopping list, ask Paul to do the shopping, remember to bring the washing in, fold that washing over there, don't forget to put more fruit on the shopping list, the grass needs cutting, the bathroom carpet needs to be hoovered.

I make a cup of tea, grab two biscuits and go though to the sunroom where my desk and workspace are. I slide the door to close off the kitchen. I am pretty good at compartmentalising when I work. But today I am not working, just remembering. I click through images on my computer, searching for photos of Dad's gravestone in West Byres cemetery; there they are. I look, then close my eyes, feel the peace that I always have felt in that pretty place, hear the birdsong and see in my mind's eye the fields of golden barley that ripple out beyond the graveyard in summer. I imagine standing by Dad's grave then sitting on the garden bench nearby, having a chat to him as I do whenever I visit the graveyard in person. Then I let my mind wander, conscious that I am only going to enjoy happy memories of Dad today. The difficult times are so dominant; the brain hangs on to the bits that spell danger, that we humans need to learn from. But he was not only the hard parts, the abusive man, the coercive husband. Today is a time for some cheerful, jolly memories, for balance, for reality, for me as much as for him.

Ormiston: Mid-1970s

Two gnarly old plum trees in the garden at Marketgate cast cool shade on a warm summer evening. The leaves of the plum tree were deep green and lush, all the blossoms had fallen and small plums were forming, a promise of autumn fruit. Our garden was large, with a high stone wall all around, private even though the main street of Ormiston was beyond the wall on one side. Jasmine covered the rear wall and beyond it the stained-glass windows of the church glittered in the sunshine. This garden was Mum's, her joy and refuge, and where she nurtured the plants which fed her family.

Mum decided to have a picnic tea on the grass, something simple, relaxed. We kids and the dog ran around as she brought out plates of food. Dad came out and sat with us on the old tartan picnic rug as we gathered to eat. His hair was longer than usual and he swept it back as he sat down. His sleeves were rolled up and his firm, fit body was in its prime. He stretched out beside Mum, relaxed and calm. We ate tomatoes, lettuce, cucumber, bread spread with butter, ham and cold boiled potatoes.

After eating we ran around and my sister and I decided to play a trick.

'We'll throw a bucket of water onto Dad.'

So we filled the bucket at the garden tap and then crept over to launch a stream of water over him.

Dad's yell was huge and vast and filled the whole garden. He was standing up and laughing and he chased us all around the flower beds and the pond as we shrieked and shouted. We fell over from our laughing, knees weak. Dad tickled us whenever he caught us, then let us go to run and be chased again.

Years later, chasing my own kids around this same garden on a visit from Australia, I realised that he knew that bucket of water was on its way all along. He let us do it and then he gave us the great joy of being chased, his voluble and exuberant reaction just the sort of excitement and intense emotion that kids thrive on.

A psychologist once told me that indifference is what children fear most because it puts them in the greatest danger. A flat, emotionless affect is more damaging that shouting and yelling – at least some noise shows care. Children prefer abundant, noisy exuberance and love but shouting and yelling will do at a pinch – at least that's some sort of attention. Being ignored and being neglected is the worst.

Be exuberant in your affection, he advised. Do not be flat in your affect. Sweep your children up in your arms, hurl them around, sing their praises, shout for joy. When you are joyous, they will be too. When you pay no attention, that's when fear will come creeping out to catch them. Be raucous in your attention, be physical and loud in your shared happiness. Kids love that.

Dad was the loud one when I was little: excited and exuberant at times, scary at others. Mum was often flat; who wouldn't have been? She was that long word I learned when I was a child: depressed.

Karachi, Pakistan: 1998

As a child, our summer holidays were the very best time of the year, adventurous and exciting. With just the six of us and our dog aboard the boat, Dad didn't get wildly drunk, was not abusive. I jumped ship at sixteen, though, and never went on a family holiday again. But Mum and Dad once came to stay with us after Jake was born, and we had a happy holiday again. I take my mind and memory back to the year our little family spent in Pakistan, leaving Scotland when Jake was just three months old, for Paul to start a job. At the time, we had a choice between Aberdeen and Karachi. Well, what would you have done?

The main beach in Karachi is nothing like the silvery strands of Scotland or the golden dazzle of Sydney sand. However, it does have snake charmers. Jake wriggled and twisted in his stroller as a snake slowly rose up from its basket just a couple of feet away from him. The flute playing of the snake wallah sounded fairly basic to my untrained ear but it seemed to be doing the trick. The snake was rising, rising, and we were just as mesmerised as it was. It lifted and swayed, eyes fixed on the flute, its tongue briskly zipping in and out. Jake's podgy arms waving towards it were the only jagged movements in the scene. Even if it struck out, it couldn't get to him, could it?

'It's a snake, Jake. Can you say "snake"?' I said.

Jake was only eleven months old and he could not, of course; in fact he didn't even babble yet. He did not turn his head towards me as I called his name. He seemed too entranced by the sinuous snake moving higher and higher from its colourful woven basket.

'How high do you think that snake can go?' asked Dad.

Winters in Karachi were clement – there are about three months of fine, warm weather, such a difference to the scorching months of the rest of the year when it was 36C daily and we ran the air conditioners night and day. Mum and Dad had come for a visit and this turned out to be the very best time that we ever spent with them. If you have a loved one with a serious drink problem, move to a dry country and invite them over.

Beside the snake, which finally seemed to be drooping somewhat, were a couple of camels, festooned with pink and purple ribbons, their handler grinning widely, if not toothily, in our direction. Our driver, Piyari, was always the man to work out these situations. He was a big man, tall and confident, with a generous chest and tummy that told of his status. Piyari was Hindu; he dyed his hair with henna and his moustache was luxuriant even by Pakistani standards. He always wore perfectly ironed stripy shirts which showed off his fine physique.

Smoke curled towards us from further along the road where food stalls were being set up, the scent acrid, oily. We were too nervy by then to eat street food in Karachi, a few attempts having ended with violent emissions from all orifices.

'You want to ride on the camel, memsahib?' asked Piyari. 'He is offering you a good price.'

'Sounds great, Piyari. What about it: any takers for a sail on the ship of the desert?' I asked.

Jake was gazing out to sea as Dad and I clambered onto the throne-like saddles of the camel.

'Look at Grandpa,' said Paul. 'That camel is going to stand up.'

And it did, but even though Paul pointed and called again, Jake was still staring out to sea.

'Maybe camels aren't his favourite,' I said.

Dad and I were all settled in when the cameleer gave the signal and whacked the poor camel. And up we went. It's a steep and sudden rise when a camel gets up, pretty exciting for beginners like us.

Dad's cheeks were bright red and he was laughing away.

'Well, hello there! This is the life, Seana. Let's go!'

And off we went, loping along the sand, not at all used to the slow and steady but still unexpectedly juddery motion of the camel. We did not go far at all, but it was fun. It was so rare to do something together, just Dad and me. We were the adventurers in the family, not a pair who would knock back a camel ride, however much the camel smelled of camel. How far we were from the seaweed-strewn beaches of Scotland with gentle waves curling over. Here in Karachi the waves were deep blue and they absolutely pounded the beach; local people drowned regularly. There were often dead dogs on that beach, once a dead porpoise, and the litter was shocking.

Dad's shirt was sweaty by the time we got off, and my legs felt stretched and a bit sore. Piyari was definitely ready to get going. Mum was folding up Jake's stroller and Paul was holding him high up saying, 'Camel, it's a camel, Jake. Can you say "camel"?'

Jake smiled as Paul tickled his tummy.

This holiday most definitely remains a highlight of my adult life with Mum and Dad. It was so simple; all we had to do was take alcohol out of the equation and all was rosy. Dad absolutely could stop drinking if he had to, there were no fits or even tremors. Not at that stage in his life anyway.

⚘

Pakistan is a Muslim country. This means that Pakistanis are not permitted to drink alcohol and there are no shops selling alcohol, unlike in Bonnie Scotland, and no huge beer barns like those in Australia. If you are not a Pakistani citizen then you are allowed to drink alcohol in your own home, and we did visit one French restaurant in our year there which sold alcohol to foreign diners. Paul had once spent most of a day in a government department with a fellow from his company's office attempting to get an alcohol permit. He had gone from desk to desk getting forms stamped but eventually had thrown his hands in the air and given up. He wasn't motivated to drink; we didn't really care at that point, not even me.

Going shopping for Pakistani handicrafts was easy and it involved not so much going out as staying in. The shops came to us. We sent out word to the chowkidars on the gate that we would love to see some brass work and later that afternoon a seller came calling.

We pulled the wicker chairs into the front garden and basked in gentle sunshine as the brass man unwrapped his wares from bundles of inky newspaper. Our garden was enclosed by very high walls, covered in bougainvillea which was frothing with pink and red flowers. It looked very pretty rather than revealing the small fortress our home was. The sharp shards of glass set into the top of the wall occasionally glinted in the sunshine.

Jake was splashing in his paddling pool, a nude cherub, the picture of glowing health with his fair curls and little teeth. This boy of just eleven months old was huge compared to the beggar babies that would be pressed against our car windows, their full set of teeth showing they were much older than my baby, but so much smaller and skinnier.

Safe behind our flowery walls, we picked up various brass

pots and intricate spice boxes, whose hinges opened smoothly to show smaller boxes set inside ready for coriander, chilli, ginger and other spices. A wide brass dish with a smooth top, polished so highly that it reflected the birds flying by in the sky, was our first purchase. Dad loved antiques and history and he told us stories of Sindh as we felt the smooth cool metal and talked about the elegant tall tapering lids of some of the other pots.

Piyari helped us negotiate fair enough prices, and our goods were moved inside where the maids would polish them daily. Dad and Mum took a couple of pieces back to Scotland, exotic reminders of a restful holiday of safe adventuring, to add to their other souvenirs from more stressful holidays.

Dad spent a lot of time reading, burying himself away in books. That was also how he dealt with the occasional weeks of not drinking in Scotland which he did sometimes just to prove he could. The returns to drinking were always spectacular and explosive. It was always a point of pride with Dad that he could stop when he wanted to. He had held back when we had a Spanish school student staying for a month one year, then gone on a massive bender as soon as her plane lifted off to return her to Madrid.

Perhaps the biggest difference the lack of alcohol in Karachi made was to Mum. She was so much more relaxed; she didn't have to worry about what Dad would do and what Paul would think and what might happen. This visit made me realise that a big part of the unease in our family home had been Mum's stress and worry and her nippiness. Without alcohol, she was much more herself, much calmer and happier. It was a relief.

What Dad didn't know was that one of Paul's colleagues had given us a bottle of Gordon's gin and it sat on a shelf in a big storeroom off the laundry, which was tucked away behind the kitchen. Since we had a maid to do the laundry, Dad never went into that room, so he never knew about that bottle of gin hiding out in the laundry. And I certainly wasn't going to tell him.

Orange

A Thursday evening, mid-August. Paul is away this week and my loneliness is building, building. The itch to go somewhere else, to be en route to anywhere, watch clouds from a plane or mountains and fields whizzing by from a train window is growing, growing.

After the twins are in bed I go to my desk, taking my glass and bottle of wine with me, and I read some news and then start to do a little search on Facebook.

You weren't supposed to be drinking during the week, Seana.

Och, shhh, would you? I feel great, and I needed the instant relax after the messy day that I've had, all that running around, and the fussing as the kids went to bed. Now it's my time. Don't be mean to me.

You're drinking on your own, you've had most of that bottle already, and you have a big day tomorrow.

Worry about that tomorrow. Come on, let's have a bit of a laugh.

My fingers tap the keyboard, slipping a bit as they go so I have to stop and type in the name again.

You know you shouldn't be doing this. You're fifty-five. This is childish.

Just a little look, just a wee check to see what they're up to.

I pick up the glass, but it slips in my hand and wine spills on the keyboard. I lift it up and try to put the wine into my mouth, make a mess and mop up.

I turn my head too fast and the world shifts, and it feels as if I am tipping myself into the screen. I'll just search for one

or two, I tell myself, but my heart is racing now and the lure of
the hunt is taking over.

You've never googled any of the Desperadoes when you've been sober,
Seana.

Wheesht, I can't pay attention to you now, too busy.

I pour another glass of wine and drink the whole lot in one
go.

That will shut you up.

I feel my head swim and slide into the screen and go with
it, don't hold back.

The Desperadoes is my collective noun for all the ex-
boyfriends of my twenties, all a bit wild, all super bright blokes,
all of them big drinkers. I was exceptionally mean to all of
these young men, punishing them one after the other for
their heavy drinking. The fact that I drank alongside them
did not compute in my emotionally messy calculations about
who to dump and who to pick up next. Oh messy, very messy
indeed. I went back to one or two of the Desperadoes too,
slept with them again months or years after being mean to
them, a way to say sorry maybe. Or, perhaps, the shame, an
attempt to keep them interested, keep them dangling, just in
case I needed to use them again, needed to borrow them like
a library book to read and then give back.

In 12-steps groups, people talk about 'taking a hostage'
and I relate to that very keenly. I snatched at these young men,
initiated relationships, wrapped them up and kept them close.
Then when I was fed up with them, angry because of their
drinking, I'd set them loose, drop them off in the middle of
nowhere, leave them to find their own way home.

I find Rico, still looking very handsome in his late fifties.
He's retired from his fund management career and I wonder
what he's up to now. Something interesting, I have no doubt.

Then I check up on Neil, who is living the life I had thought I would have, being a writer of travel guidebooks, based in Perthshire. Rob is now the stay-at-home dad of three little boys while his wife works in an embassy in Italy. He has an interesting website about old-fashioned photography. I search for my first proper teenage boyfriend too. He is easy to find since he's a Professor of English at Cambridge these days.

I wonder if they all know how lucky they were to get away. Nothing good could have come out of any of these relationships in my boozy, bewildered twenties. They were all fortunate to have avoided engagement, marriage, babies with me when I was young. It took a long hard year of therapy in Glasgow in my early thirties, a lot of tears and mental shifts, before I drew a line in the sand, stopped abusing my own body and young men's hearts. I used to say that Paul and then Jake were the rewards for that year of intense therapy.

'Does he take a drink?' my friend Rory at BBC Scotland asked me when I told him about Paul. That Scottish code.

'No, he just has one or two, not a drinker.'

'That's good then.'

I open another bottle of wine, stay at the computer for hours, knowing I need to get to bed, but drinking more and more until I start nodding off at the desk. It's a stagger not a walk to the bathroom, and I cannot be bothered brushing my teeth.

Do you feel that this drunken googling is a betrayal of your family, Seana?

No, I'd never do it sober, would I? Just a bit of escapism.

※

Oh blimey. I feel terrible this morning. I must have stayed up so late.

Oh cringe, cringe, cringe, I spent hours last night trawling the internet for the Desperadoes. Gawd, I haven't done that for a long time. I must have been really pissed.

Is there anything sadder and more lonely than late night drunken scrolling and searching, Seana?

No, there is not. You're a massive loser, do you know that?

God, I feel terrible, awful; I think I might vomit. What time is it?

What sort of a mentally unfit mother am I? How emotionally messy am I still? Does this count as infidelity?

Do I really have to get up and sort the kids out?

I do, and I end up shouting at them when they're slow. Again. Even after two coffees, two Panadols and a lot of water.

Does my breath smell? I bet it does. Do my clothes stink?

∮

I am talking to Morag on the phone one wintery late August night in Orange and I tell her that I have started writing – finally – about the domestic violence that happened in our family and how Mum managed to stop it happening, more or less, after she went to Al-Anon and learned to stop arguing with Dad and stop the fights before they started. She became quite independent of Dad, lived her own life. She did stay though. Why on earth had she stayed? The great conundrum and question of my life.

'She didn't completely stop the violence though, did she?' I say.

'Do you mean the time she said to Dad after a terrible night that if he did it again she'd call the police?' Morag asks.

Then she adds, 'No, hold on, did she actually call the police that night? Or was it another time? He was once charged, wasn't he?'

There is a lot of confusion about what happened, when and to whom in our family. There is no clarity around how often the police were called, not to mention how often they ought to have been called.

Morag and I finish the conversation, with her letting me know that the big box of Greenwheat crockery should arrive on my doorstep any day now. After Mum moved into St Olaf Care Home, her Denby Greenwheat collection was boxed up and stored at Morag's house. When she died, neither of my sisters wanted it and Callum does not use his own crockery in his care home. I couldn't bear the thought of it going into my nephew's student flat or being given away, so a box full of it was on its way to me now.

The Denby factory in Derbyshire first produced stoneware in 1809 and still does today. Denby Greenwheat was manufactured for twenty years from 1956. The design features a stylised wheat design hand-painted on an off-white egg-shell glazed background with deep green highly glazed saucers, lids and bases. Mum and Dad were given many coffee cups, bowls, plates and serving dishes by their friends and family as wedding presents in 1960. I have a quick look at the Denby website after I put the phone down and see beautifully coloured, solid and practical crockery there for sale. There's even a factory shop to visit. One day I will get there.

I look up Denby on Google Maps and see that it is only seventeen miles south of Chesterfield, which is where Mum's own mother was brought up. That must be why Mum and Dad were given the Denby Greenwheat pottery – Granny must have known about it from her own childhood. I'm finding out new things about my parents even after they have both died.

I really am looking forward to seeing the Greenwheat crockery and I'm hoping none of it will arrive smashed in pieces. Mind you, I have myself been in pieces over an incident that occurred with Greenwheat crockery many years ago.

Ormiston: Early 1990s

'I will never, ever forget seeing your Mum out in the garden with blood streaming down her face like that,' Mr Mike told me one night when I walked down the yard to visit my favourite neighbour in his house, the Granary.

'Like what?' I asked, and he told me.

Mike heard screaming and looked out of his window to see Mum standing in the garden covered in blood and hysterical. In a drunken fury, Dad had smashed all of the Greenwheat crockery and Mum had sustained at least one cut during this crockery catastrophe.

'Oh, you didn't know.' Mr Mike looked upset, not realising that I hadn't been aware of this particular violent incident.

'No, but I had noticed there were lots of new Greenwheat pieces in the cupboard in the wall where we keep it. And I did ask Mum about it but she just said Dad had been buying more pieces.'

I wonder if it was Mike who called the police? Someone did and they carted Dad off to sober up.

Dad was charged with assault for the night of the crockery smashing incident. He didn't have to appear in court himself. His lawyer pleaded guilty and Dad paid the small fine.

By the way, it's not as if there was an utter blanket silence about disasters from Mum. She would talk to me on the phone about Dad and Callum a lot. We were not trying to pretend, by that stage, that nothing untoward was occurring, but the whole story certainly wasn't being transferred to me far away in Australia.

Anyway, let's just say that the police could have been

gainfully employed at Marketgate many more times than they were. But they weren't.

Dad spent a lot of time replacing that Greenwheat crockery, buying from a second-hand crockery website. He added to the collection, purchasing many pretty little soup bowls and vegetable dishes as well as plates and cups and mugs. By the time Dad passed away, there was a good collection of this Denby pottery in the cupboards at Marketgate.

Orange

A few days later, on a frosty morning, the doorbell rings and a courier is standing outside with a large cardboard box strapped to a trolley.

'Sign here.'

He takes the box into the kitchen and lifts it onto the bench and I thank him, then reach for a pair of scissors and start to slice the packaging tape, very gently.

A ruffled sea of scrunched-up newspaper and bubble wrap awaits me, and I find my hands are shaking slightly as I start to slowly lift out pieces. Here is a large dinner plate, with the wheat stalk image to one side and a thin dark green line around the circumference. Small cereal bowls are nestled together with padding between each, and two larger bowls will do for pasta dinners. Next come small side plates and then, ah, it's a milk jug, so round it almost looks like a ball with the top chopped off. Oh, this does take me back.

'Your mum is a real lady,' Dad used to tell us, and she really was. Milk was always poured from its glass bottle into a proper milk jug. Each day the milkman left six pints of milk at the back door and sometimes a blue tit would peck through the foil lids to sip the cream. Milk in a glass bottle was never, ever seen on the kitchen table.

I look at this one-pint milk jug and wonder if it was the one that had been completely emptied by the little pussycat Treacle on the day we brought her home from Seafield Cat and Dog Home. Perhaps it had been safely in the fridge when Dad smashed the rest of the crockery.

Oh dear, my children and Paul and I never use a proper milk jug. Great big plastic three-litre containers litter the kitchen bunker and we slosh merrily from them. Our kids would drain a one-pint jug far too quickly for that ever to be practical. Maybe I shall start to use a milk jug now, just for myself, grow more refined.

Towards the bottom of this large box I find a four-pint lidded casserole dish with a loop handle and the base of a smaller casserole dish. I tend to serve my family soup from the pan or slow cooker but maybe it is time to use these as soup tureens and smarten up the family's table etiquette. Tucked deep in the corners of the cardboard box are small salt and pepper shakers, empty for now.

I rinse and dry all these pieces of crockery and place the bowls and plates in the drawers with the crockery we use daily. The teacups go on a high shelf and the casserole dishes in the bottom drawers. I take out the last item, and unwrap a tall Greenwheat mug which I use for my next cup of Earl Grey tea. I cannot remember ever having seen this Greenwheat mug before, but it's the right size for me and I think it will become my new favourite. A sudden urge to nibble on a piece of shortbread comes upon me. I have none, but I pull out my recipe book and find Gran's recipe which Mum had written out for me many years before and which I have sellotaped in. Butter, sugar, white flour, rice flour, I have them all.

I bake some petticoat tails and then have another cuppa and place some shortbread on a Greenwheat plate and hand it round to the kids when they get home from school. They do not need to know the whole story; the sweetness of the shortbread will do.

As I wash up later I'm thinking that, to me, this crockery is not only a remembrance of Dad's violence but also of his attempt to repair what he had smashed. It is also a symbol of their long marriage, which began with these presents as they started a life together, so very young. Their marriage started with passion and with hope and joy and love. Most of that hope and love and almost all the joy was worn away during the almost five decades of the marriage but, by the very end, as Mum lay dying, some of the love and hope was found again, brighter at the end of her life than it had been for much of the marriage itself.

NINE

September

Orange

Springtime in Orange is a most marvellous season. Ornamental apple trees make my daily walk around the streets of East Orange a joy of unfurling foliage and frothing white and pink blossom.

I have a huge treat coming up, a work trip to Fiji; surely that is a massive and outrageous oxymoron. One of those miracle emails arrived just a couple of weeks ago: would I like to fly to Fiji to join the small cruise ship MV *Reef Endeavour* for a week's exploration around the Mamanuca and Yasawa Islands?

I just had to check that Paul didn't need to go away and then I emailed back at warp speed. Book me in!

My role is to take a lot of photos and videos and then write a big article for my family travel website and post lots of images and video to social media. No problemo.

So mid-month finds me packing my stinger suit and snorkel, waving goodbye to the kids and Paul, and driving down to Sydney to catch a flight to Nadi. Unlike motherhood and housewifery, these travelling and communication skills come naturally to me and I do feel competent, which is exactly what all people long to feel.

What is different about this trip is that I have not left meals prepared nor changed the sheets before I left nor made a list of who is going where and when. It is all over to Paul in his new post-career house-husband phase. Have a week of full-time proper parenting, my darling, and you are very welcome. Off I go! Trala!

Fiji

I stay one night at an airport hotel, fly north and east to Nadi and walk over to the jetty at Denarau on a warm sunny morning, immediately spotting the ship and my fellow passengers.

The first three-day loop takes us to the Mamanuca Islands including Monuriki where *Cast Away* was filmed. I am keen to get some good shots and videos in the bag and do not stay up late or drink too much, but by the time we return to Denarau to pick up and drop off passengers I know I am off to a good start and can relax a bit.

My travel blogger friend Paula has joined the cruise and I catch up with her and her husband Charles as we start the four-day loop which takes us up north to the Yasawa Islands.

'We've been given a bottle of sparkling wine as a gift. Charles doesn't like bubbles, would you like to have a glass?' Paula asks and I am in like Flynn. The sun sets purple and pink along the rim of the ocean's edge and islands turn to mauve silhouettes as the ship steams along. We sit at a table on the upper deck looking out at the churn of the ship's propellers. Paula pours me a tall glass of fizz and I practically snatch it from her.

'This is so far, so very far from what I am normally doing on a Tuesday at six pm, Paula. This is heaven. There's somebody making the dinner, setting the table and all will be washed up for us. I've gone from slavery to luxury, and I am telling you, luxury is better!'

'Yes, we're a long way from home. Cheers!'

Paula is a website whiz, so smart and generous with her discoveries. She's younger than me, in fact, but had her children young and she just seems so much more together than I am. I always enjoy being with her, and now this setting and the adventures ahead are making me positively fizzy in the brain. Or maybe it's the wine. I am on my second glass now and it's making me laugh and talk even faster than usual. And I just cannot imagine having this moment without the bubbly. We polish off the bottle as dinner is announced, and the walk down the metal steps to the deck below is more than precarious.

Next morning, though.

God, why did I drink that bubbly wine so fast, and on an empty tummy? And why did you have more, Seana, at dinner?

Why do you need alcohol to fully relax in this glorious and luxurious setting? Aren't the ship and the sunsets and the great food and the snorkelling enough for you?

Why can't you let go and sink into enjoyment on your own? What is wrong with your brain?

I don't have time for your whinging. OK, so your head feels as if someone whacked you with a mallet, and your throat is dry. Everyone is drinking on this cruise, you're no different to anyone else. Get up and go to breakfast, and then get in the wee boat for a snorkel.

Tonight, I can't do the same again. Don't let me. In fact, I really need to stop drinking for the rest of the cruise.

The evening arrives and again I buy a bottle of wine for dinner, managing not to drink all of it which feels like an achievement. I ask the barman to keep it behind the bar for me until dinner tomorrow.

And the next morning I am wishing I hadn't had that wine. Here I am in the midst of utter luxury and so very much enjoying the freedom and the ocean and the snorkelling and the beautiful views and the company of the fantastic lively Fijian crew, so large and so healthy looking and smiley and full of joy. Why make my mornings a misery?

And so it goes on. The exuberance and the impulsivity of the late afternoons and evenings and the self-recrimination and self-abuse of each morning. So familiar, so painfully familiar.

Many people just enjoy a glass or two of wine on a cruise at sunset, and then leave the bottle for a few days. Do they? Maybe they don't. If they do, I just need to become like that. To make a plan and stick to it. I am sure at the start of the day and the start of the week that I can be sensible, normal and sane, but once I start, I don't want to stop. I'm not being outrageous or causing any scenes or even being unprofessional in any way in this semi-work situation. But oh, the effort required to stop myself drinking a lot, lot more is enormous. I put the brakes on when I don't want to and my inner brake pads are wearing thin. My knuckles are white as I grip and stop myself drinking as much as I know I really want to.

I meet a warm and friendly couple from Melbourne on this cruise. Deborah and Brian are aboard the MV *Reef Endeavour* for their second time and loving it. Deborah is a writer and a very perceptive, warm and caring soul.

'I saw you for the first few days, very self-contained and looking busy. You seem much more relaxed now.'

We are deep in an outdoor pool as she speaks, washing off the mud with which we were completely plastered moments before. A muddy hot spring experience is a hilarious highlight of this cruise.

'Yes, well, I did have to do a bit of work really, and I still need to take notes and photos but I am feeling more on holiday now.'

I have told Deborah about my family and our move to Orange. I can tell she is intrigued by me being here on my own. She doesn't ask a million questions like I tend to, but slowly I ease into telling her that Mum died in January and that my emotional tectonic plates have been shifting beneath me.

'And I miss her, Deborah. I know it was better for Mum to pass away. She never wanted to live like that. Years ago she used to make us promise that we would be as kind to her as she was to the dogs and cats and the horse. "Take me to the vet and have him put me to sleep," she used to say, and we promised we would. But of course we couldn't do that when the time came.'

'We've got time now. Tell me about your mum,' said Deborah. 'I would love to hear her story.'

I blab on and on about my Dr Jekyll and Mr Hyde father, about how young Mum was when she married, the opposition from her parents, how much Dad loved her but was so terrible to her and how she did carve out her own life, learn some detachment from him. I tell her how much we had hoped for change when Dad had died, hoped she would have a long, healthy life doing what made her happy.

Ormiston: 2015

Mum turned the old stables attached to Marketgate into a small cottage for herself. She divided up her garden, retaining the part with the greenhouse and berry and vegetable patch. She installed French doors from her kitchen out to the garden. The rest of the garden was sold with Marketgate.

However, just a few short months after Mum moved into her new home, Morag called to let me know that Mum was in hospital. She had had a stroke. Later Mum told me what had happened.

'I felt weird, terrible, and I knew I needed help. I managed to call Cath but I couldn't get the words out to explain what had happened. She knew something was wrong. She walked straight round and she could tell I'd had a stroke. She called an ambulance straight away.'

'How did you feel?'

'Mainly scared, I think. Who wouldn't be?'

Mum went to the hospital in an ambulance and was given medication and had a brain scan. She was released the next day, much to my horror. Surely that couldn't be right? She couldn't talk properly or think quite right. A physiotherapist and a speech therapist did make house visits to Mum but it did not sound nearly enough.

I would call Mum and it was clear that some words were hard to find. Sometimes she would mix up words. Just talking on the phone seemed tiring.

'Hello, Mum, how are you doing today?'

'Well, I did go for a walk, but my hip is still sore you know. And I tried gardening, there are so many … oh now, what do you call them?' Mum stopped to think for a while. 'The things that grow in the garden but you didn't plant them and you don't want them there.'

'Weeds, Mum. Well done, you explained what you meant. Between us we always do get there.'

Sydney: 2016

About a year later, Mum came to visit us in Australia, together with her youngest sister Heather, who was between husbands at the time. They should not have come. Mum was unwell and seemed confused by many things. I gave her a new camera and tried to show her how to use it, but she could never manage it.

'Something's not right,' I said to Heather before they left. 'It can't be jet lag for a whole month, can it?'

Mum was very low for most of that year, but an event towards the end of it knocked what little stuffing was left right out of her. She had hardly driven at all, but told her doctor that she hoped she would start to drive again one day. He thought it would be best if she went for a driving test where she would be assessed by an occupational therapist.

'It's just to check that I'm fine to drive, he says.'

Even from halfway round the planet, I could tell Mum wasn't feeling very confident. There was anxiety in every word.

'It's my worries dear, I've just got my worries.'

I called Mum after the driving test had taken place.

'How did it go, Mum, what did they say?'

'Well, I didn't pass. I'm not allowed to drive anymore.'

Black panic dropped like a shroud. I should be there. The thought that I was too far away went racing around my head, a demon being chased by another demon. I struggled not to cry and tried to sound positive.

'That must be a big shock, Mum. How do you feel?' I asked.

'Well, it can't be helped. How are things going over there with you?'

Mum could change the subject with lightning speed. Years of practice. Remember, this is Mum, who really never, ever cried even though she had many reasons to, usually on a daily basis.

Madness, it is madness not to cry when things are worth crying about. Tears are good, they're there to soothe and help emotions flow out. But Mum just did not cry, at least not in front of us children in those years. When she was near the end of her life she did weep. But that came later.

Shortly after this blow, a psychiatrist assessed Mum and then visited her at her house in the old stables to tell her that she was suffering from both Alzheimer's and vascular dementia.

❦

I barely draw breath when talking to Deborah as we sit in that glorious muddy pool in Fiji. I tell her about the day I met with women friends and shared my worries about Mum. Many of them could empathise.

I tend to find being bossed about or being given advice very irritating, but on this occasion, the absolute conviction, the firm and definite opinion of one woman, Bel, hit the spot.

'Oh no,' she'd said. 'Your mum must move to be near your sister. No, no, no, tell your sister that she is not the one who is going to be moving, your mum is.'

'But Mum has lived her whole life in Edinburgh or East Lothian. She's been in that village since 1970, all her friends are there. Her life is there,' I replied.

'Your sister has a family, a husband with a job, her own work, her kids are all settled at school. Your mum is alone and it is much easier to move her than to move a whole family. Your sister needs to put herself and her family first. She must!'

I took a slow sip of my coffee and said, 'Poor Morag is worried to death. She's driving up and down the length of Scotland every third weekend, and it's still not enough.'

'Well,' said Bel. 'It's your mum who needs to move. You call your sister tonight and tell her so.'

And I did, I actually did. Sometimes you just need the right person to be forceful enough to clear through all the emotional static. Sometimes an outsider who has no connection to the family has a clearer view than family and friends do.

'Your Mum might forget everything very soon,' Bel had continued. 'When she's in a care home, it doesn't really matter where she is.'

'But her friends, the people she knows.'

'She may not know them for long. And how can the care home be kept accountable? How can you daughters be sure she is being well looked after if you are all very far away?'

Her words were so definite, so very black and white. I did just as she told me to, called Morag that night and said that Mum had to move north. Perhaps I was equally definite because my sister never mentioned again the notion of moving her family south to East Lothian. When I talked to Mum I also suggested that a move north to Nairn might be the best thing.

'Morag wants to take care of you, Mum. If you have to leave your house, she would love you to be close to her.'

Ormiston: 2017

In June of the year after Mum's dementia diagnosis – a few months after my conversation with Morag about Mum being the one to move house, not her – I spent six weeks with Mum in Scotland, with my son Tom accompanying me. Mum very much liked the dementia-specialist nurse who visited her at home. 'She's very down-to-earth, and she's keen to meet you now you're here.'

Short and feisty, the nurse wore a blue uniform and a warm smile. Her accent was broad, and her words direct.

'Your mum cannot live alone anymore.'

That certainly helped evaporate my jet lag. I sat up straight and asked, 'She does need help but is she really at that stage now?'

'Any morning, she might wake up and not know where she is. She might wander away from the house and get lost. It happens all the time. She needs twenty-four-hour care now.'

'I think she wouldn't go out of the house. She never ever leaves it if she can help it.'

'But that can change overnight, Seana.' The nurse was speaking slowly, or so it sounded to me, as if her words were at half speed. 'You do not want to risk her getting lost, it's not fair to her.'

'I'm here with her 24/7 now and we will get something sorted out.'

Morag and I had already been looking at the options. There was an agency that employed women from Zimbabwe and South Africa who would live in with her, promising to stay for at least six months. There were care homes in Nairn, just a few minutes' drive from Morag's house.

'If I were you, I would stay here with a carer, Mum,' I said. 'So long as she's kind and good fun.'

'I want to go to Morag,' Mum said. 'I don't want to stay here with a stranger.'

It was a massive comfort that Mum's closest friend, Cath, agreed that moving north to be close to Morag and her family was the right thing to do.

Cath told me, 'I have been saying to Alison that she couldn't spend another winter cooped up in that house on her own. She needs to go north to Nairn.'

'Yes,' I replied. 'This is a lovely house but she spends so much time on her own.'

Cath nodded. 'She needs to be with other people. And Morag is beside herself. She will feel much better if she can keep a closer eye on her mum.'

For us, it was a huge relief that Mum told us that she wanted to move near to Morag. We had never wanted to make her leave her home. But I have always wondered whether Mum was really able to give true, informed consent. Did she really understand what she was saying? Or was she repeating and agreeing with what we all said, so as not to cause a fuss?

Our oldest sister Kirsty had already taken over the role of looking after Mum's finances, managing her tax and bills and practical matters. She told us that Mum's pension could cover the cost of the care home.

Moving north really was the right thing to do in this difficult situation where all we could hope for was the least worst outcome.

Nairn: 2017

'We're staying at the Golf View Hotel, Mum. It's not far now,' I said as we drove out of Inverness and along the coast road to Nairn.

'Oh, that's a nice one,' she said. 'It's expensive though.'

'Yes, but we can afford it and they have a big room we can all stay in together.'

Morag had made some appointments to visit care homes in Nairn. But the day before we were to travel north, Mum became very shaky about the idea.

'Mum, we've made a plan and we're going to stick to the plan. It will not all be smooth sailing but we'll manage.'

I used all my skills of distraction and deflection and managed to get her into the car.

There is nothing like a bit of luxury to soothe the spirit when life is tough and I was trivial enough to find the tartan carpets, the sweeping views and the wood-panelled public rooms of the hotel a salve to the stress.

'I can't go down for breakfast. Let's just stay in the room,' Mum said next morning. That was an easy one. I had my breakfast, the full Scottish with black pudding, and then brought hers up on a tray.

As she ate, I saw a porpoise close to the beach and we both watched it together, stitching its way neatly through the water, up and down and up and down as it swam along the shoreline.

I could see that Mum was struggling with conflicting feelings. She did not want to cause a fuss yet was terrified of going to a new place and having to meet new people. She did not want to be at the hotel, she did not want to leave the room and she did not want to talk to anyone. She was biting her lip as I helped her into the lift and then the car to drive the few minutes to the care home. I had to be the sensible parent in this situation, and I was glad not to feel the emotions I knew were boiling away within.

St Olaf is a grand Victorian building on the edge of the village of Nairn, alongside the woods and rich farmlands that surround the village. It's whitewashed and looks stately with ivy growing up the facade by the tall and wide main door. I rang the doorbell and the manager welcomed us into the conservatory where we had coffee and looked out onto the garden with its huge rhododendron bushes and flower beds.

Across the car park was a new building, the specialist dementia unit and I was glad Mum never asked about it.

Slowly we went to the lift and up to the first floor. As the door slid open the scent of disinfectant wafted our way from a utility room. No one said a thing and we turned left and into a large room with a single bed at the far end. The manager showed us the little kitchen in a cupboard with a kettle and a microwave, and the large bathroom with shower.

We stayed in the room for a while and then went back down and slowly walked to the front door. On the way we met a lady whose face was only very lightly wrinkled; she was walking from room to room and singing Highland lullabies as she went. We said hello to the Singing Lady and she turned and sang to us. We passed another room where a lady sat on a chair, the top of her shoulder folded down over her chest as she slept. She came to be known as the Folded-Over Lady.

In front of the television, on plush armchairs, other old codgers dozed, snoozed or stared. Was this really the right place for Mum?

'Well, it looks nice,' said Mum. 'It will have to do.'

Saying goodbye, the manager tapped a code onto a keypad and then opened the door to let us out.

We drove down the sweep of the drive and, as we waited to turn right, we could see a leafy laneway directly across the road. There was a shady, dark tree tunnel which led down to a large house. In the shadows a small roe deer stood, still as a statue, delicate, with just the tips of new horns showing. Startled and alert, the deer stared straight at us and did not move as I slowly turned right and drove to Morag's home, just three minutes away.

'Did you see that deer, Mum? Down the driveway just opposite where we came out of St Olaf.'

'No dear, but that's nice to know they are about. And there are red squirrels around here, too. Do you know Morag's had one in her garden?'

To me, that deer was Mum made animal, gentle, shy, still. Though I am not prone to notions of celestial intervention, the message was that this was the right place for her, that she would be safe and cared for here in Nairn.

At Morag's house, we sat Mum down with a cup of coffee and placed the cat on her knee.

Later at the hotel, I had a glass of wine with Morag when Mum was back upstairs in our room. A very large one. Then another.

'Did you know there's a code to get out of the door at St Olaf?' I asked Morag.

'Yes, and Mum would not be given it. She would actually never ever be allowed out on her own.'

'Oh, why not?'

'She could wander, couldn't she? Get lost.'

I had to admit that yes, she could.

'Or she might run away.'

'Now come on, Mum would never do that.'

'Yes, well, I'd also say that's unlikely but you never know how dementia might change her.'

'But she could learn the code by watching, don't you think?'

'Seana, if she was able to remember the code, she wouldn't need to go there.'

Ormiston: 2017

Tom had come with me on this trip to Scotland and he went off for a week's holiday with Morag and her family to Durness on the far northwest coast of Scotland where the beaches are beautiful and the chocolate shop is the very place to pick up supplies after a long day of adventuring.

My little Aussie was used to driving to beaches, parking in car parks and walking only a short distance past the surf lifesaving club and down to the searing sand. There he would splash in the waves, always between the flags where the lifeguards patrolled. When the kids were little and rose early, I would pack bags and brekkie at night, and then as soon as they were out of bed we would drive into the bright white of the day, spend the morning hours at the beach and then retreat home before the blazing midday sun lifted the UV levels to newsworthy and dangerous.

Tom was used to wearing a rash vest and being slathered

in sun cream. He was used to bright cobalt blues and startling aquamarines, to snorkelling around rocks where shoals of yellowtails parted before him, where huge blue gropers stared silently and rays swooped away on the sand below. The rock pools of Fairy Bower, Avalon, Dee Why and North Narrabeen were his happy hunting ground. Beware the blue-ringed octopus at North Curl Curl! Tom loved jumping into Sydney Harbour from the netted baths at Clifton Gardens and Little Manly Cove.

In Scotland, it was a shock for Tom to go to the beach with Morag, Gary and his two wee cousins. Getting to the sandy seashore is often a bit of a mission that can involve a long walk through fields and along little sheep trails, over stiles, past Highland cows, crossing streams and rivers. Morag always takes some kindling and matches so that a little fire can be built to warm the kids after chilly swims. Some days can be hot in Scotland, but few are. Most days are a bit breezy and chilly, or sometimes even ferociously windy and totally perishing.

Dressed to withstand all weather, kids find cliffs and caves to explore and they dip their fishing nets into rock pools. There is treasure-hunting to be done along the high-tide mark, there are rocks to scramble over and hillsides to gallop up and down. It takes all day.

In Australia this would bring on a dreadful dose of sunburn and heat exhaustion. In Scotland it gives you windburn and a big appetite.

That July, for the week when only Mum and I were at the Stables, the days stretched out in sunshine and birdsong. There were just a few showers of refreshing rain, and the breezes were soft. Each morning I would wake up early and make tea to have in bed as I read my book. Mum was sleeping in, but when I heard her stir, I would pop downstairs to offer her a coffee and open the curtains of the window which looked onto the garden. Mum would wake slowly, get herself to the bathroom and then get back into bed. In her nighty, looking very like a dozy mouse, she would relax under the covers until I brought in two mugs of instant coffee and put them on the side table. Then I would hop into bed beside her.

The walls of this old stable building were almost two feet thick, with the window recessed into the wall, lined with white painted wood. Plants grew along the wall outside, their shadows dancing around the window frames. Mum was safe and secure here, sleeping right beside her garden where the blackcurrant bushes had been for decades. When she did the renovation to turn the old stables into her home, she turned the area into a courtyard for herself and her bonsai trees.

'It looks like a nice day.'

'Yes, Mum, it's warmish and shouldn't rain. Shall we rush out and climb a mountain? Shall we run around on the beach?'

'I don't think so, dear.'

I pulled out my phone to show her photos of the big boys and Alice in Sydney.

'Is Paul doing fine without you?'

'Yes, he's managing well. It's good for him.'

'Your Dad wouldn't have liked it if I had ever gone away for so long.'

'True, and neither would we have, Mum.'

These calm mornings in Mum's bed, with fresh linen and the scent of sweet peas, were precious small pockets of stillness. I longed to keep Mum there all day, didn't want her getting up to start the daily anguish over simple things. She was safe here in bed. Life's many worries only started once she got up.

'Now this morning, Mum, can I please bring you a piece of

toast with honey?'

'No, dear, definitely not. I don't want crumbs in my bed.'

'How about some muesli and yoghurt?'

'No, I'd slop it all over the sheets. Let's just have our coffees here. Don't wriggle around and make me spill mine. We can stay here until we're hungry then get up.'

Mum had made me laugh so loudly once when with us in Australia where coffee culture reigns supreme and the acme of good living for me as a mum with young kids was to go to a cafe and have a soy flat white. If I could drink it all while sitting down on my bottom, then my day was complete. Second best was to get a takeaway coffee and sit drinking it in a fully enclosed playground while the kids ran wild.

'I just do not understand,' Mum had said, 'why you want to go out and pay for a coffee when you could have a cup of Nescafé at home.'

I had collapsed in a raucous giggling fit. It was all there, the culture divide, the generation gap, our own differences. While Mum liked being at home, I felt strangled by all the domesticity and was out of the house like a shot as often as possible. Lucky for me there was a cool little cafe at the end of the road where we lived when the twins were little. I was down there very often with and without them; it was my haven, an almost grown-up-life place. Also, the coffee was good.

Mum sipped her beloved Nescafé as I pulled a pillow behind me and stared out the window.

As little kids we would sometimes jump into bed with Mum and Dad on Sunday mornings, the only day Dad would sleep in. There was that famous occasion when the cat had found a nest of baby rats in the fields and brought them up to show Mum and Dad one at a time. We all jumped around in bed shrieking as the little rats ran around the room, all creatures equally terrified.

'Do you remember the cat bringing in all the baby rats, Mum?'

A pause, a long pause.

'Oh yes, I do, that was before the houses were built, when the cowshed was still a cowshed and the fields were fields. Imagine being scared of baby rats. You kids were funny.'

We sat every morning of that week, just Mum and I, with nowhere particular to go and nothing particular to do. The later mornings passed in showers and breakfasts and a little read of the papers in the sunny kitchen, in opening and closing doors to the conservatory, in watering the plants.

Some days, there were no doctor's appointments, no visits from the nurse, no struggle to get Mum out of the house and into the car to visit the optician. There were no mischievous microwaves or obstreperous ovens confusing Mum, no worrying about the garden. For me, there were no children to feed, wash, chase around or drive to school, or asking a zillion questions. Our meals were simple and our conversations, too. We did a little bit of gardening, chatted to neighbours and friends over cups of tea and shortbread in the conservatory, and spent our evenings watching *Eastenders* and Wimbledon.

While Morag and her family and Tom ran and played over the beaches and hills of the far, far north, Mum and I basked in the lowlands' warmth and ease.

⟩E

Then came the day to farewell Mum's bonsai trees. Friends from her bonsai club were coming to take them all away to be distributed among the members. Mum had been a bonsai lover for more than twenty-five years and dozens of her little trees sat in the courtyard just outside the kitchen. Some lived in the small conservatory, too, and others in the house.

Here was a sturdy little fir tree about a foot tall, its tiny needles a deep green, its round shallow pot a clay brown. There, a small oak tree with a thick stem and lots of exposed roots stood small but tall in a forest-green dish as wide as the little tree's branches.

Mum had started her bonsai adventures after all her children had left home. I remember worrying that she had made life hard for herself by taking on more responsibilities instead of enjoying her freedom. But that was simply my escapist and irresponsible perspective. Mum loved her house and her garden, and her new hobby was a pleasure to her. She won many prizes for her bonsai but her favourites were the few that she keep closest to the house.

'These ones are just my pets,' she had told me, but she cared for them as patiently as she did all the others, perhaps more so. Bonsai trees need a lot of love: they must be carefully trimmed, repotted, fed and given water and food; some need to be shaded from the sun, others need to be kept warm in winter.

'You have poured so much love into these trees, Mum. Is it hard to let them go?'

'They are a worry to me. It's all been far too much for too long now. I can't manage them.'

The day was warm and there was a gentle wind blowing the scent of mown hay around the garden and ruffling up the leaves of the strawberry plants. Sparrows hopped and pecked on the grass, and bees hummed around the roses. The garden looked a bit bedraggled, not nearly as well looked after as it used to be, but it remained a haven of peace and quiet, tranquillity and calm.

Jim and Cath McRae and Charlie, a close friend from the bonsai club, arrived. They opened the boots of their cars and Mum told them which bonsai she would like them to have themselves and which could be given to others. Cath was wiping her eyes now and again but being brisk as she carried a bonsai which had been trained to turn and grow sideways.

'I've always loved that windswept fir with the miniature cones, Ali. I will take good care of it.'

Mum just smiled and turned away. I could tell that all this movement and chatter was swamping her senses. She seemed remote, cut off. I was expecting some sort of emotion at the loss of her beloved bonsai, but she seemed blanked out.

'I'm just relieved,' Mum said as we had a cup of coffee after all the bonsai were gone and her friends had driven away. 'I couldn't care for them anymore.'

'I thought you might keep one, Mum, to take with you.'

'No, dear, I can't look after anything anymore.'

'But Mo would have helped you, Mum.'

'No.'

For Mum everything had become too much and she was relieved to let it all go. She wanted to collapse and be looked after herself. Having cared for husband, children, garden, friends, horse, dogs, cats and bonsai for most of her life, she was ready to slough them all off and take her turn at being cared for.

As July and the best of strawberry season drew to a close, we started to pack up things for Mum to take with her to St Olaf. Most of Mum's clothes were in her bedroom and she was clear about what she would like to take and what she did not need anymore.

'Charity shop,' she called out. 'I'm taking this one, not that one, the green shirt there. And that blue one can go to the charity shop, too.'

Mum was sitting on her bed, waving her walking stick at me imperiously and rather enjoying bossing me about, I thought.

'Mum, are you sure? You do wear that one a lot.'

'Yes, yes, I know what I need and what I don't need.'

It was hard to know whether Mum really could make these decisions for herself or not. If she couldn't remember how to use the microwave, could she really be clear that she didn't want to take all her nighties? What about the blue one? Wasn't that her favourite?

'Isn't this one your favourite, Mum?'

'Not anymore, I've gone off it,' she said and tutted. 'Really girls, my eyes are still working, and I know what I like and what I don't like. What we have packed is plenty.'

Right, well, that was more forceful than Mum's usual statements, so I was happy to take her at her word.

'Can you girls please sort out the clothes that are upstairs by yourselves, whilst I go and boil the kettle?'

Upstairs under the eaves of the house were hanging racks full of clothes. Mum had always loved wearing fine clothes though she did not buy a lot. Sometimes Dad would take her shopping and spend much more money than she would ever have spent on herself. As kids we'd loved touching Mum's clothes, loved seeing her out of her gardening garb and wearing her 'princess dresses' as we thought of them. And here they still were, long flowing silk skirts, the lambskin jacket and the velvet cape. There were evening dresses from the 1970s and '80s that she had kept all these years. What to do?

And there were cardigans, mostly bought in Marks and Spencer. There were literally dozens and dozens of them; after we had gone through them and taken a few down to check with Mum, there were still more than thirty left over.

I took a heavy knitted cardigan for myself, as ever having underestimated how chilly some Scottish summer days can be. A pale wheaten colour, with a thick cable knit, it was almost rough to the touch, but large and cosy.

'Can I have this one, Mum?'

She said yes and my sisters didn't mind so I tucked that one away for myself.

During these days of packing up the house and sorting out clothes, Mum was in good spirits. She seemed to enjoy feeling competent to decide what to take and what not to take and we were happy to be her willing slaves. The bags were being packed and the piles of clothes to be sent to charity shops grew higher and higher and it felt like the end of a long era because that was exactly what it was. A life at Marketgate had begun in 1970, and was coming to an end now, after forty-seven years

A few days later Morag and I were driving Mum and her suitcases, plus boxes of photo albums and papers, north to Nairn. We stopped at Pitlochry at the cafe beside Loch Faskally for a cup of tea and a piece of cake. Swans glided by alongside the trees that line the foreshore: beech, Douglas fir, larch and spruce. The air was soft and still and the sunshine soothing.

Mum was looking upset and a bit scared as we helped her out of the car and walked with her to the cafe.

'Have we been on this road before, Seana?'

'Yes, Mum, we stopped here when we drove up to visit St Olaf about two weeks ago.'

'Oh, did we?' Mum said. 'So I have been to see St Olaf. Did I like it?'

Morag and I looked into each other's eyes, tears brimming.

'You did like it, Mum. And you loved our new cat, too,' Morag replied. 'And you were pleased when they offered you a room there. You'll be staying there tonight.'

Mum was watching us, her face showing confusion and concern, but she did not say anything as she sipped her coffee and glanced over the loch towards the hazy heather-covered hills.

Mo and I helped Mum back to the car and then stopped for a moment before opening the doors to climb in ourselves.

'I feel so responsible. She isn't really the one who's made this choice to move,' I said.

Morag looked as if she was about to break down and howl. 'I know. But we're on the way now. Can I drive? I need to concentrate on something to keep myself together.'

We got into the car, put our seatbelts on, and I turned around and squeezed Mum's hand. We pulled out and the road led us north.

〉ϵ

In Fiji, for the last couple of days of the cruise, Deborah is a patient listener. As I talk and talk and talk to her about Mum, she says only a few words, just telling me a little here and there about her own parents. I feel I have freed up so much brain space by recounting everything about Mum's last months and years, about how I felt through it all.

For some reason, I find myself drinking less on the last night of the cruise. Is it because I'm getting up early to join the first snorkel trip of the day? Is it because I have found someone to pour my heart out to – all these memories of Mum and the huge sadness for her as she declined in her late seventies? Far, far too young. She was just seventy-nine when she died in January. She deserved so many more years and her grandchildren would have loved to get to know her better.

There was sadness and grief to express, but what a gift to be able to talk about it with a warm, loving person who started the week a stranger and ended it as a friend.

Orange

I arrive back home to Orange just after the middle of September.

'Did you work hard?' Paul asks.

'I did,' I reply, noticing the huge piles of clean washing on the dining table and the muck on the kitchen floor. I'm home.

'I have heaps of great material to write up and photos and videos to edit. I'm whacked.'

'I'm whacked, too,' says Paul. 'All this domesticity has really worn me down. It's the same every day, it never ends.'

'Trust me, Paul. I know.'

Yes, I'm here. The filter on the dishwasher is clogged up and in need of a major clean, there's hair caught all around the roller of the vacuum cleaner, the aircon filter light is flashing, it desperately needs a wash. The hidden things. The filters and rollers that, in this household, only I can see and only I clean. Messy, messy. No cruising here at home. Lucky I've got the photos to edit and the words to write, reminders that light up the brain as I work; work, my reward for the burden of domestic duties done.

Towards the end of September, Paul goes away to a yoga retreat for a couple of nights and I buy two bottles of wine to drink while he is away, mid-week. Don't I deserve a little relaxation, a pick me up?

After a week of daily drinking, I am feeling deeply depressed. I listen to a podcast in which a sleep expert gives advice for getting the best night's sleep. He mentions that even one or two units of alcohol disrupt REM sleep considerably. So the sleep I am getting is not real sleep. No wonder I'm tired.

But I'm more than just tired. I feel depressed, slow, sad, under the weather, under grey skies of grim weather. Flattened, miserable.

But you do know, Seana, that alcohol is a depressant? Everyone knows that.

Yes, I do, I know that. I know it can calm my racing brain, slow down the urge to dash everywhere all at once, stop me from impulsively going away even more than I do. Stop me from escaping this domestic grind permanently. Depressing my brain isn't all bad.

This is bad, though, isn't it? Look at you trying to be bright when you really feel like a steamroller has given you a good going over.

Leave me alone, stop this.

The ratcheting of the cogs in my brain is wearing me out, the grinding of gears, forward and back and forward and back, the regret and remorse and a terrible feeling that I will always be like this, stuck, pulled this way and that.

And still, and still, just like during the entire year when I didn't drink, even then when I had been sober for months, the thought of letting go of alcohol forever is unbearable. The loss would be too much. I would not survive that. It would be too much for me. The end for me. Just the act of considering never drinking again causes a great pain to engulf me like a wave smashing into a Sydney rock pool, with a backwash of teariness and despair. I just cannot. I could never. I need alcohol. Friend, companion, instant relief from life. I couldn't manage without it. I just need to learn not to overindulge, that's all. Just try to get to that goal of just one or two, moderation.

But Seana, it's the attempts at moderation that are knocking you flat. You are trying and trying and trying. Every single time you pour a glass of wine, you're attempting to just have that one. It's the moderating that's killing you.

Should I just go the whole hog then? Should I give in to these crushing urges and drink as much as I truly want? What will that look like?

Or you could stop.

No, not that, I never could, I'd be alone, bare, naked, I would not survive that. Not ever.

TEN

October

Sydney

I drive down to Sydney for a couple of nights at the start of October, arriving in the evening at our wee flat where our son Jake lives. Next day, after an early morning beach walk, I visit my old Scottish pal, Isabel. My head is sore and I would love to chat through my conflicted feelings around alcohol and my distress at all the harsh things I was saying to myself this morning as I walked at Manly. I want to be healthy, I really do. I want to be fit and active for a long time so I can be there for the kids as they grow up, be a useful granny if they have children. I eat well and I exercise. Then I write myself off with alcohol.

I know this is called cognitive dissonance and I've been reading about it lately. Cognitive dissonance is the technical term for doing things that are the opposite to each other. It's the cause of most of my emotional messiness and all my self-abuse.

Isabel and I have similar Scottish stories. We both have

221

deceased dads who were problem drinkers. We both met our partners in our early thirties, both had babies very quickly and both moved to Sydney with toddlers. Isabel has always enjoyed a glass of wine, or two, but found it required effort to stay within the government harm minimisation guidelines. I have lamented to her in the past that the number of units of alcohol that is considered low risk for women keeps getting fewer and fewer as we get older and older.

Isabel and I have talked too about my struggles to keep my drinking within some sort of reasonable parameter, about my Fear and my Thirst and how I worry that one day I might just go the whole hog, the full swally, as we Scots say. I feel she has some understanding of my alcohol push and pull, even if she had always managed to keep her own wine habit lower-risk – unlike me.

Who can I talk to now that Isabel has stopped drinking?

I am riveted, fascinated and slightly appalled by Isabel's managing to stop. Just like that. How does she do it? How can she just switch it off like that? Could I? No, I definitely could not, I am very sure about that. I think that my life would be easier and better if I stopped drinking – I just do not believe I can do it.

Isabel had a medical issue and was advised by her doctor to stop drinking. And she did it. Just like that. Like me, she is an older mum and she wants to stay well for her family. A part of me wishes a doctor would tell me to stop drinking. But even then, I'm not sure I would manage. Could I? Isabel has.

I rap on her front door and then open it and go in, scratching her beautiful dog Bailey behind the ears as he makes me welcome. Isabel and I go for a walk around Manly Dam, catching up as we amble: kids, school, partners, exercise, our health, our mental health. When we return to the house,

I sit down on one of her comfy sofas.

'I'm going to show you a drink I've been trying.' Isabel goes to the cupboard and brings out what looks like a gin bottle. 'It's called Seedlip Garden.' She pours a measure into a glass.

I move to snatch the glass up but Isabel waves her hand at me and then takes a bottle of tonic from the fridge and adds a long splash.

'It smells like pea pods,' I say. 'My mum used to make pea pod soup from an old wartime recipe book.'

I take a sip, sniff again and have another drink.

'I like it.'

Isabel pours herself a glass and then sits on the sofa, breathing out as she takes in their wide view of the suburbs running down to the pines that line the beach at Manly.

'Try the Heineken 0.0 as well. Corin and I both have one of those in the evenings. He says it's almost better than the alcoholic version.'

'I've never been a beer drinker, at least not since I was really young and used to love one after days at the beach when we were all salty and boiling hot. I've only drunk wine, wine and more wine in the past twenty years. But I'll try them and see if I can ease myself off the wine a bit.'

I do not discuss with Isabel the terrible morning I've had with myself. If a man or indeed any other human talked to me the way I talk to myself, I would stand up and walk out. But it is all me talking to me, recriminations and inner verbal abuse the likes of which I last heard from Dad when I was bailed up by him as a teenager.

There is no discussion of all my alcohol woes on this sunny spring Sydney morning with Isabel. What could she say to me anyway except 'Just stop drinking'? And that is advice I do not want to hear.

Instead I talk to her about the box of Mum and Dad's letters that Morag posted to me from Scotland. These are letters that Mum read when she was living at St Olaf. They opened up a door into the past for Mum; they took her way, way back to much happier times.

The Whitehall Secretarial College
Fairfield Court
Meads
Eastbourne
Sussex

11th Jan 1960

Dear David,
I don't know where to start. I don't think I have realised yet that I shall be away for 3 months. But leaving you on the platform last night was terrible. You looked hurt and I do wish I had kissed you goodbye. I am an idiot.

The girl I was sleeping with was about my age and was quite friendly, and so we shared a taxi to Victoria station & had breakfast together. I didn't sleep much as the compartment was alternately hot & cold, my blankets fell off & I lost the sheet completely. I felt hell of depressed in the train.

However I got here in one piece. David, the girls here are on the whole sickening. Most of them have been to boarding school: all of the ones in my room have. There are three others, one from near St Andrews called Monica, an Australian (she's the nicest) called Marjory and Anna Franklyn-Smith. A lot of them are terribly elegant and are highly intensive types, and Anna has just told me she knows nothing about jazz.

I'm really glad I can 'pour out my heart' to you.
I love you,
love you,
I love you.

All my love from,
Alison

6, Coillesdene Crescent
Joppa
Edinburgh 15

Monday 11th Jan

My own sweetest Alie,
I hope that you arrived safely in Eastbourne unmolested
by any wandering wolf or soldier after leaving your broken-
hearted fiancé behind you.

I didn't really feel so bad when your train actually went,
there have been a few incidents during today which have
reminded me of you and brought me often to the verge of
tears when I think of how far you are from me. However, I
don't suppose the reality of your absence will really strike
me until I really miss your warm embraces next Saturday
(when we always are together). So I beg you, please think of
me a lot on Saturday as I'll be thinking of you.

Believe me I do wish thought could be willed to
reality as I would will you to come to me, and I would be
rapturous loving your warm, soft yielding lips and tender
body close to me now, forever.

However I really must try and cheer up as I'll just have
to forgo the sensuous warm pleasure of your proximity for
12 more weeks.

Ted and I had a fairly hard day's work at Galashiels,
however it was great fun having the car. I've determined
that I must take you with me on business trips when you are
here on holiday or at least when we're married (before the
family arrive).

Your faithful, adoring fiancé,
David

Mum and Dad had been courting in 1959, but my upper-
middle-class maternal grandparents did not approve of Dad, a
working-class apprentice quantity surveyor who played banjo
and trombone in a jazz band at the Royal Mile Cafe. On a
Sunday. The horror.

The stress of this affected Mum greatly and she had some
sort of nervous breakdown and dropped out of university at
the end of the year. In 1960, she went to Eastbourne to attend
a secretarial college for a year. Her parents hoped to split up
the lovers, not knowing they were secretly engaged. The year
in Eastbourne saw literally hundreds of love letters sent from
one to the other. These letters stayed hidden in boxes for the
forty-nine years of my parents' marriage and then the ten
years after Dad died.

I smile as I read the letters, remembering Mum in her
chair at the care home in Nairn in the summer of 2018, taking
the delicate pages out of their small envelopes, reading them
and then letting them flutter back into the box. Back then,
I was worrying about all the letters and envelopes becoming
muddled up and out of order. Mum was not at all concerned
about that; she was just reading.

Mum read another letter and dropped the pages back into
the box. She looked up at me.

'Are you sure these letters were written by the same man I

was married to?' she asked, her face a soft query.

'Yes, Mum, they were written the year before you got married when you were sent away to the typing school in Eastbourne.'

'It really doesn't sound like him at all,' she said as she pulled another sheet of blue writing paper from an envelope and began to read.

'It's definitely his writing,' I say. 'But I've never seen this box of letters before. Where did you keep them?'

'I don't remember, dear.' Mum rummaged around and picked up another envelope, gently easing the letter out, fine as tissue paper. Her face softened as she read, her eyes wide.

Young love triumphed. Mum and Dad were married on 27th December 1960, just after Mum had finished her course in Eastbourne. They married in the church Mum had attended since childhood. No alcohol was served at the reception: Mum's parents were teetotal. This did not go down very well with Dad's jazz musician friends so they brought their own hip flasks, as did Dad.

With dementia, Mum's confidence in the present slowly evaporated and her ease with the past deepened. The past was reliable in a way the slippery present with all its knobs and buttons and remote controls was not.

Mum read and re-read her box of letters and she talked about Dad as he was before they got married, their adventures together in the canoe he built, their nights out dancing and the jazz music they loved. Mum felt comfortable and safe reading the letters and looking at old photos of when she and Dad were very young, so innocent and looking deeply happy together.

13th Dec 1960

My darling David,

Do you realise that a fortnight tonight we'll be together?
I've said it before, I know, but just can't believe it. It will be
wonderful to be with you again.

We had quite a few presents today. Mr & Mrs. I. M.
Campbell have given us a picture. It's of Majorca (I think)
– boats, sea, etc. It's quite nice. Then some aunt of Mum's
sent a hideous tablecloth.

I was Christmas shopping too. I got presents for all your
five nephews. So that's cleared up. I must start thinking
of something for your mother. Did I tell you I met her
yesterday? Oh yes, I did. I told you on the phone. I'm going
for a lesson on the sewing machine tomorrow after I have
been to that damned-crook-of-a-dentist.

I really am sorry I didn't write last night because I said
I would, and you'll have been expecting a letter. Do you
know what stopped me – the television of course! It's a
damned nuisance. However, I saw a good play on it tonight.
But I'm having to write this in bed at 12.

I had my wedding dress fitted today. It looks all right.
I think it does anyway. I hope you do too. Margaret and
Heather's dresses are ready as well, and they are a lovely
red colour. I don't know what your mother will think, as she
thinks red & white is unlucky. I'll have to warn her gently.

I had a phone call from a man tonight. But don't get
jealous. It was only Ogy telling me what he got for us.
They have started a new thing at Jenners. There are six girls
waiting to take your car away after you have driven up to
the door. They go and park it in a special place, and bring
it back when you want it. And all for nothing too. It's quite

a good idea, except you may not know when you're wanting
it back if you're like my mother who always takes about
twice as much time as she needs to do when she's buying
things.

Ooh. It's cold. I'm sitting up with just my nighty on, and
there's a draft blowing in the window. Thank goodness
I'll soon have my very own, super special hot water bottle.
Wouldn't you like to keep me warm in bed? A rhetorical
question perhaps. Oh, I love you. Have the table & chairs
arrived yet? And do they make the room look squashed?

What have you been feeding yourself on? Boiled eggs?
Mum bought us some more pans and dozens of other
things today. You have got a long-handled brush, haven't
you? I thought I noticed one in the wee back room.

All my love,
Alison

19th Dec 1960

My dearest Alie,
This is, believe it or not, the last letter you'll get from
me during our long separation while you've been in
Eastbourne. It really seems fortuitous that we'll be together
again. I just can't really remember what it was like when we
did see each other three times a week. Can you?

At the moment, I'm all choked up with the cold and
thus I'm quite miserable as I have to keep blowing my nose.
Last night I was at a party with Stewart and got wildly drunk.
Thus I was late for the office this morning and I've not
been feeling too well today.

The boys in the office have given me a super present of

a Prestige Potato Peeler. You've probably seen one, you put the spuds in the pot, close the lid then turn the handle at the side. This peels the spuds quickly and cleanly. Good eh? I'm not bringing it up to put on display though, as it's too bulky to carry.

I got your wee note tonight when I came in. I should hope that you did behave at Meta's party. After all, you'll be an old married woman in a week's time.

Well, my darling, I'll close now and say goodbye to letters of this type anyway. I'll see you on Friday in Waverley at 6.42 pm, remember. I love you very much.

Your lover,
David xxx

After reading the letters, when Mum and Morag discussed what sort of a funeral Mum would like, she asked for a humanist celebrant, and that her ashes be buried alongside Dad's body at East Byres. After ten years of saying she would never be buried with him, reading the love letters changed her mind.

Orange

October is passing all too quickly in Orange. Term 3 ends and school holidays begin. The twins tell me they're tired, but they're full of life, movement. Their long legs flash as they throw balls around on the oval, their bodies starting to change, childhood being left behind as they launch into the teenage years. These beautiful bodies are sprouting and stretching, muscles forming on smooth backs, as firm and solid as the Sydney blue gum trees I walk by on my favourite bushwalk, in awe at their sinuous strength as they stretch effortlessly skyward.

I am thinking a lot about Mum, wishing she were still alive and that I could talk to her about the garden here in Orange, get her advice. I ache thinking about how fast she declined just one year ago. Too fast.

Mum had gone from walking slowly and chatting happily when I saw her last August to incontinence and being unable to walk or talk by December. She was having little strokes, and then some bigger ones.

During October and November last year I listened to Morag's distress and heard the blow-by-blow account of daily diminishment, of Mum's confusion at night about why she was wearing incontinence pads, her attempts to get to the toilet. The only upside was that by the time she was incontinent she did not feel embarrassed or upset about it.

As December rolled around just under a year ago and the kids' school holidays began, my heart was sinking. I was buying Christmas presents for the kids and making my usual attempts to feel Christmassy in 30-degree heat. I remember a call I had with Morag.

'Hey, Morag. How is Mum today?'

'It's awful. She can't speak at all, she's stopped trying.'

'Oh no, poor you and poor her, Mo.'

'I went in earlier today and she was propped up in the lounge with all the people who can't move at all. She turned her head to look at me and she began to cry.'

Morag stopped for a bit and I filled the gap.

'I'm so sorry, Mo. It's not fair that you're there without your sisters living close by. Just at this time, I would do anything to be living there.'

'All she could do was cry and all I could do was hold her hand. I was saying things to her and often she would just look away. She's really bad, Seana.'

231

There was an unscalable wall in my mind; I could not bring myself to know that Mum was going to die. Not until Christmas was over.

Scotland: December 2018

As Mum's body was collapsing, my older sister Kirsty and her husband did a very kind but difficult thing. A heroic thing: a long, long journey.

Callum had not seen Mum since she had moved to Nairn. Since moving into his care home ten years before, Callum had only been away when he had stays at Queen Margaret Hospital's psychiatric unit in Dunfermline. He hadn't travelled long distances or had any weekends away or holidays elsewhere.

Driving long distances is easy in New South Wales where the weather is generally fine and the days are long. Scotland in the winter means rain and wind, sometimes snow; these are treacherous conditions and the A9 from Perth to Inverness is a notoriously dangerous route.

Nonetheless, Kirsty and her husband drove over from their home in the west. They stayed a night in Fife and then drove Callum the three-hour journey north to see Mum. They did this in the face of some opposition from staff at his care home who felt that the trip might be too much for him, unsettling.

Callum sat with Mum in the conservatory at St Olaf. They talked a bit, they had tea and biscuits. Just before leaving, Callum helped Mum walk through to the dining room, gently holding her arm then pulling the chair out for her as she sat down.

Kirsty popped in to see Morag and then drove Callum all the way back to Fife in the dark. They spent another night in a hotel and then drove west the next day. This was a journey of kindness and of love. It was the last time Callum saw Mum.

Orange

Now in October, ten months after Mum died, I know that it was better that the decline she began to hurtle down one year ago was a steep one, precipitous. She had only weeks, not months or years, of being unable to talk or to walk. She would not have wanted to hang on, immobile, being spoon fed. No one would want that – Mum certainly didn't. Her decline took just a few weeks, her death a few days and, now, I know that I might well wish such a death for myself when the time comes.

Still, how I wish she had lived longer, had more healthy years, been able to come out and help me with this garden. Her fingers were so green they almost glowed.

'Start with rhubarb.' The thought comes to me fast and definite. OK, Mum, I will. Your rhubarb at Marketgate was a mighty beast of a plant, plentiful, bountiful. I shall buy a rhubarb plant at the local garden centre, bung it in and see whether it will survive our Australian summer. Will my rhubarb plant put roots down firmly and flourish the way your rhubarb always did? Shall I pick stalks of rhubarb and then dip the ends into a cup of sugar before taking a bite, the way you taught us? Thank you, Mum.

❦

School holidays rip by. We explore the local area with friends who have come from Sydney for a visit. The goldfields of Ophir Reserve with their clearly visible mine workings, water runs and dug-out caves are a treat to explore, the sound of the river rumbling along and the warm sunshine filtered by tall eucalypts. We visit the caves at Borenore – the soaring ceilings of the main cave provide a cool haven – then we stop at a farm shop on the way home.

In mid-October Alice and Tom return to school for the fourth term of their first year of high school. I am so grateful that all four of my children have generally loved going to school, because I loved dropping them off there. Seventeen years of school drop-offs and seventeen years of school pickups and seventeen years of parent-teacher meetings and seventeen years of school newsletters and seventeen years of morning teas and seventeen years of packed lunches and seventeen years of school uniforms. And five more years of all of these to go.

Just thinking about these cumulative twenty-two years of school parenting is overwhelming. Thank God I am no longer doing most of the domestic duties and the school parenting alone anymore. Thank God Paul stopped working in oil and gas. Paul gives me respite and, next week, I have a massive treat to enjoy: a week in Cairns to attend the Australian Society of Travel Writers conference and annual general meeting. Paul is almost finished his studying and he is able to hold the fort in Orange while I sally north.

Cairns

I get to Sydney airport and enjoy the luxury of the Qantas lounge as I wait for my flight, congratulating myself on not having any of the booze I could help myself to. Well, it is only 9 am. I settle in and read and watch movies on the way north, check my itinerary and plot how I will not go over the score with alcohol this week.

I won't make a complete idiot of myself the way I did at the conference I attended a couple of years ago. No, I will not. That was a bloggers' conference, and at the final party where bubbly wine was handed around free I ended up stumbling around, barely able to get any words out as I tried to tell a much younger and shy female blogger just how much I love her heartfelt and ever so beautiful website. This woman has a gift for connection and I adore her design skills. I fell on the floor in front of her. Looking embarrassed, she just walked away to chat to someone else and I was mortified. That night I had certainly failed to connect with her as I crept away to my hotel room and cried, before pouring myself another glass of wine. Oh dear. Next day, I was absolutely beside myself with shame and my self-recrimination was furious.

So no, there will be none of that. I must and shall have a glass of water between each drink. I must and shall delay the first drink until after others have finished their first one. I must and shall stick with the travel writers who are less boozy. Mind you, many travel writers are boozy people. Surely I can find a more moderate soul and stick close to them, both physically and glass by glass.

I do really well, too; on the first night of the trip at least.

When I join a group of friends and acquaintances on the first night at the bar beside the huge resort pool, as the sun sets and the sky lights up with pinks and corals and orange, I watch the others, watch their drinking. I have a fizzy water first of all.

Ten out of ten, Seana.

I watch two writers who are the solid drinkers in the group. They drink as fast as I usually do and it doesn't take long before I notice them start to talk very quickly, waving their arms around. Their eyes begin to glaze over, their conversation goes blurry around the edges.

I only drink three glasses of wine that night, and next morning I wake up feeling very proud of myself and head out early to board a boat trip to the Great Barrier Reef. All around the boat the sea is crushed diamonds and sapphires, sparkling in the sunshine. At the first snorkel site the sea is glassy and deep, deep blue. I slip into a wetsuit, grab my gear and stand at the stern. One hand over my mask, an arm over my chest, I jump and cross my flippers, hitting the water with an almighty splash, and I'm there. Wide views of coral gardens all around, batfish the size of dinner plates hover close by and tiny aquamarine fish dart in groups in and out of the coral. This is my holy grail, this warm sea teeming with life, and I feel totally at ease, at home and elated. I duck dive and kick my legs hard as I knife down, stretching my arms before me, finning down deeper and deeper, until I know I have to turn. Looking up as I fin to the glittering surface, I see the sun beaming through the water, push one arm up with my fist clenched and rise high as I hit the top, jubilant, breathless, alive.

꽃

My restraint with alcohol does not last. As soon as I have completed my speaking stint, as one of a panel talking about SEO (search engine optimisation) for travel websites (update your old content!), I feel the wash of relief and the slight twist of madness, the urge to let loose. For the last party of the conference, I wear my Birkenstocks instead of sandals with heels: this is my subconscious way of giving myself permission to drink a lot, with less chance of falling into the pool at this sunset-drinks party.

We stand on the walkways through and around the several pools which make this hotel, the Crystalbrook Riley, one of the very best in Cairns. Waiters are circulating and I take a glass from the first I encounter, trying not to snatch. Paying for drinks really does help slow drinking down. The tyranny of the round. This fizzy wine is free and waiters keep bringing it to me. I have to drink it, of course. It's free. I drink fast.

I must not fall down tonight. I must not drink so much that I embarrass myself or, worse, embarrass someone else.

Also, Seana, you have to get up early in the morning so don't get totally trashed.

But look, here comes a waiter with a tray full of glasses glowing gold in the last of the north Queensland sunshine, beads of condensation sparkling. I must help him fulfil his duty. I must drink.

Seana, look at all these boozy travel writers, see the flushed cheeks, the red noses. Have a look for the older people who have been drinking too much for too many years. Slouched shoulders, hand on another's arm. Do you really want to age as they have?

For goodness sake, it's the last night, calm the farm and enjoy yourself. Home and family and domestic duties resume very soon. Drink it all in, drink it all up.

Hey, look over there, Seana.

Where?

That writer over there, you know her. She definitely has a drinking problem.

How do I know?

She's drinking just as fast as you are.

⚡

The journey home from Cairns involves a long flight to Sydney, a night at the flat and then a four-hour drive home to Orange. Throughout, I am feeling seedy. It was a busy week but the alcohol intake night after night was too high and, after a week of daily drinking, I am feeling depleted and depressed.

It is time to get home and dry out, I tell myself as I listen to the Corries on the way home. I ask Siri to play 'Wild Mountain Thyme' and she kindly does. We sang this song at Mum's funeral and it always brings me to tears. I feel that I need a good cry on this journey and the song helps me to sob out the tensions and the sadness about what happened to Mum's brain and about what I am doing to my own brain.

The stress of it all. I did not do anything ridiculous, there was no falling over, I didn't vomit down anyone's dress, there was no rudeness or aggression. But still, too much, too much. The drama and distress might be all contained in my own head, but it's pretty bloody wild in there, and threatening to explode out.

Overall, my very own personal drinking problem is not really the amount of alcohol I am throwing down my throat. I am rarely falling around drunk, or drinking every day, or hiding my drinking or driving drunk or not being able to get up in the morning. Not never but rarely.

It is the massive effort that I put in to keep my alcohol intake under control; that is a big problem. It is the huge demands made on my brain by not drinking as much as I really want to. It is the constant stopping myself, the white-knuckling. I am suffocating. I am being utterly exhausted by my heroic efforts to not go off the rails. I know very well that alcohol wants to take me somewhere I do not want to go. It wants me to follow Dad into appalling behaviour and an early grave. The effort to stop that happening is the killer, not the real-life glasses of wine I pour down my throat.

The road west feels endless and neither podcasts nor audiobooks can distract me.

Orange

Back in Orange I manage not to drink for a few days. I have taken a scunner to alcohol. 'Scunner' is a terrific Scottish noun meaning that something has made you sick to your stomach and you now have a massive aversion to it. A big hangover can give you a scunner to alcohol that lasts a few days, like I'm having now. People often say, 'I'm not having a beer today, the drinking yesterday has given me a scunner.' My scunner is deep in my guts and for these few days I truly do not want alcohol. The thought revolts me. Long may it last, I think to myself.

It doesn't.

After a hectic week, I feel stressed. By Friday afternoon, the scunner disappears and I can feel the tick-tock-tick-tock of my craving for alcohol reverberating around in my head. I decide that it will be fine to buy a bottle of wine. And I will be super environmentally friendly and go to a winery and buy direct. I drive out to the cellar door at Highland Heritage and taste a couple of wines and then buy two bottles even though I had gone there strictly intending to buy only one to last the whole weekend.

I am a very good girl and only drink half a bottle each night on Friday, Saturday and Sunday. I put the half-empty bottle of red at the very back of the cupboard and decide to use it when I cook a spaghetti bolognese later in the week.

When later in the week rolls around, I use half a glass of red in the bolognaise and knock back the rest of the bottle.

Quick, quick before you notice, Seana. Even though your plan was not to drink at all during the week.

I drink the rest of the bottle so fast that I have a rush of dizziness as I drain the pasta and I stagger while I set the table.

Should have taken it slowly, Seana.

Should have put it in a travel cup and taken it to sip at the movies tonight, a favourite trick of mine. I do love drinking wine at the movies from my Tupperware travel cup. I just have to be careful that I can still drive home. Mind you, it's only a five-minute drive and I've never seen a police car yet on that short drive home. But still.

'I'm just going to drink for two nights at the weekend,' I say to Isabel the next day on the phone. She doesn't say anything and I feel such a fool to be talking to her about this plan at all.

Then the alcohol creep starts up again. I wake up in the mornings working out how many days until I can have a drink. I feel real physical cravings for alcohol in the middle of each afternoon. I have to clench myself so hard mentally and physically, white-knuckle it, white-knuckle it, until I allow myself to have a drink, or two or three or four. I have all sorts of cunning and conniving ways to stop myself drinking as much as I really want to.

They do work.

I am not falling about.

They don't work.

This is killing me.

Alcohol creep has happened hundreds of times. I have stopped and started and stopped and started. When my kids were little, babies and toddlers, it was easy not to drink too much. Occasionally I would have a wee mini-bender, but rarely. But as the kids have got older, as life has got less demanding, the drinking has come roaring back. I used to moderate and be healthy for a bit, especially when taking loads of exercise or spending lots of time outdoors. But sooner or later the mental obsession returns and I am thinking about drinking, obsessing about alcohol in a way that wears me out. All through my twenties, I just drank and drank and drank, I never tried to moderate, ever. But ever since I turned thirty, when I did stop for a while, before I met Paul and had Jake, ever since then, the past twenty-five years, it's been all stopping and starting, and attempts at moderating. Again and again and again and again and then that one year off alcohol, and then I started and stopped and started and stopped again and again and again and again.

It is the stopping myself, the holding back, that causes the most anguish. My mental health is plummeting with the stress of keeping alcohol within some kind of limit. The constant thinking about it, the worry and the endless deals that I make with myself, all to keep my drinking within some sort of boundary. The devious plans, the trades and trade-offs, the cunning notions. The wanting to stop is all in my head but the craving for alcohol, for ease, for relief, is all in my body. Tick-tock-tick-tock starts the metronome in the late afternoon: feed me, feed me. My chest feels tight, it's as hard to breathe as when I was in the final months of my pregnancy with the twins.

Just wait, Seana, just wait until the weekend. Go out for a walk.

I can't, you fool, I have to dash to the shops, collect the kids then start cooking.

What you need is a swim, a break, a rest.

What I need is for you to stop wittering at me and pour me a glass of wine as soon as I start chopping veggies for dinner.

Come on, you promised yourself you would not drink at home during the week for this whole month. You can do it!

Midweek I find myself suggesting all sorts of activities to Paul and my friends. Out to dinner. Let's see a movie. Let's go to a comedy night on Tuesday. All to sneak in a glass or two or three of wine. And then to feel as if that's not enough and that I need to drink more.

I am running out of excuses for all these excuses I keep giving myself. I am running towards a precipice that I truly want to jump right off. Mental itchiness, inner discomfort. It's so very physical, so very overwhelming.

Stop the world, I really do need to get off. I can feel a

scunner growing again, not just to alcohol, but against myself, my whole life. I'm totally scunnered with it all.

⚘

At the very end of October, Mum's ashes are interred above Dad's coffin in the graveyard at West Byres near Ormiston. Morag organises the date with relatives and friends and they make a ceremony of it. She sends me photos from the day and tells me about it.

Morag and Kirsty were there with their families. They collected Callum and brought him to the graveyard. Mum's sisters and brother were there and a niece and nephew too. Mum's best friend and neighbour Cath was there with her husband Jim.

'What were Mum's ashes in, Mo?' I ask on the phone the next day.

'The undertaker gave them to me in a nice wooden box. It was screwed down. I had thought of having a wee peek to see what ashes look like but the box couldn't be opened.'

'And did you dig the hole for them yourself?'

'Oh no, the council does it. They did tell me I could dig the hole but I wanted it to be done properly.'

Morag goes on. 'Cath brought flowers and put them on the grave and then I said some words. Gary read the little speech that you sent and spoke his own farewell. He was very emotional.'

The family then went to the Goblin Ha' Hotel, a historic pub and hotel in the small village of Gifford. Mum used to drive Kirsty and me there for riding lessons on shaggy Highland ponies when we were little. I heard all this and a pain started in my chest, a sharp thin dart hot in my heart.

Envy, feeling left out, regret, far too late. Exiled.

Over the decades I was not present for three of my grandparents' funerals, was absent for friends' weddings and the birth of so many babies. Emigrants miss these milestones, these rituals; we hear about them only.

'What should we have engraved on the tombstone, Seana?'

'How about something like Dad's? We could put: "With love we remember Alison Mary Smith, mother, gardener and lover of animals" and then the dates. But will there be space on the gravestone for Callum's name too?'

'Oh no, there definitely wouldn't be. We had only left space for an inscription for Callum.'

'Well then, maybe we will need to get a new headstone for the three of them?'

'Poor Callum, here's us so sure we will be organising his funeral for him. He's still alive and we're already planning his burial and headstone.'

'Just being practical, Morag!'

'Let's do nothing for the moment. Mum and Dad are there now and they're not going anywhere.'

'That's just their bodily remains, isn't it? Dad's off sailing and Mum's off planting carrots and thinning cucumbers in the great greenhouse in the sky.'

'How lucky we are that we can visit them in the one place.'

And yes, we are. That graveyard is a very beautiful and special little corner of Scotland. That lovely little wooden garden seat close to Mum and Dad's grave. I hope I can visit many times, remember them and the best of times, until I am a very old lady myself.

October is mid-autumn in Scotland and the leaves are turning red and gold. It is mid-spring here, halfway around our spinning planet. So far, so far away. Far away again from a family gathering. I am upset and I have more than a few glasses of wine on the night when Mum's ashes are placed on top of Dad's coffin.

Next morning, I wake up early with a racing heart and a galloping mind.

Done it again, let yourself down, never be free of it, trapped in this drinking.

I'm not like Dad, but really, I'm just like Dad.

ELEVEN

November

Orange

November is traditionally the most stressful month of the year
for this mother and even with a mere two children at home
and in school, I can feel the tension building.

The end of the year in Australia is always all too much. The
school year ends, Christmas looms, the calendar year ends.
Until November, the year tootles along but then suddenly it
tilts up and we all start sliding downhill fast. I feel as if I'm on a
tray and some evil soul has picked up one end and everything
is flying down. I'm heading for an edge which I'm about to
tumble off into God knows where. Mostly likely towards the
stress of Christmas and the beloved relief of New Year (new
me).

I'm reduced to tears by the thought of writing Christmas
cards and finding presents for the family in Scotland before
the dreaded last post day. The changes in our school routine
cause mental potholes. Something new happens every week
then every day. Sports days, school picnics, rehearsals for

singing, speech day. I love social events but there can be too many of them. I want to buy gifts for teachers because my gratitude to them is overwhelming, tearful, profound. But the kids are in high school now. Do parents give presents to all their kids' teachers in high school? Surely not?! That would be creating yet another rod for my maternal back, wouldn't it? I decide not to buy any teacher gifts at all. Self-preservation in action.

Over the past five years I really have tried to simplify, to pace myself so as to not end up in floods of tears or flumes of fury. But November has come crashing into us and the twins' school has all sorts of activities and demands. An emailed invitation to a school Spring Soiree almost brings me out in hives. How much does it cost? Does that cover a whole evening of wine flowing free? Hope not. Hope so.

I am doing my best; I have been on this mental health helter-skelter before. I take walks in the warmth of the spring sunshine. I literally stop and smell the luscious roses that adorn the gardens of the houses in East Orange. Mindfulness? I'm all over it. Well, at least for that moment when my nose and lungs fill with the scent and my brain stills and settles. But you can't spend all day with your nose stuck in somebody else's rose bushes.

⸙

It's a week into November and I pull into the car park at the pool around 10.30 am. It's a warm, still day, the end of spring is close and there's a tinge of ferocity in its warmth; it feels like summer is coming early. The sky is a crisp arctic blue high, high above. Some foamy white clouds waft along slowly, low on the horizon.

An early start to the day means that some writing work has already been done. The twins went off to school with all their necessities: books, lunch, sports bags. Mid-morning at the pool is usually quiet and when I pay and walk out the back, I see there are several free lanes. A lane of one's own: it's something Sydney pool swimmers can only dream of.

I pull my hoodie towel over my head, then sit down at the end of the lane, slide on my fins, my cap and my goggles. I slip in, breathe deep and push off from the end of the lane, dolphin kick as the water draws me in, arms straight, head down, eyes closed. I slowly kick and wish that I would never have to lift my head out of the water ever again.

Why am I feeling so jittery this morning?

Yes, why are you, Seana? There is actually nothing wrong.

I feel so much pressure. My insides feel all wobbly.

But everything is going fine. The work has started well today, the kids are happy.

It's the alcohol, isn't it? Drinking too much these days. But it still doesn't feel like enough.

What happened to the idea of never drinking during the week, Seana?

Oh, that went west sometime in October. And I don't even know why.

Stop thinking, just swim.

Two hundred metres of front crawl, I'm trying to warm up but keep moving faster and faster, longing to hear my heart thumping so my thoughts are drowned out in the puffing and panting. A rest and a deep drink from my water bottle and then I start to swim again, taking long, slow pulls through the water, enjoying watching the ripples on the bottom.

I swim slow breaststroke, loving the views of the vivid green poplar trees reaching for the morning blue of the sky. I swim backstroke and see a plane flying overhead. I wonder where that plane is going and who is flying away on it. I wish I was up there on that plane, too. I put my fins back on and lift my kickboard, turn onto my back and stretch my arms then my board over my head so that I am one long straight line in the water, my legs moving up and down, core and arms taut, head back so that I look up at the sky and the dazzling sun. All that air above me, oxygen, life-giving; the water below me, carrying me, supporting me. I am between the two, made of water and in the water, lungs full of air, blood full of oxygen, of both and neither; and I'm crying.

Slowly, slowly, I move up and down in the lane. Tears slipping out, turmoil roiling in my head and washing all through my limbs. I know that exercise helps both body and mind. I want to be healthy, I really do. I don't want to feel on edge all the time. I want my body to work well and to carry me into old age. I need to be active in old age, partly for myself but also for my children. There's the love for them, yes, and there's also the responsibility that comes from choosing to have children in my forties. They will need me into my sixties and seventies and, God willing, into my eighties. I want to be there for them, it's the right thing to do.

I clasp the kickboard to my chest with one hand, kick along with my other hand trailing, fingers tapping on the lane ropes; red, white, blue, yellow, white, primary colours within the pale blue water, the Oxford-blue stripe of the pool lane below me.

Then I swim front crawl again, slow rhythmic pulls through the water of the outdoor swimming pool. This act of doing what is best for body and brain does calm my seething thoughts. That one hour in the pool, among the trees and the sloping grass, with the sun overhead and the soothing warm water. By the end of an hour, the shakes have gone and the tears too. I am hungry. I think about trying to carve out an hour a day for swimming.

Then you'd only have the other twenty-three hours a day to get through, Seana.

※

I'm drinking at least half a bottle of wine daily and feeling worse and worse for it. Depression is coming for me, blacker than usual. The old blanket is covering me, draped from head to foot. Some days it's a fairly light wool blanket that drapes softly over my shoulders, but other days it is soggy, heavy, suffocating. And underneath the blanket I am a slippery, slidey, gooey mess of distress. My heart feels as if it's sitting just under my left collarbone, in the wrong place. It feels compressed, flattened, struggling to beat blood through its thin walls. It's working too hard and my blood pressure feels high. All up and down my legs and arms and into my hands and feet I feel pumping, hard pumping, but not enough blood is getting through and it can't get to my lungs for more oxygen.

※

I am sitting at my desk in the sunroom one morning towards the middle of November when that feeling of being weak and shaky, of not getting enough oxygen, comes over me, washing through my body and my bones like a chill Scottish wind through winter trees, through bare branches reaching skywards like claws.

I have to get out of the house. I need to leave. Ten deep slow breaths. Count backwards from twenty to zero.

'Paul, I'm just popping out to the shops, picking up some

milk,' I call as I grab my bag and bolt out the front door. I sit down in the car: where to go, what to do? Somewhere new; I need to go somewhere where I will not bump into anyone I know. The cafe by the adventure playground. Don't think, just go. Car windows down, try to breathe deeply.

I am shaking as I turn the car off and swing my legs out, lift my bag up. I feel as if I have no insides at all; everything I am is humming in my fingertips, and on the outside of my skin. Just go slowly. Just breathe.

I order coffee and sit down at a table beside a wall painted with pink flamingos, their heads dipping into sapphire blue water. My heart races and my limbs feel sore and panicky and all wrong. I am light-headed, dizzy. And now there's that old plum stone stuck in my throat and my oesophagus is swelling around it. I want to let that plum stone float up my throat and come out as tears but it is stuck there and, as I try to take deep, slow breaths to calm down, only tiny tears can slide out.

I've had plum stone throat before, a couple of years ago in Sydney. Plum stone is a term used in Chinese medicine and it feels just as it sounds. Back then, I went to the doctor and had an upper endoscopy. There was nothing stuck in my throat, just a hard plum stone stuck in my head. And here I am again, with an even bigger plum stone lodged in my oesophagus.

Around me are graceful drooping palms in pots and I move to hide behind one so the people at the other table cannot see me. I try to take sips of coffee but the plum stone blocks the way. What I need is a drink. Just one glass of wine swallowed down fast. Even a standard-sized glass would do the trick. Even a little glass might wash that plum stone away, away.

That's the thing about booze, Seana. It works so bloody fast and yes, at first it does relax you, your head, throat, shoulders, back.

But you know the booze is affecting you a lot right now, especially your mental health. It's a bloody fickle friend; it's not a friend. You know it's making you suffer, causing this stress that you then drink to escape from.

I know, yes, maybe I do know that. But at least I'm stopping by 8 pm and I go to bed early in an effort to get a good night's sleep and to wake up feeling better.

That might help if you hadn't started drinking earlier in the afternoon. You are being a total fuckwit and you know it. You're not fooling anyone, not even yourself.

Your cunning plans and latest ploys are not working.

Why do I keep writing myself off with alcohol? Why do I drink so fast and furious?

Yes, Seana, why do you do that when you say you want to stay well?

⚘

The drought has been ferocious and living in the country means I understand this much better than when we lived in Sydney. Friends talk about their sheep, their cattle and their lost crops. So when rain pours down on the evening of the school Spring Soiree, no one is complaining that we cannot stand and sip our drinks outside at this vineyard. Instead, the crowds gather in a massive shed where towering vats hold the fermenting grape juice, turning it into red, white and rosé wine. Each parent receives two tickets for a glass of wine and then pays for the rest. Paul didn't come so I hold his tickets too and then am offered more by someone who is driving. I have told myself this is not going to be a big night, that I will be up and about to watch Tom's cricket the next day. But I hold those tickets in my hand very tightly.

Many people I know are here and also many I have never met. Ideal! Now, I bustle towards the table where the wine is served, hand over a ticket and decide to start with a tall glass of bubbly wine.

'In fact, give me two. That'll save me from queuing up again too quickly.'

The silvery gleam of metal is all around and the people in this shed are reflected in odd ways in the round and angled surfaces. I see a group of friends who are nattering close by and join them.

'How's the week been? How are the kids?'

'Mad and maddening. It's always this term when they start to act up.'

'It's been tricky getting mine out of bed this week, too.'

'A pal of mine always takes her children out of school for a week in November. She says it's a lifesaver.'

'We all need that, but the term ends so soon, a holiday wouldn't work for us.'

'I know, they finish so bloody early in December. Nightmare.'

I am multitasking, watching all the glasses of all my friends as we chat. The usual suspects, the drinkers, the ones I relate to and love to death, are drinking so much faster, so, so much faster than the steady friends, the ones who are driving, the ones who can and do just have one or two. Just one or two.

The legacy of watching Dad drink gave me the survival mechanism of being very alert to how much everyone around me is drinking. (Except me, of course.) It was important to keep an eye out as Dad drank glass after glass after glass so that I might have some idea of what could be coming, what probably was.

Caroline chats, one little finger curled around the bottom of her wine glass as she gesticulates. She has two small sips while I slurp down my first glass. And there's Maz with no glass in her hand at all. But Cass is keeping up with me. She slurped her first one down as fast as I did then her husband gave her another and she's drinking that now. I finish my second glass and excuse myself to head to the bar again. Caroline has not even drunk one third of her glass of bubbly. Lightweight.

I didn't have much to eat so a warm buzz is settling in and around me. I'm getting a taxi home, I know where my bag is and I have a fistful of tickets to use.

And then it starts, that inner nag, perhaps my conscience, who I didn't expect to turn up to torment me before the morning after.

You could just float for a bit here. Why do you feel you need to immediately get another glass in your hand? You're an idiot and you're weak. You can't manage without that crutch, can you?

There are echoes of Dad from this inner bitch witch. He used to drunkenly abuse Mum for needing the crutch of her cigarettes, while missing the fact that alcohol was being used as a scaffold around his entire life. Mum stopped smoking one day, just like that. That annoyed him.

Dad used to corner us and shout when he was drunk, and now I have a drunk shouting at me inside my own head.

Seana, you really are pathetic, you should be able to drink less. Look at all the other people here who are in control of their drinking. You're a sad case.

Look, you nasty piece of work, I've got an emotionally snapped femur, a greenstick fracture on my mental tibia and several torn psychological tendons. My emotions need a crutch, everyone needs support. So piss off and leave me alone to hobble along on this one crutch in peace.

Weak, pathetic, you pretend to be healthy and then damage your brain, your body. Haven't you seen the research on cancer and alcohol? Denial, pretence, your life is a sham.

The voice in my head is sharp, a shriek.

Well, thanks for that support and I love you, dearest inner critic. How busy have I been? How much crap have I got done? How stressful is the end of the school year? Fuck off tonight and leave me alone and I'll catch you when I wake up in the morning.

Two quick glasses of wine later there is no inner critic, in fact, no inner anything. I am nattering nineteen to the dozen, laughing and high. A wee while later, my words are slurring and I pull back for a while until I feel my body coming back into itself and I can talk again. I calibrate my drinking pretty well; there's no getting too messy tonight.

✻

Sunlight forms a bright stripe in the centre of the two curtains in my bedroom when I awake the next day. I'm squinting and confused at the brightness, then realise I must have closed the curtains badly last night, pulled them roughly when I came in, no care.

As I come to, my inner witch is up and waiting, sharpening her kitchen knives and digging down sharply into my skull.

Now then, what day is it? Saturday. So don't worry, you can have more wine tonight.

Look, I feel shocking, I don't think I should really drink tonight at all. Sore head, dry mouth and what crap came out of my mouth last night? I can get up, I will watch Tom's cricket, but then I think the best thing is just to get to bed super early.

Well, if you don't drink tonight then tomorrow is Sunday and you shouldn't really drink during the week.

Yes, I know, I know. Each week I try but each week I've been failing.

If you don't drink today, that's Saturday gone, and surely it'll be OK to drink on Sunday instead? It's still the weekend. How about making risotto for Sunday dinner? That needs white wine. Buy a bottle, make the risotto and have a glass or two.

It's a stressful time of year. Maybe I deserve it? Maybe I need it?

I manage to watch Tom's whole cricket match. Wide-brimmed hat. Dark sunglasses. Lots of water. I stew with my hangover, hiding in the shade of a tree, trying to avoid the too-bright heat of the sunshine. I'm not able to get at all comfortable on my camp chair and I am not up to chatting to any of the other parents. I try to read the paper at times but can't concentrate. Hungover; two aspirins do not shift the headache. I'm parched all day however much water I drink, however many ice cubes I suck. It's a lost day, a day I don't want to be awake in at all.

I do get to bed early on this Saturday. Close the curtains and lean a pillow against them to stop any morning light getting in. I don't talk to Paul or the kids in the evening, do not eat the Indian takeaway they get. I am avoiding them and am sure they're relieved.

And then on Sunday, off I go to get the ingredients for risotto. I pass by the tiny single serve bottle of wine that would be the ideal amount for a mushroom risotto, grab a bottle of sav blanc instead. When I get home and start cooking, I pour a glass before I get the mushrooms out of the fridge, the onion, the arborio rice, the butter. I chop and I drink, I sauté and I drink, and the last glass is there on the table as we all sit down to eat.

※

It's just past mid-November and the day has started out warm and dazzling as I meet my friend Sue for an early walk around East Orange. I am giving her the full bore; my lamenting about this morning's hangover and my end of year overwhelm is bending her ears backwards.

'Do you think all working mothers feel this way?' I ask. We both collapse laughing because everyone we know feels this way. The mental motherlode of mothering.

'Do you think I drink too much?' I ask.

'Well, you're not someone I think of as being a huge boozer. You're not falling around drunk ever, not that I see.'

'Is that the bar we're going for? If a person can still stand, their drinking is all right? What about my poor brain? I force myself not to drink. I white-knuckle it. I really want to drink a lot more than I do. So I do drink, but it's never enough and I'm exhausted and I feel my ability to rein myself in is crumbling. I want it to crumble.'

'Does being too busy make you drink more?'

'Yes, for sure. Maybe if life was calmer the urge to drink vast quantities would ease. And when my brain gets too fraught I like to drink *a lot* and make myself hungover so that I really cannot do much at all next day. It's a depressant isn't it? I think I like to use it to depress myself, flatten the internal frenzy and quiet the mental chatter.'

'Do you think it's having other effects on you too?'

'Yes, bad sleep, eating too much, feeling depressed and thinking about drinking all the time. I did have some days or weeks when I was feeling great and whole days used to go by with no urges but I started to feel overburdened and now I want to drink daily and it is so hard to stop myself. I don't want to stop myself. Or it's getting too difficult to stop myself.'

※

A morning at the pool again and an acquaintance is swimming in the lane next to me. She asks how we're going and I almost vomit all over her, so many words and rancid feelings pour out. I know that I am talking too much, being inappropriate, embarrassing. But I cannot stop as I lament my worsening hangovers and creeping mental health collapse.

'Can't you just stop?' she asks as she pulls herself out of the water. Is she leaving early because I'm talking too much, being too much?

'I've tried and tried … but there seems to be no "just" in "just stopping" for me.'

I push off and swim a lap, turning words in my mind as I turn my arms. I cannot do it. I cannot do it.

There is a very high and thick brick wall in my brain and it has massive graffiti sprayed on it: 'You will never survive without alcohol.'

I stop that idea of just stopping before I even get started.

Even when I did quit alcohol for that whole year, over five years ago now, my stopping drinking was always and only just for that one year. During that year of sobriety whenever I thought about never drinking again, I felt physical pain; tears welled in my eyes. The emotional and physical reaction to the very thought of extending beyond that one year was intense and immediate.

Meanwhile I feel constantly harassed and too busy. There's too much going on and most of it is caused by me saying 'yes' to too many things. And I have booked a holiday for straight after the end of term. Why did I do it? It'll be good when we get on that plane, but until then, there is too much to plan and organise.

And I need to get so much work finished before the school holidays start. Why do I work? Just running the home and family and looking after myself could easily take up all my time. I wouldn't be twiddling my thumbs. Of course, if I didn't work at all I would die of boredom but now I'm dying of harassment instead. There's no balance between the mental stimulation of working and the mental implosion of being overworked and overwrought. Exercise and self-care reduce according to how much work I'm doing. The domestic work, the housework, the cooking work, the washing work, the cleaning work, the organising work, the managing schoolwork: all that work always gets done. To add my writing work on top of that means that my non-work, my good living, relaxation, walking, swimming go down and down and down. When I have a big writing job on, I barely move my old carcass. What is that doing to the poor, tired brain which is supposed to be managing the whole lot of everything? Nothing good.

But adding alcohol into that messy mix is not helping you in any way, Seana.

Silence! Do not add to my stressed-out state!

৵

Three am, alcohol and stress shake me wide awake and keep me wakeful. Again. Theoretically, this is not the end of the world. When I was pregnant and had babies and toddlers, I learned to make my peace with 3 am. Instead of freaking out and winding myself up even further, I learned to relax. Often I would read a book, or I might get up and do something useful. Then all the next day, I survived by doing everything slowly and repeating to myself. 'I'll be in bed by 8 pm. I'll have a lovely, early night tonight.'

Still, now, at this particular 3 am, after two or three weeks of waking at 3 am several times a week, I am feeling awful, so anxious. Bloody anxiety. Before menopause, I did not experience it too much, never in a debilitating way. But now

I have sweaty palms and pounding heart and brain shutdown.

Seana, you never understood people who had anxiety before. You found them irritating.

Yes, I did. Anxious people tend to fanny around and some do nothing to help themselves. And they make me feel anxious.

Well, here we are at 3 am. What are you doing to help yourself?

What I am doing is moving to the spare room to read my book and then hopefully I will get back to sleep.

You're in a mess, Seana – all this shaking and worrying and the circling thoughts.

Circling anxiety demons. I miss my old bull-in-a-china-shop approach to life.

꙼

And it is the next day, the very next day, when I find myself in the garage, putting together the steel shelves and thinking about hiding a bottle of wine in the welly boots. And although I'm laughing at myself as I think about it, I'm startled that the thought has come upon me. Imagine thinking that! Over decades I've heard so many stories of husbands, always husbands, who hide their alcohol in the garage, popping out at night just to sort some things out, or to whittle or build things, but really to tipple.

Tipple is such a good word, isn't it, Seana? You could hide a cheeky bottle of wine over there in that welly boot and just have a little tipple now and again and what harm could that possibly do?

You've got to be kidding me! Hiding alcohol is a big step down in the downward spiral staircase. Only people with a serious drink problem need to do that. Even Dad never, ever hid bottles of booze anywhere. His were all out on display, as was his drinking. Come on, who hides their alcohol? Why would you do that?

I'd do it so I could drink more and nobody would see, of course. Just like all those boozers who used to say they did it when I went to AA during my year off the bevvy. Always, always men.

Come on, Seana, lighten up. Hiding alcohol in the garage as a woman could be seen as a strike for feminism, don't you reckon?

Don't be ridiculous, you maniac. Stop this thought immediately. Anyway, there's probably a family of deadly spiders living in that welly. Give up on that idea.

I know, I'll hide my wine bottles in suitcases over there.

Why would I want to hide my drinking? Paul is not worried about me. He has never, ever said that he thinks I'm drinking too much. Mind you, I tend to do more of it when he's away and he's been away many weeks this year. And I'm not telling him anything about what's happening inside my poor, exhausted head; the brain that feels like mashed potato with the stress of this time of year and the stress of holding back on the drinking; about reining myself in, putting the brakes on when I really want to go for it in a big way. A spectacular way.

Paul doesn't see that I am enduring my very own variation of a drinking problem because I am never falling around drunk (well, rarely). Yes, this week I am drinking a bottle of wine a night rather than the half bottle it used to be. And, yes, I always, always want to drink more. I always, always, always want to drink more. But I am not talking to him about it, not honestly. Why not? Because if I was honest with him then the only next step is to try to stop – and that feels terrifying.

My head is sore today, the hangover is still with me, even after three coffees earlier this morning. And I can feel The Thirst starting to wiggle around in my guts. I walk into the house to get a glass of cold water, add in some ice. I chug one down, and pour another. There you go, you bloody Thirst, does that help? Suck on that ice water!

It doesn't really help, does it? Taking huge swallows of chilled water feels excellent in the mouth and the throat, marvellous as the cold hits my stomach. But the daily Thirst is deeper in my guts, a long worm unravelling itself, starting to squirm and wriggle. Discomfort deep in the pelvis and itchiness inside my skull.

There is no bottle of white wine in the fridge because I drank it all last night. Shall I buy another today? Shall I pop quickly down to the IGA and grab a local wine? Anything will do. Or can I grit my teeth and have a night off? What to do? What to do?

I walk back out to the garage and start to bolt the shelves together.

Maybe you should just let go, Seana. Go wild. Drink and drink and drink and drink. Then Paul would notice, then he'd have to do something to help you. He'd be forced to do something about you if your behaviour got really terrible.

I wish I could get a small breast cancer, just a little one. Would a shock like that stop me? Remember when a Sydney swimming friend said that she didn't drink as she had read the cancer stats and was keen to reduce her risk as much as possible? I was astounded at that. Surely the rewards of alcohol are worth the slight risk, I said to her. It's not slight, she replied, and I changed topics swiftly. I didn't want to hear more then. But surely if I was ever ill, had cancer or heart problems, surely then I would stop, surely?

Or could you, Seana?

And these thoughts are making me nauseous. Tempting fate. The lack of respect for my friends who have been sick, for the loved ones who have died too young. I'm wishing for illness. I feel sicker still because I don't think that I could stop, not even if I was sick myself. Oh, messy mess. I cannot believe

I'm even thinking this but I am. Shit.

I never do hide bottles of wine in welly boots, thank God. But I do go out that night and buy six bottles of wine, making the excuse that it would be nice to take a bottle or two to the last meeting of the Parents and Friends group at school. I offered to bring some wine, but how many bottles to take? I take all six to the meeting and only two people have a glass when I do. After the meeting, I finish the bottle I opened and put the other five in the cupboard in the sitting room. I can feel them throbbing in there. They are calling to me as I go to bed that night.

Next day I wake up with a bastard behind the eyes, a term picked up from the hilarious cult movie *Withnail and I.*

'If you've had one, you know exactly what it means,' my ex-boyfriend used to say when we watched the film.

My head feels hot, sharp pains jab from the centre of my brain to my face where the skin feels dry and itchy. The back of my skull feels as if sharp talons are scratching at it. It's hot there too, and when I try to lift my head from the pillow, the whole world lurches to one side and I feel vomit rising in my throat. I swallow it down.

Don't worry, Seana, there are more bottles in the cupboard. Just have one a night until they're all gone.

Man, I will feel so terrible and so depressed if I drink a bottle a night.

But the afternoons will go very smoothly, don't you think? Start tippling when the twins come in, a glass of wine as you finish working at your desk, another while you cook dinner. Have a red one night and a white the next. Just finish what's in the house, get rid of it all and then start again. Take a break then.

It's so hard to control myself when there are bottles of wine in the house. I'm a bloody idiot, why did I buy so many? Maybe I should give them away?

But Seana, you love these wines! Come on, don't worry so much. Just off this lot and take it from there. Don't worry about what day it is or what's happening tomorrow, sink into relaxation now. Come on, this is a shocking time of year. Be good to yourself.

I am effing well trying to be good to myself by NOT drinking. I'm trying to be healthy, I'm walking and swimming and trying to eat well. This wee devil is sitting on my shoulder, though. He knows and I know and everyone knows that drinking is totally not good for you, not for the body and not for the brain. Stop kidding yourself, Seana; come on, what are you doing?

I am not, not, not going to drink that wine tonight. I am not going into that sitting room and I am not opening that cupboard. I will keep away from it.

)€

Of course, I do take a bottle of wine that night. I go into the sitting room and I open the cupboard, take out a bottle and drink it all. And the next night, I do the very same thing, and then the next night after that.

Just drink the wine! It's shouting and yelling at you. Put it out of its misery. Drink it all.

Just keep the red in the sitting room and pour it from there, when Paul is not around.

And don't let him see you pour more than two glasses on any one evening. Make those really huge glasses.

Keep the white wine behind other bottles in the fridge so that he doesn't notice how quickly they are being emptied and replaced.

Yes, just drink it up. Get rid of all this wine from the house and start trying again. Come on, it's always shitty keeping wine in the house. You're not seriously thinking of pouring it away, are you?

No, I didn't think so. Just drink it up, get rid of it.

I drink a bottle of wine a night, and by the last week of November, I feel appalling. On 28th November I've drunk so much that I've got a massive scunner.

Time to get up, Seana. Get out of bed and into the blinding light of the day.

Man, hangovers are so much easier in Scotland in the winter when the skies are grey, the light is dim and the days are short. This scorching end of spring is a killer.

I feel ill, my poor guts are churning all day and the alcohol cravings do not arrive in the afternoon. It's not even that I don't want to drink: I can't drink. My tummy feels as if the insides of my intestines have been scoured, peeled off, as if they're bleeding. I am nauseous all the time.

I call Isabel. 'I'm scunnered,' I tell her. 'Totally scunnered.'

I spend the whole day in bed. Just me and my laptop, covered in a blanket of shame and misery, pain and self-loathing. Paul makes the dinner and I stay in bed. If I were an Irish mother, I would just turn my face to the wall at this stage. But I am a Scottish–Australian mum and so I dive into my laptop and numb out scrolling through my feed on Facebook.

I am tutting away as I see advert after advert for Black Friday sales in my feed. So American! Rampant commercialism! It makes me feel even more unwell, all that pushing to make us consume and consume and consume. Barf. I want to see what my friends are up to!

Then I see it.

There's a Black Friday price reduction on a thirty-day alcohol-free challenge from a UK company. They offer daily emails, video training and a Facebook community to connect with. A bargain is so tempting to this canny ex-Scot. The impulsiveness that sees me crack open a bottle of wine on a whim on so many of the days I'm supposed to have 'off' alcohol now sees me signing up for this thirty-day alcohol-free challenge. No one could be more surprised than myself.

'Guess what?' I say to Isabel on the phone the next day. 'I've signed up for one of those month-off alcohol challenges. If I can stop for a month now, then that gets me through the holiday in Vietnam and through Christmas and New Year so I can start the coming year afresh.'

'Do you think you'll be OK over Christmas, and for the whole month? Can you manage it?'

'Well, I've paid for it, and that's a big incentive to do it properly. I hate wasting cash. And I really, really need it.'

'And do you think that will help you slow down your drinking next year?'

'Look, I hope so. Surely it will? Surely!?'

I have never done a month off alcohol before. I never, ever signed up for a Dry July or a Sober October because I never thought I would manage it. Never thought I could survive it. But I did survive that whole year off, and I am feeling as desperate now as I was then. I'm feeling worse. I have never felt so shaky in my life, physically, never mind mentally.

Can I use this massive scunner I have given myself as a catapult into a whole month off alcohol?

How hard can it be, Seana? It's only thirty days. Lots of people manage a month off alcohol.

But what will you do instead, Seana?

I'll swim and I'll be on holiday and I'll listen to health podcasts and I might find some books to read. I can do this!

Can I?

I log on.

TWELVE

December

Orange

I would love to report that my first sober week is a piece of cake. But sadly, no. It is not all beer and skittles, not even all alcohol-free beer and skittles. This first week of December is hectic, being the last week of the school term. To distract myself I keep busy, busy, busy, even busier than normal. I run around like a headless chook, to the pool, to the shops, to the post office, here, there and everywhere, running, running, running around.

Each morning I receive an email from the UK company running the alcohol-free challenge with information to read and questions to answer. Each afternoon, I pour myself a tall glass of diet tonic water, clinking with ice and sharpened by a slice of lemon. And then another. Each evening, I write and write and write.

Q. What is not going well in your life at the moment?
I feel constantly harassed, too busy, too anxious, too stressed.

Too hungover.

I have been forcing myself not to drink as much I want to drink. My urge to drink a lot more than I do is very strong. When I do drink, it is never enough. The white-knuckling – it is killing me.

Q. What would you like to change about how you live your life?
I need to stop impulsively over-committing to too many things. I need to stop feeling so harassed. Would the urge to drink vast quantities then ease? Or would I just have more free time to spend drinking?

Q. What are the consequences of the way you are drinking?
Bad sleep, eating too much, feeling depressed, and thinking about alcohol too much. I feel overburdened and want to drink every day and it is so HARD to stop myself.

My terrible sleep is a nightmare. Alcohol and stress find me at 3 am and keep me awake.

Anxiety. I have been feeling anxious and stressed and I need that to STOP!

Q. If you were drinking less or nothing, what would you gain?
Freedom from cravings and from white-knuckling through my urges to drown myself in alcohol.

Q. What are the things that trigger your drinking?
I drink when I feel stressed. Life feels overwhelming and I need an escape and to numb out. I need to quickly calm myself so I drink and stop caring about whatever it is that I am stressing about. But I never sort things out!

Wine is also a reward for my hard work. I use alcohol to relieve the tedium of routine, to rebel against housewifery, overwhelm and boredom. The wine I pour when I start cooking dinner is all about that. It's about knocking the edges off my daily resentment, too.

Q. Are there rewards in the drinking?
The reward of wine is that I calm down, numb out, de-stress. Alcohol is so quick, and it feels like a treat. But it's a treat that ends up kicking my arse.

Q. Why is it just not possible for things to stay the same?
I feel so upset, sad and stressed and also angry and tired. I have a good life and I want to feel good in it. Which I definitely do not at the moment. Life is so much easier and better this year, but I feel terrible a lot of the time. I'm wasting my life, this one precious life.

Q. What daily changes could help?
I need a more structured way to chill out, like doing meditation or sitting in the garden for a while or reading a book or numbing out watching TV. All these take time though. I need to get into the habit of these alternatives instead of pouring a glass of wine. A large glass. And then another.

I need to get into the habit of noticing low-level stress and being vigilant about not letting it get too bad. Maybe I run around and get stressed out so that I have an excuse to drink? Or maybe it's all a vicious cycle, on a very bad-tempered washing machine.

Q. How could you celebrate without drinking?
I could buy some good alcohol-free drinks, spend as much as I did on wine, etc. I could enjoy a meal out with friends and actually focus on the food instead of the wine. I could buy a new swimming cossie or some clothes. I could chill out at a lovely cafe, all on my own, just me and the newspaper.

※

By day, I am baking like a maniac and eating vast quantities of cake and biscuits. By night, I drink bottles and bottles of tonic water. But in this first week of December, I do not drink any wine at all.

I deliberately keep a low profile and avoid all social activity. Then comes our school-mum-friends dinner at a pretty restaurant in a vineyard. I am not sure whether to go. Will I be able to stay sober? I'll take the car, I will. I put on a floral frock and drive there.

I walk into a room full of antique furniture and golden evening beams filtering through lace curtains. There are bottles of wine on the table already, but I pour a glass of water for myself and put my hand over the top of the wine glass when the waiter tilts the bottle in my direction.

I summon all my strength and ask, 'Can you take this glass away, please?'

He lifts the glass as I say, 'Do you have any non-alcoholic drinks?'

'Yes, we have various cocktails. I'll bring you the menu.'

It's a revelation! Menu? A menu for alcohol-free drinks?!

Minutes later I am brought an espresso martini in a shallow coupé glass. It has a foamy coffee crema on the top and three little coffee beans. The scent is divine, a feast in itself. I take a sip of my first ever espresso martini, mocktail not cocktail, and a mix of sweet and bitter washes over my tongue. And there are more cocktails to try on that menu too, not boring fruity ones but more sophisticated cocktails using alcohol-free spirits. This is all new to me!

What is not new is the rush I am feeling, the excitement and the pleasure.

But you're not drinking alcohol, Seana. How can this be?

Oxytocin? Serotonin? I love being with my pals, love hearing them chattering, love listening to their stories. They are a funny bunch and we know each other well now. There's community and intimacy among us; we have helped each other and held each other close this year.

You seem to be getting pretty high just on that, Seana.

Yes, I am, and also the delight of a new flavour, a zinging taste on my tongue as I drink from this elegant glass. It's a treat and it feels like one. Something's certainly happening to my neurotransmitters.

'You're not having any wine, Seana?' asks a friend.

'Oh no, I'm driving, and I've got a big day tomorrow.' I have all my lies and excuses ready.

No one notices or cares that I stay sober. Why would they? They're all having a jolly time and we're all old enough to be living our own lives. No one seems to feel judged, no one is judged.

This is not my first sober rodeo, of course. In the past I have had to explain myself, been criticised by people who do find it threatening when one person is not drinking. As a long-term people pleaser this made me feel anxious. But being in my fifties has meant a loosening of the clutches of giving a rat's about what people think.

Vietnam

Paul, Alice, Tom and I fly to Vietnam for a two-week holiday. Each day is busy with sightseeing, the food we eat is wonderful and there are no bottles of wine to tempt me in the cafes and restaurants we visit. I am wakeful at night but read that this is normal when you first cut out alcohol. It takes time for your neurotransmitters to settle down and stop anticipating the depressant effects of booze.

On planes and in cars and on buses, I am devouring books about quitting and sobriety. I'm learning there is a whole genre called 'quit lit'. The first book I read is *The Sober Diaries* by Clare Pooley and I often find myself laughing out loud at her antics. I am seeing myself reflected in her middle-class angst and misbehaviour. She is a bright, well-educated and successful woman who drank too much; whose three children can drive her to drink, even when she has switched from beers with alcohol to Beck's Blue, an alcohol-free beer. She sounds like me.

I read *The Outrun* by Amy Liptrot, which brings back a few too many memories of drunken misbehaviour in my twenties, and *Alcohol Explained* by William Porter, which helps me understand how ethyl alcohol affects the brain and the body. Yikes.

I read *Dryland: One Woman's Swim to Sobriety* by Nancy Stearns Bercaw and *Woman of Substances* by Jenny Valentish and *High Sobriety* by Jill Stark and *Quit Like A Woman* by Holly Whitaker and *Dry* by Augusten Burroughs.

Some of these writers make me look like a complete lightweight with my drinking. Yes, I was wild in my twenties, but I never lost jobs or was thrown out of shared houses. And I never was a drug taker. I read the term 'grey area drinker' and little fireworks light up in my head. That's me, it's me!

There are plenty of treat drinks to enjoy here in Vietnam. Fruity mocktails decorated with tropical blooms, lime and passionfruit tingle on my tongue. There are all manner of weird and wonderful coffees and teas, hot and cold: egg coffee, coconut coffee, mint tea, pandan tea. The exotic is all around me, scents and tastes and sounds and sights.

I remember my late twenties when I finally managed to stop smoking. It took two years of stopping and starting and stopping and starting, then – a big click in the head – the mind shift occurred. I went from feeling I was missing out when I watched people smoke to feeling that I had been saved, that I was so grateful that I did not have a cigarette in my mouth, staining my fingers, making my breath stink. A massive mind shift from loss to gain, from missing out to attaining something.

On our last evening in Saigon, Paul and I walk to the Heart of Darkness brewery and bar. This is a bit of a franchise operation, with outlets in Singapore and London. But guess what? There's no alcohol-free beer. How lame is that? If there had been an alcohol-free beer, I might have tried it, although I've rarely drunk beer in my life. But there isn't. So a fruit juice it is.

I congratulate myself on this hangover-free fortnight in Vietnam.

Very well done, Seana.

I am running my finger down the condensation on the side of my glass. Licking the finger.

I am not craving the sensation of alcohol. I am not dreaming of the taste of a glass of crisp white.

What's wrong with you, Seana?

What's right with me?

Paul drinks his beer, his one glass of beer, and we walk back through the lights and noise and clinging heat of the Saigon night.

Orange

In the run up to Christmas, I continue my walking around Orange, venturing out to Bloomfield Park and to the paths alongside the river behind the swimming pool. I may not have a dog but I do have some new companions. I have blundered into the world of sober podcasts, and there are dozens of them.

I now have friendly voices broadcasting through my ears and into my brain, giving me information and sharing stories I can relate to. I listen to Janey Lee Grace's *Alcohol Free Life* podcast as I walk into the grounds of the hospital precinct, passing the mob of kangaroos on the golf driving range. I listen to the *This Naked Mind* podcast from Annie Grace and then buy her book on Kindle, not wanting to waste a day before I read it. I listen to Dr Rangan Chatterjee's *Feel Better, Live More* podcast, picking out the episodes that discuss alcohol, horrified to hear how much sleep is impacted by even a glass or two of wine.

I am hearing stories of people just like me. They chat about their lives when they were boozers; many are ex-party people, always up for a laugh. Some drank a lot and some drank less, but all found their life was impacted by alcohol and they now chat about how much better, easier, simpler life is without booze. Who knew all this was out there? In the few years since my one year off there has been an explosion of drinking less.

Time and time again, I relate hard to the term 'grey area drinker', meaning someone who was not at all at rock bottom, was functioning pretty well, but whose health both mental and physical was affected by alcohol. So they stopped. It is all very different to the AA rooms I have spent time in. I certainly relate more to the ex-grey-area drinkers, who are out and proud now. No anonymity here.

Can I even dare to call myself a sober rebel? Am I starting to feel like I am part of a movement, a wave of people who do not have to get to where alcohol might take them, who stop before reaching whatever their version of rock bottom might be?

I am a sociable person, an extrovert: it feels both comforting and exciting to hear so many different voices. To know that I am not alone. Far from it. I am in most excellent company.

\#

A sober Christmas period turns out to be hunky dory. Who knew? Paul and the big boys drink some beers. I make a visit to our local bottle shop and find all sorts of alcohol-free spirits and wines which I bring home in great volumes. This trip is different from my scurrying visits to bottle shops in the past, when I used to grab just one bottle of wine at a time and whisk it home.

Now, for Christmas, I am heaving cardboard boxes full of pre-mixed fake gin and tonics, zero per cent wine and a bottle of Lyre's Italian Spritz – what even is that? It turns out to be a deep-orange colour and flavour and when I mix it with sparkling non-alcoholic wine and garnish it with a slice of lemon, I have a yummy drink to enjoy. I have never had an alcoholic Aperol spritz in my life but now I mix up the alcohol-free version in huge glasses and drink them down good style. Refreshing, delicious, and there's no hangover to follow. Who knew there were so many new options for booze-free drinks? I hadn't noticed when I was busy throwing wine down my throat.

Christmas with young men in their twenties and the twins aged thirteen is different, far more relaxing. The children have embraced gift-giving, and enjoy thinking about what will be enjoyed. So that's chocolate gingers for me and Turkish delight for Paul. Ben has made a present for Paul and me: it's a stencilled picture of a tree and the words 'Family: like branches on a tree, we all grow in different directions yet our roots remain as one'.

Christmas Day is not too hot, and we walk around Lake Canobolas in the late morning, chattering as we go, enjoying seeing the glossy cows, the ducks taking off and landing, the orchards and vineyards around and then the shimmering blue water. The kids help prepare a feast, set the table, and we sit for a long time at the table. It has been many months since all six of us were together.

In the free and easy days after Christmas, I am enjoying waking up each morning with a clear head. My first thought on waking is 'Thank God I didn't drink yesterday, and hooray for feeling good in the morning.' No headache, no hangover, no regret and not a single nasty voice yapping in my head. The relief.

Inevitably, though, life tosses up challenges. There comes one terrible day when I really, really crave a drink to get me through a crisis.

Lola is our fluffy, grey lop-eared rabbit and Eric is a tiny black velvet bunny, rescued via the RSPCA. They live in a large enclosure in our garden, a salubrious establishment which, in this heat, is made even more comfortable by the large flat freezer blocks that we place under their straw. Like all rabbits, they do not help themselves, often trying to escape by burrowing or by jumping out of our arms when we play with them.

On a very hot day between Christmas and New Year, I give them some dandelions and speak sternly to Pluto the black and white cat who is standing stock still outside the cage, one paw out in front, staring at the rabbits.

'You look ridiculous, Pluto, pretending to stalk those rabbits. You'd be terrified of them if they came near you. Behave!'

There had been a huge thunderstorm in the early hours of the morning and the grass is still wet.

'Did the thunder and lightning scare you, bunnies? Or

were you all right tucked up in your hutch?'

The bunnies just twitch their noses and carry on nibbling the grass. They're not great conversationalists.

I leave the house. Paul has gone to Sydney with the older boys and Tom. Alice is still snoozing in bed: she is a champion teenage sleeper, just as I was myself. I pop into town to meet up with two friends at one of our favourite cafes, and much gabbing and eating of avocado toast keeps me busy until around 11 am when I drive home.

All is quiet when I open the door and walk into the house. As I reach the kitchen I hear barking from the garden, run to the door and look out on a scene of destruction. A solid brindle dog, squat and fierce, is rushing around, barking and growling. It runs towards me, stops at the glass door and barks, baring its teeth, foam-flecked. I am paralysed. The dog barks and growls at me again, then turns and dashes back into the garden. I start to shake. The bunnies' cage looks a bit mangled and I see their bodies lying long and flat inside, as if they were running and were shot and fell as they bolted.

What to do? What to do? I am too scared to go into the garden. Dogs have never scared me but this one does. My hands are jittery as I try to dial the council, ask for rangers to come to help me. A drink, I need a drink, just to settle me down.

Then I think of Alice, who is still in bed and unaware of all this. But if she had been here on her own, if she had woken up, she might have gone out there. I can imagine her panic, her fear, can picture the dog attacking her if she had tried to help. All these thoughts jabbing inside my head and I can barely stand, I feel so shaky and weak. The poor rabbits. A glass of wine would steady me.

When the rangers come, it takes them a long time to catch

the dog. Finally, they use a long pole with a loop hanging off the end.

'The storm last night caused this,' they tell me. 'We've been out to catch several dogs already who escaped their backyards in terror.'

The dog, a Staffordshire Terrier, more or less, has come from three gardens away. I can see it is hot, thirsty, still scared, as the rangers take it away.

'It doesn't take a bad dog to kill a rabbit,' the older ranger says as he leaves. 'And your cage would never have stopped it. There's no cage in the world that could stop a Staffie getting to a rabbit.'

Alice gets up and she weeps and shakes too. I take the bunnies out of the cage; there is no blood on them. I tell her that they died of heart attacks because they were so scared of the dog and I hope that that is true. I place their soft, limp bodies into a cardboard box and take them to the vet to be cremated.

Home again, I am overcome physically and mentally. Mind taut as a tightrope, heart sore, body still shaky. The sight of that dog growling up against the window, its teeth bared.

I need a drink. *I do.* One hefty glass of wine would ease these feelings immediately. A second could lull me into calm waters. Ah, I do need a drink. But no one needs to point out that a third and a fourth would follow. And the self-loathing would restart.

I can stay strong, I can. I think I can. Just get started, Seana, make something to drink, not wine. Try it. Start with that.

I go to my large stash of non-alcoholic drinks and mix myself a Gunner. This is a recipe given to me by a friend who first tried one in Hong Kong: ginger beer, ginger ale, juice of a half a lime and a dash of Angostura bitters, built over ice. A

Gunner is an indulgent sweet drink with a serious gingery kick. And guess what? It does the trick.

As I sit with it in the garden, in the afternoon sunshine, I feel myself relax, slow down, let go. I did need a drink, and it turns out the drink didn't need to be alcoholic. Oh, my goodness, who knew? Why wasn't I told? It is the ritual, the taste, the sitting still, that slakes the sensation of needing a drink. Perhaps I could have meditated or taken a bath or gone for a walk, but look, a drink does the trick. Revelation!

I think back to family life when I was a child at Marketgate, about the rituals around Dad's drinking. The dripping of the pink Angostura bitters down the side of the crystal glass. The slow pour of the gin, then the cracking of the cap on the tonic bottle, the feel of it heavy in the hand, the fizzy splash. And when Dad drank whisky, he would open the bottle, would always smell it first then pour a big dram into the glass, lift the water jug and pour that in. The perfect ratio. So much of drinking is ritual and so much of that ritual is soothing, comforting.

❦

It's the last day of the year, December 31st. I take a tray of tea and biscuits out into the garden, set it on the little table and settle down into one of the soft cushions of the old cane chairs. The scent of summer jasmine is on the soft breeze, sweet and luscious. I look at the red bottlebrush flowers, at the native bees swimming in the air among them, at the busy ants on the path popping in and out of their nests. At the far end of the garden, I see the rhubarb plant growing well, wide green leaves covering the long stalks, deep colours bright in the sunshine.

It's been a whole month of not drinking, and a whole year since I woke with a hangover, packed up the kitchen and then flew to Scotland to sit with my dying Mum in her bedroom at St Olaf Care Home, holding her hand as she lay motionless, peaceful. Although she never seemed to be aware that my sisters and I were with her, that did not matter. We knew we were there, watching, talking; there was love all around Mum as she left this weary world.

One year later, I sit with a cup of tea, pick up an Anzac biscuit from the pile on the small Greenwheat side plate and reflect on all the visits to Scotland when Mum was unwell, two visits a year for three years. So disruptive to life with the family, but so important for me.

As a child, I had longed to be able to help my mother. She was so young, beautiful, and very much in need of a rescuer, someone to save her from Dad, even from all of us children. In my body and in my mind, for so many years, I longed and longed and longed to escape with her, to take her away from cruelty, aggression, from all of the bad parts of Dad, his Mr Hyde side. But I was a child. I could not rescue my mother and I had to make do with escaping on my own. I had to rescue myself.

How healing it was to help her at a time when she needed help again. I was able to go to Scotland and work with my sisters to set up people to visit her, to care for her, to send meals to her. Then I was able to be a decision-maker with the medical staff, help her find the care home in Nairn. As an adult, I helped my mother when she needed help. When I could help her, I did.

An old lady is so very vulnerable, unsure, upset, lost. We sisters did all we could, made sure she was safe and as happy as cruel circumstances allowed. There is great peace for my inner child in knowing that when I could help my mum, I did. The stressful emotions caused by my circumstances as a child were soothed by being able to comfort her, care for her, and make her laugh at times, too: wheeling her along past the beach and the boats in Nairn harbour, taking her to James's Cafe for an ice cream, sitting outdoors in the Moray Firth breezes, blankets around our knees. All this was a gift to the little child who lives in me, who so wanted to save her mum, but could not, and who had to leave her mother and go so far away to save herself.

I pour another cup of tea from the teapot into my mug, pour in some milk and then pick up another biscuit. Here I am. I am here. In this garden, here right now, now right here. So far away, away from Scotland, summer here when it's winter there, scorching here, snow there at the moment.

Did I really save myself? Moving to Australia certainly gave me distance, but in so many ways when I left the family home in Ormiston my own drinking took over the role of abuser. I became my very own self-abuser.

Now, finally, free of alcohol for this whole month, am I feeling the true freedom I always craved? I was so concerned not to become a martyr, not to turn into my mum, that I might have missed how I was turning into Dad.

Paul comes out to join me, picks up a biscuit and takes a bite.

'Paul, there's something about not drinking that is making me feel so differently about Dad, about the past with him. But I don't even know what it is I'm feeling or thinking. But if I stop, maybe that whole story will stop: his drinking story that became my drinking story.'

'So, what will you do next year?' Paul asks. 'Have you decided?'

'Yes, and I've been thinking about this for a while, but I didn't want to say it out loud. Still, New Year's Eve is a good day to be brave. I want it to be all over between me and alcohol. I feel strongly that my life will be better if I never ever drink again.'

'So that whole idea of moderating, just having one or two? What about the idea of trying that?'

'Trying that again, you mean? No, I have been trying to moderate for twenty-five years. I think if I was able to become a moderate drinker, a normal drinker, it would've happened by now. And finally, finally, Paul, finally, I think I can do it. Never drink again. The thought makes me feel free rather than panic-stricken.'

New Year has always been a favourite time for me. I love the sense of renewal, of washing away the past and having a scrubbed-clean fresh start.

When I stopped drinking at the end of November, I really had meant it just to be a month off, particularly to avoid drinking over the booze-heavy Christmas and New Year period when, traditionally, I have made myself feel shockingly ill.

But this time, stopping drinking felt different almost as soon as the stopping had started. That massive scunner was the start of it. I was sick and tired of feeling sick and tired, depressed about the depression and anxious about the anxiety. I lost the taste for all the trouble my drinking gave me. It was time to call last orders on all the hideous hangovers.

On the last day of this momentous year, Paul asks, 'Do you think of yourself as an alcoholic?'

'*Och*, Paul, I don't think "alcoholic" is a very useful word. But I can say quite cheerfully that alcohol was causing me problems – my drinking was a problem and I was a problem drinker. Now there's no alcohol, and there's no problem. Just for today. I cannot quite believe it.'

I end the year just over four-weeks sober, feeling overwhelming relief and the great hope, and firm intention, that the New Year and the whole of the next year and all the years after that will be entirely alcohol-free.

This sounds so simple.

EPILOGUE

You're Here Now

Ha!

You didn't think it would turn out to be that easy, did you?

Funnily enough, I did, and then got a humungous shock when I started to struggle and to doubt and to wonder and to worry in the early parts of the next year. So many emotions, and no alcohol to numb them with. Instead of drinking wine when I had a problem, I actually had to solve the problem. Such a hard thing to do. You need to be a real grown-up to do that. And I still had a lot of growing up to do.

The good news is that I did not start drinking again. A huge mental shift happened and, with many struggles and a lot of support, I have not drunk alcohol since that fateful Black Friday sale I saw on Facebook.

There were twenty-five years of stopping and starting since I first had time off alcohol when I was thirty. But by the time I am typing these words, I have been sober for four years, completely alcohol-free. Not one sip of wine has crossed my lips. And truly, no one could be more surprised than myself.

Nor more relieved and joyful.

While I know I wasn't the world's messiest drunk, and I know I didn't have a real rock bottom, my grey area drinking was so deeply engrained in my psyche that I believed I could not survive on this watery, blue planet without the release alcohol gave me, the instant relax. What a lot of crap I had in my brain for so many decades. Ethyl alcohol might be relaxing to the body at first sip, but its effects come back to haunt you, to bite you, to turn you into a zombie: poor sleep, anxiety, hangovers and all the dreadful long-term consequences we now know about, not least a sharp upturn in the chance of getting cancer.

Today I am deeply grateful that I stopped before alcohol took me all the way it wanted to, before I let go and gave in to my worst cravings. Ethyl alcohol is highly addictive, and I was susceptible to addiction. Everyone who drinks a lot regularly becomes addicted to some extent. I escaped, freed myself, before the slippery slope I was on got too steep.

And I still cannot quite believe my luck. Freedom! I never again need to wake up with a hangover in my life. I have lost nothing and gained the world, if the world is a Sunday morning that starts with a simple cup of tea rather than a multiple hangover with a side dish of self-abuse.

As a non-drinker, my guiding word is *safe*: this is the word that sums up the benefits of sobriety for me. I am safe on the roads, I am safe from getting into stupid pickles, from being mean to my friends, from being impatient, from hangovers and from self-abuse. Safe is what I yearned for, what I needed, like every other human child. I could not have safety as a child, but I am safe now, even from myself.

Seriously, I have lost nothing. Wine actually does not taste that good, as we all know, because everyone has to force themselves to drink it at first. After not drinking wine for a while, and enjoying hangover-free alternatives to alcohol, the smell of wine is off-putting and I totally do not miss the taste.

But it wasn't my change in taste that made the difference. There were many, many things and they took months and months to come good and to crystallise. Here are some reflections I would like to share:

One phrase
My life will be better if I never drink again.

I wanted my life to be better and I was prepared to do a lot to make it so. In my mid-fifties I could hear my life-clock ticking. Both of my parents died fairly young, Dad at seventy-one and Mum at seventy-nine. Did I really want to spend my final ten or twenty or thirty years waking up feeling shocking and giving myself a mouthful of vitriol? Or did I want to give myself my best chance for happiness, health, and freedom?

A mental shift
Once that one phrase lodged in my mind, I could not dislodge it. One day I felt a huge key turn in a giant lock inside my brain. I felt the shudder as that key turned, a thud when it clicked into place; and that key can never be turned back. There was never a visualisation of a door opening, just the massive clunk as my mental shift, my seismic mental shift, took place.

My life will be better if I never drink again. And I want a better life.

Acceptance
No, acceptance did not come and stay for good. There were whisperings of dissent and small insistent voices at times telling me that I could have one drink now, or that if I drank bubbly

on a flight it would not count. Nobody would ever know.

I never got to test that as the pandemic shut down all flying for a couple of years. Stopping before the pandemic was a bit of a lifesaver. Things could have got quite ugly in our house. Instead, I bundled up and watched hours and hours of comedy TV shows with the kids, and drank other things, and ate a lot of ice cream.

Keep the ritual – change the ingredients

That is a motto of Janey Lee Grace from 'The Sober Club', whose podcasts I listened to obsessively in my first year of alcohol-free freedom.

Seana, you did go a bit mad, didn't you?

Oh yes, just a tiny bit obsessive. I did.

In the January after the year I detail in this book I tried a new alcohol-free drink every day and deluged my Facebook timeline with arty photos of them. I did a fair bit of late-night impulse shopping of many alcohol-free wines, cocktails, spirits and mixers. I was building a wee defensive wall around me, bottle by bottle.

I found that there was relief and relaxation in having a pretty drink from a glass clinking with ice at 5 pm if I was on cooking duty. The taste was different, but it did still feel like a treat, a pause, a reward. And I am sure that I got a tiny buzz from having that pretty drink in a delicate glass.

Freedom

I had been chasing the feeling of freedom my whole life. As a child, I was trapped in my family home and I genuinely could not escape. As an adult, I was not physically trapped but I got caught up in my own head and I trapped myself. Well, there was motherhood, too. That can put a woman in a gilded cage, but it was never the kids I longed to be free of, just the washing, the shopping, the cooking and the effing sausages. It was only when I stopped numbing my pain that I took steps to change circumstances so that I could live in a way that suited me better. This involved getting Paul to do more of the cooking and to take up more of the parental mental load.

Letting go of old trauma

My childhood was severely impacted by my Dad's drinking and his appalling behaviour when drunk. I got out of the house as fast as I could and kept moving and moving. I had to leave Scotland and come all the way to Australia because Mum never left Dad. This is how it feels to me and there is great sadness about the loss of my home country.

Many children of aggressive alcoholics grow up never to drink themselves, but that is not my story. I was one of those who joined in the drinking as soon as I could. I spent so much time trying not to end up like Mum that I did not see I was turning into Dad. Even after his death, his drinking story continued through me. Only after I stopped drinking did I feel that his drinking and its influence on me was over. That story is complete.

I have found EMDR therapy very helpful for dealing with trauma, and I visit my psychologist when I feel my mental health dipping. My childhood, and the bad parts of it, now genuinely feel as if they happened long, long ago. Which they did. The past is not influencing the present, and I am very grateful for that. This frees me to look back on the many positive gifts my family and upbringing have given me and to enjoy remembering all the good parts of Dad and Mum and the adventures they took us on. What a relief. It has also made me feel emigrant regret, and the pain of the loss of beautiful

Scotland. But my kids are Australian, and there is much to love about this country.

In my own older age, I need to recapture all the good things. I need to reclaim the true essence of myself as a child and to live again with the positive parts of childhood, the fun and the freedom. In my older years, there will be space to play and to let go of responsibilities. I am keen to recapture the lightness, the exuberance, the curiosity and the energy of childhood. And, now that Mum and Dad are gone, miraculously in a grave together, I want to remember them for all that they were. It is time to focus more on the good as the years carry me further and further away from them, and wash me closer and closer to my own final shore.

Here's my takeaway piece of wisdom for any grey area drinker reading this book who hopes to make a positive change in their own life.

Give yourself a better life by rejecting the highly addictive ethyl alcohol which is making you ill physically and mentally. Alcohol marketing companies have sold us a lie: see through it. The alcohol emperor has no clothes. Tell it to buzz off.

Stopping completely is a piece of cake compared to the mental torture of attempting to moderate when you just can't. Make your life better, make it easier. Set yourself free.

The End

P.S. Did we get a dog? Yes, indeed, we did! Perhaps the wee black poodle called Maisie who joined our family after the Covid pandemic is the best symbol of being settled. She's certainly the one with the waggiest tail. I do not want to run away from home anymore, there are no more urges to travel all over the planet. I couldn't bear to leave my darling dog for long. And, of course, Paul adores her too; she sleeps on our bed with us. Maisie will be with us long after the twins have left home. Home. I'm here now.

Acknowledgements

Firstly, a profound thanks to my family in Scotland who feature in these pages. Mum and Dad did the best they could do at the time, caring for us as well as they were able, and better than they ever cared for themselves. Thank you, Mum and Dad, for the gift of adventures in the spectacular Scottish outdoors, on land and at sea, for the garden that fed us all, and for all the stories about Scottish history and our own family.

Thank you, Kirsty, for looking after your annoying wee sister, and more recently for the bracing sea swims. Callum, thank you for your good humour and your kind heart. Special thanks to Morag for your patience with your bossy big sister and for all your assistance with posting over letters and diaries and spending hours talking on the phone.

I know that what I have written has been difficult for some family members and I apologise for any pain caused.

I did not mean to write this memoir. It started as a collection of scenes that I remembered all too well and needed to get out of my head and onto a page, a therapeutic outpouring. An accidental introduction to Curtis Brown Creative on a Zoom interview between Clare Pooley and Janey Lee Grace led me to a six-week memoir course by Cathy Rentzenbrink. From there, reading and writing memoir snowballed during the pandemic years.

I have been privileged to be mentored by Carol Major and Kathryn Heyman, whose advice has been crucial, as have their own books. Sunday morning memoir groups with Jenny Valentish provided both Jenny's skilled editing and the comradeship of other writers: thank you Sara Musgrave, Vanessa McQuarrie, Jo Ruksenas, Jessie Alice and Brodie Jacobsen.

There's nowhere better to discuss books and writing than on Kate Broadhurst's green and white verandah, and no one better to discuss them with. Big, big thanks to you, Kate.

It is a joy to work again so soon with my friends at Ventura Press. Thank you Jane Curry for understanding this story and giving me guidance on telling it well. Much appreciation to Amanda Hemmings for her editing skills and kind support. Deborah Parry's cover design is wonderful: thank you, Deb. The enthusiasm and skill of Anna Lensky and Bec Bridges at Pitch Projects is also very much appreciated.

Thanks to the Orange school mums, Alex, Dee, Holly, Karen, Polly, Sarah and Tory, for your support and friendship; also thanks to the staff at Anything Grows for keeping the coffees coming.

Thanks to my friends in Sydney, Scotland and beyond. I have been so lucky with friends all through my many escapes and escapades. I have bent the ears of you all and been heard with kindness and compassion. Especial thanks to all those who feature in this memoir.

To the friends who stopped drinking before me, a massive

thank you for leading the way.

Finally, my deepest gratitude to Paul who is not only an ace partner and co-parent but handily retrained as an editor and proofreader. These skills proved essential as I am completely lacking in both. Thanks, Paul, for your many hours of hard yakka at the laptop, not to mention at the sink, the stove and the washing machine. Big hugs to our four offspring and especial thanks to our twins for all the music in the evenings.

Seana Smith was born and brought up in Scotland, in the village of Ormiston, just outside Edinburgh. After studying Classics and Old and Medieval English at Wadham College, University of Oxford, she worked as a TV researcher and producer for Channel Nine in Sydney and for the BBC in London and Glasgow.

She published her first book *Sydney For Under Fives* in 2001, and went on to co-author the bestselling *The Australian Autism Handbook* in 2008, now in its fourth edition.

Seana is a professional writer and a very unprofessional mother of four young adults. Seana now lives in Orange, NSW. Find her at Sober Journeys (www.soberjourneys.com).